Jubilate

P. 84 - Key statements
& 87

Jubilate

Theology in Praise

Daniel W. Hardy
and
David F. Ford

Darton Longman and Todd
London

First published in 1984 by
Darton Longman and Todd Ltd
89 Lillie Road, London SW6 1UD

© 1984 Daniel W. Hardy and David F. Ford

ISBN 0 232 51550 6

British Library Cataloguing in Publication Data

Hardy, Daniel W.
  Jubilate.
  1. Christian life   2. Praise
  I. Title   II. Ford, David F.
  248.3   BV4501.2

  ISBN 0–232–51550–6

Phototypeset by Input Typesetting Ltd, London SW19 8DR
Printed in Great Britain by Anchor Brendon Ltd
Tiptree, Essex

CONTENTS

Preface

This book is dedicated, with endless gratitude, to our wives, Perrin Hardy and Deborah Ford, who are also mother and daughter.

There are many others to thank for their contributions in various ways. We are grateful above all to the communities of praising and knowing in which we have participated, in particular the Church of England parishes of St Luke's (Bristol Street, Birmingham) and St Mark's (Londonderry, Smethwick), Hockley Pentecostal Church, the prayer group in Carlyle Road (Edgbaston), the Anchorhold, the Centre for Partnership between Black and White Christians, the Mother of God Community (Washington, D.C.), and the Universities of Birmingham, Oxford, Cambridge, Tübingen and Yale. For help by discussing with us ideas and parts of the manuscript we especially thank Alan Ford, Mícheál Ó Siadhail, Peter Hocken, John Eaton, Vi Godwin, Janet Graham, Peter Harvey, Gae Twomey and Frances Young. For their perceptive comments, editorial and publishing skills, and great encouragement and patience we thank Lesley Riddle and John Todd of Darton Longman and Todd. Joyce Lauder, Phyllis Ford, Anne Bowen and Irene Brenton have repeatedly earned our gratitude by typing drafts and chapters. And many have given their encouragement, ideas and prayers, among whom we specially thank our families, where we have learnt much of the richness of life in praise.

Acknowledgements

Unless otherwise stated, the Scripture quotations in this publication
are from the Revised Standard Version of the Bible, copyrighted
1971 and 1952 by the Division of Christian Education of the
National Council of the Churches of Christ in the USA.

The authors are grateful to the following for permission to quote
from copyright material: the Bible Society, from the *Good News Bible*,
copyright American Bible Society 1976, published by the Bible
Societies/Collins Publishers; Bluett & Co Ltd, from *Springnight* by
Mícheál Ó Siadhail; Mrs Katherine B. Kavanagh and Martin
Brian & O'Keeffe Ltd, from *Collected Poems* by Patrick Kavanagh;
Penguin Books Ltd, from the translation of Dante's *Divine Comedy*
by Dorothy L. Sayers; SCM Press Ltd, from *Letters and Papers from
Prison* by Dietrich Bonhoeffer, enlarged edition 1971; SPCK, from
*Vision in Worship: The Relation of Prophecy and Liturgy in the Old Testa-
ment* by John Eaton; Washington Square Press division of Simon &
Schuster Inc, from the translation of Dante's *Divine Comedy*, copy-
right 1966 by Louis Biancolli.

1

Introduction: Twin Explosions

Most of us know things, values and people that evoke our wonder and admiration. They draw us into wanting to do justice to them by responding appropriately. This universal human experience of wanting to praise is one of the roots of this book. People do the most extraordinary things and make all sorts of sacrifices in honour of what they praise. The dynamics set in motion by such enthusiasms play a large part in shaping history. On a more everyday level, the way in which recognition and respect are distributed in families, groups and societies determines a great deal both in the identity of each one of us, and in what we find worthwhile doing.

Religion has always been deeply involved with the way praise, recognition and respect create the atmosphere in which we live and the values we live by. We are concerned in this book to follow this line through in relation to Christianity. We hope to be of interest both to those who praise the Christian God and to those who do not. But we are not concerned to argue with the latter. Rather, we want to make a constructive statement of one way of understanding and affirming Christianity by concentrating on the themes of praise and knowledge. There is (quite rightly) a vast debate and literature about the truth and defensibility of Christianity. Yet it is possible to be so occupied with protection against anticipated attacks that one's energy is spent mainly on border disputes and frontier wars. These are important, but they can easily detract from development of the heartlands, where food can be grown and ordinary life carried on. It is not a matter of first securing one's borders and the proper international exchanges, and only then building up a rich domestic life; the two must go together, and the home affairs are often impoverished by an obsession with security.

At the heart of ordinary Christian life is recognition of the love of God. All creation is a work of God's love. Jesus Christ is God's giving of himself in love to restore and fulfil all creation. The Holy Spirit is the pouring out of this love in endless transformation and fresh creativity. Praise of God recognizes all this and first of all enjoys and celebrates it. Praise is therefore an attempt to cope with the abundance of God's love.

We aim to explore and cultivate these heartlands. For those who do praise God day after day, we hope that we might help them to think through their practice, with benefit to both their practice and their thinking. For those who do not praise God, but are curious, we hope that they may have a glimpse of what happens beyond the border battles. It is only by going deeper into the country that one can grasp what is at stake in the external conflicts. Too often the impression is given that the internal life is not worth the effort of exploring it – it may be defensible, but it is not very vigorous or interesting. We are trying to present a life which is lively and convincing enough to be well worth vigorously denying or affirming.

Straightforward statements such as this are quite rare in current theology, and for good reasons. They lay the authors open to such dreaded accusations of the academic world as naivety or failure to consider all the alternatives. We would have liked to consider more alternatives and to leave our flanks less vulnerable. For example, the relation of other religions to Christianity and its understanding of God could have been brought in at almost every point. But, if this were to be more than fashionable lip service, it would have multiplied the size of the book, and as our own position differs considerably from most of those at present available, we could not simply refer to a body of acceptable literature. So that has been left for the future or for others who know far more about it, along with other attractive subjects such as Church, culture, economics, ethics, language, and prayer and spirituality. Yet there are positions on all of these implicit in what is said, and, as far as our understanding stretches, hints are given about what a more explicit treatment might look like. These, as well as the theological subjects that are treated at some length, have been conceived as parts of a position that by its nature can never be completed, yet allows definite statements. It suggests one mode of doing all theology. It unfolds in a way which will be summarized below.

Something which has been present throughout the book's conception and writing but is not explicit in it is the city of Birmingham. One of us (D. W. H.) came to Birmingham twelve years before the other, and we have now been there together for eight years. We had previously had very different experiences of worship and Christian life in various countries, but in Birmingham we found a concentrated diversity on which we could reflect together as we participated. The three main streams of twentieth-century Christianity – the Catholic, the Protestant and the Pentecostal – have all had major contributions to make to our experience both in other countries and in Britain. In Birmingham we found them interesting in unusual and promising ways, often not obvious or well known, and all in a context that contained most of the problems and possibilities of modern urban living, not least in its pluralist religious form. Between the religions too, we have seen in Birmingham new types of dialogue and co-operation.

Through all this we have, on the one hand, been acutely aware of the unprecedented explosion in the twentieth century of critical and constructive intellectual activity in relation to Christianity and other religions. University-level study of them has blossomed, and besides (and often within) major historical and theological works there has been a massive effort to examine the relation of religion to the whole range of arts and sciences and to the special conditions of modern living. On the other hand, we have also been aware (often by seeing its living results) of the explosion of praise and worship in many forms which has characterized the Christian Church of this century – in, for example, the renewal brought by the liturgical movement (issuing in thousands of new forms of service), the rise of worldwide Pentecostalism, the openness of many Churches to influences from a variety of cultures, the creativity that has served new communications media such as films, television, radio, tapes and records, the vigorous and irrepressible worship of the Church in communist countries, and the widespread exploration of fresh forms of prayer, frequently drawing on other religious traditions of East and West.

Yet it is remarkable that those most involved in these twin explosions have often had little to say to each other, to the point of indifference, or have despised, feared or ridiculed each other. The atmosphere of suspicion that surrounds each can be a source of great tension for those who take part in both. Yet it is a tension well worth sustaining, because each side has something that the other desperately needs. So we have tried in this book to make a twofold movement into modern thought and into the praise of God, combined in the attempt to find out what Christian life and thought might be in contemporary Western society.

The plan is to begin with a description of praising God as it is experienced today (chapter 2). This includes a keynote discussion of the idea of praise, a brief account of the ways in which praise is threatened and distorted in modern culture (a theme taken up again later, especially in chapters 6, 7 and 9), an introduction to the four main modes of Christian praise, and an appreciation of the intimacy of solitary praise.

The next two chapters gather up some past experience of praising and knowing God. Chapter 3 uses the theme of praise as a key to the Bible. It does not do this chronologically, but starts with Paul's Letter to the Philippians, which powerfully expresses early Christian praise as it tries to take up and transform basic experience. After that the central inspiration of Christian praise is described through the Gospel of Mark, which is shown to give the dynamics of the new praise. Then the roots of all this are traced in the Old Testament, which is seen as a book sustaining and sustained by a powerful stream of praise century after century. There is a similar approach to the Christian tradition in chapter 4. It begins with a climactic literary work, perhaps the supreme Christian poem, Dante's *Divine Comedy*. From Dante's final canto it takes up the theme of the Trinity. God as Trinity is the distinctively Christian focus of praise.

Chapter 4 traces it backwards from Dante into its origins in the worship and thought of the early Church, and forward from Dante through the Reformation to today. The Trinitarian conception of God is the product of an unfinished revolution whose continuation is vital for Christian life and its involvement with a living, interesting God. Finally, the chapter engages with the main new twentieth-century dimension of the Christian Church, Pentecostalism.

Chapters 5 and 6 relate the brighter and darker sides of human existence to praise. Chapter 5, which perhaps expresses most clearly the spirit of the book, sees praise at the heart of our human identity. The 'logic' of laughter, overflow, freedom, generosity, respect and blessing are the theme of this chapter. It also offers a praise-centred view of creation and of human maturity. The negative side of existence is explored in chapter 6, showing how evil, suffering and death can be faced in the context of the Christian God. Two key ideas are developed: the neglected experience of shame is seen as the dynamic negation of praise; and the concept of non-order, as distinct from both order and disorder, sums up a great deal in previous chapters and helps deal with the problem of evil. Then the historical reality of evil is discussed, with hatred as the focus. The final position is that only if God vindicates himself and the good can the problem of evil be answered, and this is the pivot of Christian praise.

The final three chapters take complementary perspectives on God, roughly corresponding to God as Trinity and as Creator (chapter 7), God incarnate (chapter 8) and God the Holy Spirit inspiring prophecy (chapter 9).

Chapter 7 puts forward a position on knowledge of God, the role of imagination in it and the way in which one can go about testing the claim to know God. The main conclusion is that God as Trinity, developed beyond the traditional form of this doctrine, is the most satisfactory way to make sense of the cosmos, human existence and Christian experience. The final section on revelation tries to answer the question: how could something of universal importance happen in one particular time, place or person? That prepares for chapter 8, Jesus is our Praise. This tries to point to the dazzling yet puzzling person of Jesus, and understands his teaching and death as showing a way through the dilemmas and vicious circles of existence. The new life that results is described mainly in terms of a new responsibility marked by the freedom of praise. Finally, the themes of the book are drawn together in a prophetic chapter that proclaims the God of joy as the message for the present. Each appendix is an attempt to work out our theme in relation to a major way of doing theology. Appendix A is a concentrated systematic theology, pointing the sort of conceptual system implied by the book. Appendix B surveys a vast area in the history of theology and other thought in order to indicate the relevance of our theme.

Throughout the writing of this book we have tried to be open to an expanding vision of what praise is and to represent that. The joint authorship began through our work as colleagues in Birmingham University, sharing teaching in the areas of philosophy, modern theology and systematic theology. As we grappled with the main modern philosophers and theologians (and also with the very varied positions of our colleagues) we developed many shared analyses and criticisms, but felt that what was most needed was a constructive statement. Over the years the theme of praising and knowing God emerged as one of the most fruitful and so we began to think through its implications.

New contributors continually joined in (some of whom are mentioned in the Preface) and the result is far more a symphony than a duet. It has been a constant pain having to exclude so much, especially the artists and musicians who lend themselves less to expression in writing. But some of the poets have had their say, and we are especially grateful to the late Patrick Kavanagh, an Irish poet far less well known than he deserves, whose work often left us feeling: Why say more? But, in a way, the whole art of praising *is* saying more, yet without inappropriateness. We risk trying this in what follows, and hope occasionally to help the subject have for the reader what Kavanagh called

. . . a life with a shapely form
With gaiety and charm
And capable of receiving
With grace the grace of living
And wild moments too . . .[1]

---

[1] 'The Self-Slaved', *Collected Poems*, London 1972.

2

The Experience of Praising God Today

When the importance of praise becomes clear, there is likely to be, as with many other significant discoveries, a sense of obviousness, an 'of course'. If God is God, then of course praise of God is central. Of course it should be the tone of the whole of life, and of course Christian tradition has always said so. But what does this involve? The rest of this book is the beginning of an answer to that, and this chapter offers a condensation of it from the standpoint of the praiser.

The Idea of Praise

We begin with the very idea of praise. It has a strange logic. Praise perfects perfection.

When we find something of quality and express our appreciation, that very expression adds something to the situation. This is even more so in the case of praise of a person. To recognize worth and to respond to it with praise is to create a new relationship. This new mutual delight is itself something of worth, an enhancement of what was already valued.

There need be no end to this: there can be an infinite spiral of free response and expression of it in look or word or act. Like lovers writing letters or just looking into each other's eyes, the expression of appreciation is not an optional extra in the relationship; it is intrinsic to its quality, and is also a measure of all behaviour within it. There are always great dangers in this of unreality, dishonesty and manipulation: but these are not inevitable, and despite its risk of misuse, praise remains a remarkable phenomenon. When free people are in a good relationship, then the sort of recognition, respect and mutual delight that are at the heart of praise continually overflow, and become the normal way of self-transcendence in thought, word and act.

Most people have experienced at least moments of such delight in another person. In this there is an awakening of new responses, a yearning for larger capacities of expression and action, and an inspiration for all sorts of generosity and creativity. It stretches us beyond our limits, and often confuses and deeply disturbs before taking some simple form, of which 'I love you' is perhaps the favourite down the centuries. Amazement and commitment are evoked by this new vision of the other, who is seen in complete particularity and distinctiveness. It is not basically a matter of comparison with anyone else: the focus of fascination is this person in all his or her individuality. The appreciation that is poured out is concerned to do justice to what seems like a unique miracle, which has a rightness and perfection that can only be responded to with astonishment. It has simply to be recognized for what it is, quite apart from any consequences or intentions. There may be all sorts of hopes and fears but the essence of the matter is being true to what is there to be amazed at, quite apart from oneself.

None of this is strictly necessary, nor can it be demanded of anyone. There is no mechanical logic about it, with one thing entailing another. There is no law of praise, and perfection would not be perfect if it had to require praise for its completion. Yet the odd fact is that in this way perfection itself can be perfected, and the more perfect it is the more wonderfully it evokes new forms of perfection. The logic is that of overflow, of freedom, of generosity. This logic of overflow will appear at many points in subsequent chapters, and its meaning will be filled out there. It is the secret of living perfection which continually generates more rich life. Praise which freely responds becomes the environment and vehicle for fresh creativity. Its thrust is towards taking up into a higher level of relationship all the elements of life and reordering them, sometimes simply playing with them and exuberantly enjoying them. This new order and overflow of order (what we later call non-order) is a realm of freedom yet definiteness, creativity yet precision (the agony of finding the right word or note), and it aims to celebrate the best by both discerning what it is and letting it overflow in surprising new ways.

Thanks is the companion of praise, and shares the same strange logic. Just as praise perfects perfection, so thanks completes what is completed. When something has happened that is good then thanks is one way (and perhaps the most fully personal way) for that to overflow into the present and the future. The greater and more decisively complete the event, the more thanks are appropriate. Thanks is the mode of praise directed to appreciating past events, and likewise deeply affects the nature of relationships. It is possible for gratitude for one past service to sustain years of friendship. The immense creativity of thanks in social and personal life has been recognized by most societies, and is part of the wider significance of memory and history for human identity.

The operation of the logic of thanks and praise can be noticed in most good personal relationships. It is explicit perhaps rarely, but it is the essential structure of respect, personal worth and identity. Its form and content are vital clues to the character both of individuals and society. Whom do we respect and why? To whom are we grateful? Whose presence is a delight? In what does our own value to others consist? How are we affirmed by others in what we are and do? The answers embrace the whole network of meaning and reality in society, and the key times of each life – birth and mothering, childhood and schooling, adult life, work, friendship and marriage, old age and death. We need to be affirmed and affirming, and yet it is a necessity that must be achieved in freedom.

Christian Praise of God

How does Christian praise of God relate to these basic features of life? It sets up a single massive affirmation as the one which should condition all the others. This is the affirmation of God. The central thrust of the Jewish and Christian tradition is to take up the whole of life into praise of God, making him central to everything and his glory the goal of the universe.

What is God's glory? Its logic is that of overflowing, creative love, which freely perfects its own perfection and invites others to join this life through praise. The only affirmation of God that is adequate is his self-affirmation. The key Old Testament name for God, Yahweh, means just this: 'I am that I am.' God acts 'for his name's sake,' and it is he who inspires people to worship him. As Richard Rolle said: 'My heart thou hast bound in love of thy name, and now I cannot but sing it.'

When Christians saw God's culminating self-affirmation in Jesus Christ, this involved a transformed understanding of God's glory. So Paul wrestled with the scandalous idea of God's glory expressed in a crucified man, and John makes the cross central to his concept of glory. One of the most concentrated expressions of the new Christian glory is in Paul's Letter to the Philippians, and we analyse it in chapter 3 to discover the radical consequences for praising God in ordinary living. All the lines in Christianity converge on the Christ-centred worship of God. Renewal has always come through people whose first interest in life has been adoring and realistic attention to God. Any experience of Christianity that does not participate in this has missed the point. But it is one thing to agree on this, and on the main outlines of the idea of praise, and another to say what is involved in experiencing it.

There is first of all the praiser's experience of accepting that his or her basic reality is of being always before God and loved by God.

This is so amazing that it is only by constant reminders that it can become a daily reality. To wake up every morning and to know that no matter what the state of the world and of oneself, God is this loving God and so there is cause for joy: this is the highest Christian realism, besides which all other realisms are partial, but it is not one that is achieved all at once.

Even to begin to accept it, to arrive at a faith that can affirm God in any way is to have taken one among many possible roads. The reasons for and against taking it are exhaustively argued in philosophy and theology and, less formally, by people in general. There are rational, moral, aesthetic, psychological, social, historical, scientific and all sorts of practical considerations, and their relative weight in a particular case will vary greatly. Our concern now is not about how or why some people come to believe in the Christian God, but about their situation once they do so. This situation is itself, of course, partly the product of the way they got there, and the problems faced en route often continue in different forms. Yet conversion to the Christian God for whatever reasons, and whether gradual or sudden, is itself a new factor to which the fresh reality of worshipping God is intrinsic. As Gerard Manley Hopkins wrote, using Paul and Augustine (Austin) as examples:

> With an anvil-ding
> And with fire in him forge thy will
> Or rather, rather then, stealing as Spring
> Through him, melt him but master him still:
> Whether at once, as once at a crash Paul,
> Or as Austin, a lingering-out sweet skill,
> Make mercy in all of us, out of us all
> Mastery, but be adored, but be adored King.[1]

Hopkins is writing inside the experience, and there are few poets who have expressed more strongly or with more theological precision the taking up of everything into praise of God – nature, culture, celebration, disasters, himself, his own sufferings and joys, and his faith. Through it all runs the strange experience of faith: that what seems like oneself finding God is seen in retrospect to be recognition that one has already been found by him; and one's knowledge of God is wrapped up inside being known by him. Praise brings this to its extreme. All that one has and is, all one's energy, freedom, imagination and thought are tested and stretched in adoration of God; yet this supreme effort only rings true as it also acknowledges

---

[1] 'The Wreck of the Deutschland', *Poems and Prose of Gerard Manley Hopkins*, ed. W. H. Gardner and N. H. Mackenzie, Oxford University Press for the Society of Jesus, London 1967.

that God is its initiator and inspirer. All glory goes to God, but as it does so, God works his never-failing but never-to-be-taken-for-granted surprise: freedom is returned as a gift which can once again be used to thank God and offer itself joyfully back in amazed praise. The coming together of the freedom of God with that of man is not experienced as a reduction of human responsibility; rather, the call to free self-giving is intensified and empowered, and praise is the experience of this, to which all the rest of life needs to be conformed.

This mysterious life of all-getting and all-giving is only known by participating in it. This is another basic feature of praising God: there is no simple sequence of recognition of God followed by expression, but expression can lead the way, and often recognition happens in the very act of expression. There is a knowledge of God that can only come in praising him. As one acts out in praise the implications of God as the one 'than which none greater can be conceived', so the mind is prepared for an enlargement of under-standing of him. All our faculties play a part in knowing God, and any can take the lead – the imagination by entering into the symbolism of worship, the voice by singing and expanding one's conception by its soaring, the arms by lifting up and freeing one's whole self for something larger than it, the feet by dancing, taste by eating and drinking, and so on. Faith in God is an experience that lives and grows by praise. There is continual spiral reinforcement: praising God helps us to appreciate what one is praising him for. The most explicit acts of worship are times of active receptivity open to a God who can give in a flash what will take a lifetime to work out, apply and conceptualize. Praise is always overflowing where we have got to in thought and action, as it risks greater and greater receptivity and response, and so it becomes the catalyst of prophetic knowledge of God and his will.

Another hallmark of the experience of praising God is that it is intrinsically linked with other people. The right place for it is always alongside other people before God. This is so even when one is not physically with other people. There is always an inextricable social dimension to praising God. It is obviously there in whatever form of expression is used, for that is something learned socially, mediated through others, just as faith itself has come through the communi-cation of others. There is also the sense of identification with other praisers across time and space, in past generations and around the world today, an overflowing of boundaries as solidarity with others before God is acted out. There is a wealth of other social benefits which can come from good praise too: the joy that can overflow mutually, confidence for new ventures and relationships, recognition of the need to face the devastating, joyless consequences of sin and evil, enrichment of culture and personal expression through powerful language, music and gesture, achievement of a common framework for thinking, feeling, imagining and acting, and even an understanding of group dynamics.

The supreme social benefit of praising God is, however, that it helps in discovering the strongest of objective bonds with others: the link through the reality of God. To praise God as Creator and Father giving himself for everyone through Jesus Christ in the Holy Spirit: that is to route all one's relationships through God, and to open them up to his future for them. Praise actualizes the true relationship between people as well as with God, and it is no accident that in the symbols of heavenly bliss the leading pictures are of feasting and praising.

Those also give the clue to one of the most basic things of all about the experience of praise: it is about pleasure. Christianity has been understandably reticent about the joy, bliss, delight and sheer pleasure at its heart. But it is so, simply because its God is the God of joy. Christian hedonism is the holy intoxication of pleasing and being pleased by God, and that sums up the experience of true praise. *self-indulgent pursuit of pleasure*

The Threats to Praise

To all this there is of course a shadow side. Praise of God is continually threatened at all points. There are head-on attacks which try to eliminate it physically or to shame it into silence. There are numerous subtle ways in which it is discredited, undermined, or made to seem unfashionable or childish or ridiculously unreal.

In a society dominated by efficiency and a functional assessment of everything, the whole ethos supports the despising of praise as futile. Praise of God is not necessary, it is an overflow, a generous extravagance of response which is easily seen as useless and deluded. Often the Churches co-operate by making sure that religion stays discreetly in its traditional forms or is simply about morality. But when Christian faith in God does appear powerful and effective the threats against it take on more teeth. Then the worship of a power beyond society, state and civilization is easily characterized as dangerous, insidious, subversive. The perversions of religion are such that there is always plenty of ammunition, just as there is for those who suppress sexuality or democracy or free speech. The best things invariably attract the most devastating corruption, which becomes so inextricable that the easiest thing is to dismiss them completely without trying to distinguish the genuine from the perverted.

Among the threats there are some that are especially dangerous to the roots of praise. Perhaps the chief among these is the atmosphere of suspicion in which we live. Just because we live in such an open society, with free spread of all sorts of beliefs, theories and world-views, we tend to be more wary of wholeheartedly adopting any of them. In a confusing situation 'safety first' dictates extreme caution, and rightly.

This commonsense suspicion is supported by more sophisticated elements in our culture. Freud, Marx and Nietzsche have been called the 'masters of suspicion', and in their popularized forms they have been immensely influential. After Freud, how can one not wonder whether worshippers are not simply projecting on to reality an illusory God who is a fulfilment of their wishes, fears or needs? It may be in some ways a beneficial illusion, with psychological and social benefits, but once it is seen through, it loses even this advantage. Marx has done something similar for the communal and institutional aspects of religion: are they not ways in which certain groups keep power and influence, using God as a guarantee of their own privileged position and as a focus for energy that would otherwise find more dangerous outlets? Nietzsche too saw God as an insidious fiction, and his own particular effect was to undermine confidence in a morality which had been based on Christianity.

The widespread suspicion of God as a human projection goes even deeper in its assertion that this fictitious God would be intolerable even if he were to exist, because he would make human freedom and autonomy empty. So God is seen, even in projected form, as in competition with man, a threat to his dignity as a mature human being. The result for praise of God in this atmosphere is that its confidence is eroded, and even when there is no denial there is doubt.

The doubt does not stop at such comprehensive suspicion. It must face all the evidence lined up against the reality of a good God – the evil, suffering, ignorance, despair in the world. These can be traced in the Churches too, so what benefit have the centuries of worship had?

Then there is the existence of many religions with conflicting claims. The most elementary move of suspicion is to line up all the options, show their similarity as well as their incompatibility, then suggest that they are all wrong in their absolute claims and that it is far wiser to explain them in other terms – most commonly a combination of psychology, sociology, anthropology and philosophy. There are God-centred approaches to comparative religion too, with some of which we would agree, but on the whole the result of comparison is hostile to praise of God within any particular tradition.

There are libraries full of books trying to deal with the problems we have raised here. Many of them will be treated in later chapters of this book, but we do not intend a comprehensive solution, which would need a systematic philosophical theology. Hard thinking and analysis are necessary in relation to each issue, and we, with many others, deal with the arguments on either side in our academic work. Through such work we are convinced that, while there are no knock-down arguments that will neatly and neutrally settle the issues, the praise of God is not only rationally defensible but also rationally commendable.

Yet it is also clear that decisions in this area are not just taken through rational argument. The reality of God is an issue that involves every level of the self and the whole ecology of our social, intellectual and historical context. We are concerned to present a position that does justice to these dimensions. Different options in life will always call each other in question, and the life of praising and knowing God in its turn raises doubts about other ways of living. But the alternative to leading a life open to objection is not to live at all, and we do not want dealing with objections to overshadow the positive statement of our way. We will now restate this way in relation to the prevailing suspicion of it.

At present the 'conventional' wisdom of our society is certainly not that one's life should be based on the reality of God. The hypothesis that mostly operates in practice is that God is a human projection. This is omnicompetent to deal with all religious phenomena: it grants their reality but explains them in purely human terms. There is no strictly logical proof of this, but its practical acceptance has a host of important consequences. It leads to the living of a life that is in practice atheist. How can an alternative to this be posed? To argue that, on the contrary, God is Creator of man is not a very effective challenge. There is needed an alternative way of life in which this option is experienced. The activity in which this alternative is at its most drastic and explicit is praising God. If God is, then he is to be affirmed appropriately and appreciatively throughout the ecology of existence, and the truth, goodness and beauty of God are only likely to have a chance of becoming clear in the process of doing this. Above all, the joy of God needs to be celebrated as the central and embracing reality of the universe, and everything else seen in the light of this. So our way is an attempt to evoke a life which can take many forms but whose essence is that it lets God be God for us, in thought, feeling and practice.

Modes of Praise Today

Praise of God has its ramifications in a multiplicity of ways throughout reality, as later chapters try to show. Even the formal, explicit acts of praise in Christian churches have enormous diversity, and we will conclude this chapter with a brief survey of the main modes. We find four that seem fundamental, and they are best seen in two pairs.

WORD AND SACRAMENT

The first pair broadly correspond to word and sacrament. These represent two basic ways in which we relate to reality and are shaped by it: by language, and by our ability to appreciate and use things.

Language is not only a means of communication with others. We are intimately formed by it, we communicate with ourselves through it, and our capacities to think, remember, plan and hope are inseparable from it. Our very consciousness and identity, as individuals and groups, live through the medium of language. A large part of our reality (memory, values, intentions, knowledge, laws, government, culture, religion) is constituted by meaning, and most of that is embodied in language. We are in continual interplay with these and other forms of language. They are our world of meaning in which we have some freedom, and every day we contribute new events in thought and speech which in turn affect this world and ourselves as part of it. The phenomenon of language is so amazing that whole theories of human and divine nature are focused on it, and an enormous amount of energy is spent learning it, using it, reflecting on it, writing it, reading it, singing it and playing with it.

Praise of God is part of this life through language. Praise acknowledges God in his relation with creation, history, ourselves and the future, and through all that it stretches language to appreciate God himself. Language overflows, old expressions are renewed and filled with fresh meaning, and new expressions are inspired. Traditional language can give cups for meaning which are gradually filled up over the years as experience and knowledge grow and the key words and concepts (such as glory, salvation, holy, grace, cross, resurrection, Lord, wisdom, Spirit, love, confession, peace and many others) grow in content.

In the Christian Church word-centred praise is in line with the Jewish Synagogue worship that had such a great influence on Christianity. It focuses on the contents of the Bible, on preaching to stir response to the 'word of God', on prayer, and on psalms or hymns gathering all of this into praise. In the Catholic tradition in East and West, this was expressed both in the first part of the Eucharist and in the monastic offices. The Reformation saw a great renewal of it, especially in prophetic preaching. The aim of this was above all to glorify God by proclaiming what he has done, with the response expressed supremely in lives of thanks and praise. There was a fresh sense of freedom with God and this included a surge of musical creativity and hymn writing.

Singing is worth special comment as an instrument of praise. What does it do with the crucial Christian medium of words? It does with them what praise aims to do with the whole of reality: it takes them up into a transformed, heightened expression, yet without at all taking away their ordinary meaning. Language itself is transcended and its delights and power are intensified, and at the same time those who join in are bound together more strongly. So singing is a model of the way praise can take up ordinary life and transpose it to a higher level without losing what is good in other levels. The social power of music in general (for good or ill) is well known, and it moves at levels and in ways that nothing else can. It can also combine discipline and precision with great liberation of body, feeling and imagination, beautifully exemplifying the 'sober drunkenness' which the early Church saw as a true mark of being 'in the Spirit'.

The word-centred approach to God is at its most direct in prayer. In the best established division of prayer into five types, priority is given to the two which combine our theme: adoration and thanksgiving. From within the experience of adoration and thanks the relation of praise to the other three types becomes clear.

The third type of prayer after adoration and thanks is penitence. The praise-centred way of understanding penitence is to see sin as whatever hinders or prevents adoration, the highest communion with God. All the saints, the experts in adoration, have tended to become more aware of their sin as they go on, because as one gets involved in wholehearted appreciation of God one becomes more sensitive to 'wrong notes' and to everything that spoils the harmony of God's freedom with human freedom. The simplest and healthiest way of identifying sin is by giving oneself to praising God and then following through the consequences into every area of life: does it all please God or does it make the praise hypocritical? Praise can provoke a crisis in which one either gives up in despair at what one discovers about oneself or else lays out everything for forgiveness by God and so becomes able to go deeper into love and praise. Acceptance by God beyond the limits of self-acceptance is the new understanding that liberates self-forgetful praise.

This leads to the deeper connection between penitence and praise: because of the nature of God confession itself can glorify him, because it is made in the confidence of his forgiveness, and thanks for forgiveness is one of the strongest roots of praise. The classic expressions of those connections are in the Psalms, such as Psalms 51 and 103. In Christian history the outstanding example is

Augustine's *Confessions*, in which the original meaning and associations of 'confess' (to 'proclaim, glorify, praise'), are primary, and Augustine's own sins are confessed only to show the goodness of God. The whole book is addressed to God in praise, and sin is fundamentally the misery of not being one's real self, the frustration of one's deepest desires because one is not enjoying God:

> Can any praise be worthy of the Lord's majesty? How magnificent his strength! How inscrutable his wisdom! Man is one of your creatures, Lord, and his instinct is to praise you. He bears about him the mark of death, the sign of his own sin, to remind him that you 'thwart the proud'. But still, since he is part of your creation, he wishes to praise you. The thought of you stirs him so deeply that he cannot be content unless he praises you, because you made us for yourself and our hearts find no peace unless they rest in you (*Confessions*, Book 1).

After adoration, thanks and penitence comes the prayer of intercession for others. In this one tries to listen for what God's will is for a person and then ask for it. That is yet another example of the logic of overflow and non-necessity. Why bother to ask God for his will to be done? Could God not just do it himself? That line of questioning leads straight to the final one: why did God create at all and not just exist without it? The starting point from within the experience of praise is that God is essentially one who gives, shares, loves and encourages meaningful separate existence, so the logic of overflow, generosity and freedom is the very life of creation. Intercession is the giving of oneself, primarily in prayer but very often involving other follow-up, so that others may have their real needs and desires met. It involves believing that God's respect for human freedom can go so far as in some sense to put himself at the disposal of people's requests, and it is by no means out of line with this to see him having a will which respectfully waits on human asking and other co-operation.

There can be no better prayer for others in intercession than that they may come to praise and enjoy God more, and such prayer tends to spill over into praise itself both in anticipation and, on those occasions when the results of prayer are discerned, in thanks. This is the logic of overflow again, and it applies equally to the fifth and final type of prayer, petition. 'Even the prayer of demand is not truly prayer except in so far as it is also adoration' (Henri Brémond). Petition is a recognition of God as loving and involved in creation, and is a participation in the give and take which is the way creation works. Like intercession it is exercising the privilege of being a cause in a universe sustained by a God who respects our freedom and wants our discerning co-operation. This is not

'necessary' any more than the existence of the universe itself, but if
it is the way things are, then it is yet more material for praise.

The second great mode of praise is the sacramental. We look at
this first in its broad sense as the taking up of any aspect of the
material universe into being a sign or symbol of its Creator. Hopkins
celebrated this superbly:

> The world is charged with the grandeur of God.
> It will flame out, like shining from shook foil;
> It gathers to a greatness, like the ooze of oil
> Crushed . . .
> There lives the dearest freshness deep down things . . .
> Because the Holy Ghost over the bent
> World broods with warm breast and with ah! bright wings.[2]

He makes our point explicitly in 'Pied Beauty':

> Glory be to God for dappled things –
> For skies of couple-colour as a brinded cow;
> For rose-moles all in stipple upon trout that swim;
> Fresh-firecoal chestnut-falls; finches' wings:
> Landscape plotted and pieced – fold, fallow and plough;
> And all trades, their gear and tackle and trim.
> All things counter, original, spare, strange;
> Whatever is fickle, freckled (who knows how?)
> With swift, slow; sweet, sour; adazzle, dim;
> He fathers-forth whose beauty is past change:
> Praise him.[3]

A great deal of this book is about the sacramental in this wide
sense. We try to grasp how basic existence can be seen as praise
(chapter 4), how the negative experiences of evil, suffering and
death can be understood in this way (chapter 6), what sort of view
of God and the cosmos results (chapter 7) and what it means
for human responsibility and the future (chapters 8 and 9). The
sacramental concern is to enter into God's way of using and enjoying
his world. God uses all media to draw the universe into his network
of knowledge and love. In the sacramental, the media are both
appreciated in themselves and also as pointers to God. There is no
competition between the 'dappled things' and their deeper significance, or between respect for other people and the honouring of
God: matter and action are perfected in a new expressiveness. For
an existence immersed in the complexity of the interplay of word,
action and material reality, the habit of praise can proportion and

[2] 'God's Grandeur', op. cit.
[3] Ibid.

shape one's pattern of perception and response, so that one is both more likely to perceive and more free to respond appropriately and, perhaps, creatively.

Sacramental praise in the narrower sense is centred in the Eucharist (or Lord's Supper, or Mass, or Breaking of Bread, or Holy Communion). There is also the initiating sacrament of baptism as practised by most Churches, and the Catholic tradition officially recognizes five others – confirmation, confession, anointing of the sick, ordination and marriage. But the main focus is undoubtedly on the Eucharist, originating in Jesus' last meal with his disciples before his death. It has been celebrated with extremes of simplicity (even, by Quakers, subsumed into every meal eaten) and of elaborate ritual, and with a vast variety of interpretations. Is it to be seen mainly as an historical memorial, or in sacrificial terms, or as a sacrament of human fellowship, or as communion with the crucified and resurrected Lord, or as a source of spiritual energy?

We find all these in seeing it as the most distinctive Christian act of praise. At the heart of Christian praise is the relationship of Jesus with his Father, which John's Gospel sees as a mutual 'glorifying'. This is the explosive nuclear centre whose Spirit powers all praise, and at the centre of this nucleus is the death and resurrection of Jesus. The Eucharist allows participation in this death and life in a sacramental way (open to many interpretations) and imprints its pattern on all Christian praise. It takes up the main Old Testament forms of sacrifice (of thanks, communion and atonement) and focuses them through this historical event. Through the 'cup of blessing' the worshippers take part in the overflow of the mutual blessing of God and man. They remember a history, with the vital difference that the main character of this story is believed to be alive, present and communicating his life and words. And in all this the bonds between them are strengthened, in ways already suggested, with the praise of word and sacrament inextricably interwoven.

In recent years the Christian traditions of word-centred and more sacramental worship have been more open to respecting and learning from each other than they have been for centuries. Helped by major developments such as the Ecumenical Movement, the World Council of Churches, the Second Vatican Council and the flourishing of scholarship across the boundaries of denominations, there has been widespread liturgical renewal, new Protestant exploration and appreciation of sacraments, and Roman Catholic acceptance of many Reformation insights. But this peaceful progress is in danger if it ignores the disturbing contribution of the second two modes of praise.

SPONTANEITY AND SILENCE

1- Spontaneity

The second pair are spontaneity and silence. In the worship of the early Church, as reflected in the New Testament, it seems that, at least in some of the congregations, the celebration of the Lord's Supper, together with preaching, praise and the use of Scripture, were all embraced in free charismatic worship. Characteristic of this was spontaneous response to the stirring of the Holy Spirit, with various people contributing speaking in tongues, interpretations, prophecies, teaching, songs and various other gifts. It was some centuries before the eucharistic prayer was formalized rather than said extempore (though it always had certain obligatory elements). Everything points to a vigorous intensity of free praise in which all could participate. The novelty of Christianity in relation to Judaism was not just its belief that Jesus was the Messiah but also its claim that the Holy Spirit, quenched for centuries, had been poured out again. It was this which inspired fresh and spontaneous praise and proclamation, with evangelism as the horizontal dimension of praise – the content of praise repeated and explained to others so that they can join the community of praise. The Holy Spirit was for all Christians, and so there was bound to be a transformation of worship, as whole congregations reached a new level of free expression in praise and various gifts.

This mode has always been present in Christianity. Often it has been confined to private prayer, frequently it has flowered afresh in movements of revival and renewal, and it has been present in some form at the origins of many denominations. This century has seen it spread in unprecedented ways. The phenomenal growth of the Pentecostal Churches, and the influence of charismatic movements of renewal in traditional Churches have changed the face of world Christianity. What is offered is not an alternative to word and sacrament but a new life and power to both of these, with an atmosphere that actualizes the 'logic of overflow' in various ways: in the expectation that God will act and speak, in the freedom to express adoration in a wide range of bodily as well as verbal behaviour, in the physical contact between worshippers (kiss of peace, handshakes, holding hands, laying-on of hands), and in the exercise of various gifts. The gift most associated with Pentecostalism is speaking in tongues, and it is a good symbol of the movement.

One description of this is that it creates a 'cathedral of sound' in which to worship – the soaring of tongues, especially in singing, is a verbal rival to arches, stained glass and a hallowed place. Another description is as the 'sabbath of speech': when the tongue can run on, with no worry about making sentences, leaving the speaker free to concentrate on God – rather like the effect of Latin in the old

Roman Mass, or the Jesus Prayer in the East. One can also see it as a verbal abstract art, or the laughter of praise, or the babbling of babies, or a linguistic dance, or the weaving of a rich material (with interpretation as the dressmaking). But perhaps the most helpful approach is to see it as a sacrament of speech. It is physically embodied in sound, and, as in the definition of a sacrament, it is a sign that effects what it signifies. It signifies free speech in relation to God and received from God, and this is achieved (in faith) in the very act of speaking in tongues. It greatly helps in understanding classical Pentecostalism to see the sacramental affinities of speaking in tongues, for it is one of many ways in which the movement mediates between the Catholic and Protestant emphases. Character-istic of its mediation is not compromise but taking up both poles with greater intensity – in this case, the emphases on word and on sacrament.

We see the primary significance of Pentecostalism in its recovery of the authentic Christian impetus of praise. This has resulted both in new patterns of worship and evangelism, and also in the renewal of older patterns. As always, the power of the real thing is paralleled by awful examples of what its imitations and perversions can do. Yet the difficulties that have been facing it are mostly problems of life and growth rather than those of weariness and death, as is the case with much traditional worship. The often-used labels of 'enthusiasm', 'emotionalism' and suchlike should not be allowed to deceive those with no experience of mature praise in Pentecostalism. Good free worship always has a pattern and requires an immense amount of sensitivity, discipline, experience and preparation for it to ring true. It also requires deep roots in real life, and it is no accident that the origins of Pentecostalism are in the black slave Christianity of the U.S.A. Emotions are of course liberated in this worship, but as most musicians or artists will agree, the appropriate expression of feeling is one of the most demanding tasks.

Yet this should not let Pentecostalism be seen as just another pattern of worship. At its best it is distinctive by being able both to combine pattern and dispense with pattern. It revels in improvisa-tion, innovation, an ability to play with themes in the Bible or in music. It has 'the jazz factor' (and jazz has the same black American origins), which we develop later in the idea of something that is not order or disorder but what we call 'non-order'. This is a threat to much of the tradition, perhaps most of all because it demands trust both in God and in the worshippers as a group: anything might happen when freedom is granted; but if it is not, some of the most liberating and relevant activity of God is excluded.

The twin of spontaneity is the mode of silence. The experience of silence in worship is, by definition, hard to put into words. There are many qualities and levels of silence, just as there are of language and gesture, and good silence is at least as demanding as spontaneously expressive forms of worship. Often the two go together, and in world Christianity there are signs that just as the old divisiveness over word and sacrament is being healed in many Churches, so the difficulties over the relation of the charismatic to the contemplative are being solved in groups and individuals that value both. Early Quakerism is an example of the two combining with great power. Silence can be many things: an act of humble waiting and adoration that lets God have his way without hindrance; the necessary prelude to right hearing, or acting; the best way to follow hearing, speaking or acting; the excess or overflow of speech into amazed love, delight or conviction; the form of freedom best suited to let everyone in a group worship at his or her own level; a medium through which people are strongly bound to each other; and the ultimate in spiritual realism before a God who is simply beyond all we can say or do.

Only the Quakers have followed through such insights to the extent of having silence as the dominant feature of their public worship, and even they have lost much of the charismatic that was part of their origins. In the monastic tradition in both Eastern and Western Christianity there is also a wealth of experience of silence before God and its climax in adoration. This has worked like an underground stream down the centuries, penetrating and nourishing the Church far more deeply and widely than its usual hiddenness might suggest. It is also a tradition which by long experience has developed a wisdom in discerning and using the charismatic gifts of prayer. This confirms the proper partnership of spontaneity and silence. 'The quietude of jubilation' is Poulain's name for the state of prayer where both combine in praise. The two modes appear together frequently in other contexts in the mystical tradition and in numerous records of personal experience in prayer. In both Pentecostalism and the charismatic renewal in the historic Churches there is a similar convergence on the value of the interplay between silence and spontaneity.

The theological point in this is simple: God is free and one cannot make rules for how he may speak and act. Yet the complementary point is that God is faithful and consistent, the sort of God who takes part in liturgies as well. The further perspective that embraces both these is that God is above all to be praised, and that he is well able to guide individuals and communities as regards how to do so. This century has seen an unprecedented interplay of the four modes of word and sacrament, spontaneity and silence, but their awareness of each other in most Churches and beyond the Churches has hardly begun, let alone the immense possibilities for the full praise of God.

Face to Face

Finally, there is the matter of private, individual praise. Each of the four modes is relevant here – even the essentially communal Eucharist has always been surrounded by a variety of individual practices, whether in preparation or contemplation. The priority of the communal has usually been maintained, because even in private one is still a member of the Church and is affected by and affects the rest of the body. Yet the quality of one is deeply linked with that of the other and solitude is the only place where much of the training for and practice of praise can happen. There, certain features of Christian praise are clearest.

This is true especially of the interplay of intimacy and mystery. The structure of dialogue is central to the Judaeo-Christian knowledge of God, and the contents range all the way from 'Abba, Father' to 'Holy, Holy, Holy, Lord God of Hosts'. In private prayer the intimacy can be freer, more experimental and playful, less self-conscious, and more open to change of modes, moods and content. The awe and mystery may likewise be freer in form and content, and can unite with the homely in enjoyment of the presence of God: 'Heaven in ordinarie, man well-drest' (George Herbert). But the rigour can also be more intense in private, and the most important battles are fought there. The logic of sacrifice becomes unavoidable, and also the truth of suffering, sin and evil.

Above all, there is the model of the face-to-face relationship between the individual and God in Christ: 'For it is the God who said, "Let light shine out of darkness," who has shone in our hearts to give the light of the knowledge of the glory of God in the face of Christ' (2 Cor. 4:6). It is only possible to look into the eyes of one person at a time. That experience symbolizes love. There is a book of the Bible which concentrates on this: the Song of Songs. It is a love song, and its use through history demonstrates in extreme form the capacity of faith and love to take up and transform material into praise of God. The Song of Songs is full of the praise of lovers, and their ecstatic experience of mutual recognition, honour and delightful self-surrender. 'My beloved is mine and I am his' is the ultimate state in which praise in its fullest sense is the perfecting of perfection.

Summary of ch. 2

The Experience of Praising God

Praising God has been described in this chapter as participation in something with the logic of love, freedom, generosity, amazement and thanks, which is at the same time the most appropriate relationship with reality. It has been traced in some of its implications for the whole of experience, and seen as a way of life which explicitly and radically challenges a culture which lives in practical atheism. Its keynote always is to let God be God and to celebrate this, and it draws on the basic human capacities of speech, use of things, spontaneity and silence. All of these can interact in the explicit praise of the Christian community, and today they are in powerful new interplay, some of whose characteristics are explored in later chapters.

What idea of 'experience' can contain all this? A dynamic notion of experience is needed which can cope with constant development and openness while at the same time continually grasping afresh its basis and principles. Finding God and letting him be God changes a person's experience in cumulative ways. There is a constant but non-coercive making and re-making of the self in community, a new proportioning and energizing that at each stage opens up to further transformations.

This developing experience, which we view from the perspective of the praise of God, embraces intellect, will, feelings and imagination, as well as the social and corporate dimension of life. It poses critical questions in all these areas, some of which will be discussed in later chapters. It also has deep historical roots without which it dies. These are the subject of the next two chapters, in which the Bible and the centuries of Christian tradition are examined as living roots of praise today.

3

Past Praise Now: The Bible

The contents of the Bible are very varied. It can be read for its history, its language and literature, its world-views, its ethics, its religion, its sociology, its wisdom, its prophecy and much else. Some ways of approaching it catch more of its substance than others, though none can claim to be comprehensive. Our own key to interpreting it in this chapter (which is only the most concentrated instance of a use of the Bible that runs through other chapters too) is as a book primarily related to God and written by people who were engaged in praising him. It was produced in a context of active commitment to God over many centuries, so the dynamics of this relationship are vital for understanding it.

The fact of praise of God is a particularly good way of getting to the heart of the Bible because in praise there was the supreme attempt to acknowledge to God what was most fundamental for the community: God himself and his activity. The explicit praise of the Bible concentrates in itself what was most distinctive and important for Israel and, with the addition of the New Testament, for the Christian Church. Praise was the time of ultimate directness, of most active recognition of the presence and character of God.

This was not just stated but also acted out, using the body as well as mind and feelings. It also focused the whole of life: everything should be subject to this God, and nothing ought to be out of harmony with this praise. Praise is therefore the perfect vantage point on the whole, and contains in essence the characteristic patterns and structures informing the community. These are likely to have been the 'deep structures' through which the identity of the community was shaped over many years. We can also expect that major transformations in praising God will reward careful study, as they will probably express changes at the heart of the tradition.

Explicit praise is the symptom of something much deeper. The more the Bible is read with this in mind, the more the dimensions of its praise become clear. Praise of God is one of its formative principles, and the relationships of various elements are determined by their being taken up into the fundamental movement of response to God in worship. The many stories of God's involvement in

Israel's history are recorded as the material of praise and thanks; the lengthy regulations about holiness and ethics are intrinsically related to proper praise of God; even the Wisdom literature is pervaded by that complex relationship so inadequately translated as 'the fear of God', which is the attitude of worship; and most of the New Testament is about the new act of God in Jesus Christ, the content of fresh praise.

Add to all this the process of writing, collecting, testing, sifting and editing that went into the formation of the canon of Scripture as it slowly accumulated: all of that happened in communities permeated by praise, and aware of the distinctiveness of their relationship to God. In each generation the tradition was learnt and modified in the context of praise of God, and knowing God was inseparable from praising him.

Is there something simple at the heart of all this praise? Simplifying is a dangerous activity, but there will be no shortage of qualification and complexity in later chapters, so we risk asserting that the multiple forms and elements of praise do cluster around two key acts: recognition and respect. Because it is God who is being related to, the recognition and respect overflow into forms appropriate to their object – adoration, thanks, petition, delight, prophecy, obedience and much else. Yet the key to understanding the dynamic of praise is still in those two complementary acts.

Paul's Letter to the Philippians

We start with a document which shows the way in which praise of God through Christ is worked out at many levels of Christian existence. Philippians is perhaps Paul's last surviving letter, and it is a mature expression of his faith in concentrated form. Its chief themes are joy in the Lord, the glory of God, and the way of life that expresses those in faith, rejoicing, loving, honouring, thinking, suffering and practical living. In brief, it shows the transformation of an existence taken up into the praise of God.

'. . . through Jesus Christ, to the glory and praise of God' (Phil. 1:11). That is not just a conventional phrase to round off an introduction, but shows the relationship within which the Letter is written. It is one of astonished joy in God's glory seen, without qualification, in Christ. There is an other-directedness in this joy, an objectivity in its appreciation of God in Christ, and a knowledge of its basis and content, all of which are properly gathered up in praise. There is a constant overflow of 'prayer with joy' (1:4), thanks (1:5), hope (1:6), grace, thought and feeling (1:7f) and love, knowledge, discernment and righteousness (1:9ff). All of this, culminating in future perfection (1:10), Paul sees embraced in the glory and praise of God through Christ. He is describing a new level of existence which, as will become clearer as the Letter continues, is pervaded by communication with God and takes up all human faculties into its free movement of joy in him.

What about the awful things in life? These too can be taken up into joy when experienced through faith in the gospel. Paul talks of how his imprisonment has helped the gospel, and as he reflects on his own position he even rejoices (1:19). The reason is that he is confident that it is all a contribution to the glory of Christ, that 'now as always Christ will be honoured (magnified) in my body, whether by life or death'. This shows everything in Paul being drawn freely and joyfully into an event of powerful communication called the magnifying of Christ, over which Paul is not in control, but in which he has complete trust. The future he sees as either being with Christ in glory or serving the Philippians' 'progress and joy in the faith, so that in me you may have ample cause to glory in Christ Jesus, because of my coming to you again' (1:25f). The whole Letter reinforces this message that praise and joy are not optional extras in faith, but its very life, and that it is possible to grow in them through suffering (1:29f) as well as blessings.

The understanding of Christ in the past hundred years has perhaps been more deeply affected by Philippians 2:1–11 than by any other single text. It locks together the new content of Christian praise with the conduct of ordinary relationships. It begins with a statement of the depths of love and encouragement available in Christ and makes a passionate plea for the Philippians to shape their lives accordingly and so complete Paul's joy. Then in two verses Paul says what this involves. It amounts to an ethic of active recognition and respect which is the inter-personal counterpart of the praise of Christ which follows: 'Do nothing in selfishness or conceit, but in humility count others better than yourselves. Let each of you look not only to his own interests, but also to the interests of others' (2:3–4). This remarkable way of regarding other people sees the standpoint of equality, considering oneself on the same level as the other, as inadequate to describe what happens in relationships of goodness. Rather, there is always a looking up to the other, seeing oneself as at his or her service. Interpersonal space is seen as asymmetrical: the fundamental reality of the situation is that I must always look up to the other in service. There is a revolution of habitual understanding of ourselves and others here which Paul sees demanding a new sort of mind. It is not a matter of having a permanent inferiority complex; it is the privilege of taking part in God's own way of life:

> Have this mind among yourselves, which is yours in Christ Jesus, who, though he was in the form of God, did not count equality with God a thing to be grasped, but emptied himself, taking the form of a servant, being born in the likeness of men. And being found in human form he humbled himself, and became obedient unto death, even death on a cross (2:5–8).

This is the same transformation that Mark makes the pivot of his Gospel, the new astonishing form of God's glory in the world. It becomes the content of a praise, initiated by God, that is to be the supreme activity of all people:

> Therefore God has highly exalted him and bestowed on him the name which is above every name, that at the name of Jesus every knee should bow, in heaven and on earth and under the earth, and every tongue confess that Jesus Christ is Lord, to the glory of God the Father (2:9–11).

This is for Paul the new state of reality, in which Christians are anticipating that final crescendo of praise. It has happened through a new differentiation in God: one who could have been equal with God has gone one better! This does not mean that Jesus ends up higher or lower than his Father. Rather, it leads into a realm where the category of equality is inappropriate. It is replaced by the category of mutual honour or praise or exaltation or glorification. In this Christ gives up equality in obedience to his Father, but is then given supreme honour, which is yet all 'to the glory of God the Father'. This may be the least inappropriate way to talk of the life of God, reaching beyond the quantitative language of, for example, the subordinationist controversy in the early Church about the relative greatness of Father and Son. But Paul's concern here is for the conduct of ordinary life, and one way of putting his point is that he locks Christian ethics firmly into the life of praising God through Christ.

This is developed in the following two verses which have often been used in the perennial discussion of the problem of nature and grace: what is due to my efforts and what is due to God's grace? These verses state 'the paradox of grace', that common Christian experience that it is exactly when one's own freedom is being exercised to the full that one most clearly recognizes one's complete dependence on God. 'Work out your own salvation in fear and trembling' (v. 12) but also 'for God is at work in you, both to will and to work for his good pleasure' (v. 13). What is not usually remarked about these verses, however, is the way they are both shot through with the reality of praise. 'Fear and trembling' is the response to the presence of God in worship. 'For his good pleasure' is not just a conventional phrase but expresses the overflowing of life in the Spirit, the delight in being pleasing to God which becomes the main motive for being and praising, the quintessence of joy. Something becomes reality in this wholehearted other-directedness, and Paul calls it 'your salvation'. The lesson for the controversy over nature and grace is that there is an approach through the concept of praise which is interpersonal in a way appropriate to both ourselves and God. This helps us to conceive of a non-competitive, wholly derivative, yet fully personal relationship of our freedom to God's through consideration of the mutual pleasure of praise.

Paul's next concern is for the purity of communication of the good news that gives such joy. Personal life and the use of the tongue are to conform with the gospel, so as to enable the supreme joy of mutual honour and glory 'in the day of Christ' (2:16). But the way to this is according to the pattern of Christ – there is a radical self-emptying as the condition of glory, and Paul uses the language of temple sacrificial worship and four times repeated rejoicing to give the meaning of his life:

> Even if I am to be poured out as a libation upon the sacrificial offering of your faith, I am glad and rejoice with you all. Likewise you also should be glad and rejoice with me (2:17–18).

The theme of joy and honour continues through the Christian family news of the rest of the chapter, and is repeated at the start of chapter 3: 'Finally, my brethren, rejoice in the Lord'. It leads into some hard-hitting controversy about the necessity for circumcision. Paul's case against it is based on the new content of Christian worship:

> For we are the true circumcision, who worship God in spirit, and glory in Christ Jesus, and put no confidence in the flesh (3:3).

Paul supports his point by telling of how he himself experienced the transformation of what he gloried in. It used to be religion, race, zeal for the law and moral blamelessness, but all that became worthless to him because of 'the surpassing worth of knowing Christ Jesus my Lord' (3:8). This overflow of knowledge, to participate in which it is worth leaving everything that has given meaning to life to date, is yet another way into understanding the new life of joy in Christ. It is not any intrinsic defect in what he has given up that is Paul's point, but the transformation of self in trust and praise due to recognizing someone who is worthy of all trust and praise.

This gives a new angle on one of the toughest problems of Christian history, the relationship between law and faith in Christ. Paul talks of being found in Christ, 'not having righteousness of my own, based on law, but that which is through faith in Christ, the

righteousness from God that depends on faith' (3:9). The parallel
to 'faith in Christ' is 'glorying in Christ' (3:3). Faith is the transformation of our lives through response to a new object of praise. The
content of that object is a person who has completely pleased God,
has been proved righteous, fulfilling the law, has been resurrected
from death, and who shares his life with those who glory in him. The
new life is therefore one of trust and praise (inseparably intertwined
because of the nature of Christ, righteous and glorified), and
overflowing in love (cf. Phil 1:9ff where overflowing love is linked
with the fruits of righteousness and the glory and praise of God).
There is also a reiteration of the theme of suffering in conformity
with the focus of praise:

> that I may know him and the power of his resurrection and may
> share his sufferings, becoming like him in his death, that if
> possible I may obtain the resurrection from the dead (3:10–11).

That an apparently miserable existence can be one of joy is the
measure of the power that flows through the channel of faith and
praise of Christ. In short, there is a relationship in which this power
and joy are available, and it is that of glorifying Christ.

This relationship is one of growth and progress, and Paul is aware
how far he himself has to go 'pressing on', 'straining forward'. Yet
even in this the stress is on the fundamental reality of the prior
action of God which can only be praised – he presses on 'because
Christ Jesus has made me his own' (3:12). The growth happens
in the orientation of worship, towards the 'upward call of God in
Christ Jesus', and the basic fact is that 'our commonwealth is in
heaven, and from it we await a saviour, the Lord Jesus Christ, who
will change our lowly body to be like his glorious body, by the
power which enables him even to subject all things to himself'
(3:20f). That is the culmination of chapter 3, and it completes the
new setting of the concept of righteousness, which we can now see
as just one way Paul has of pointing to the worth of the glorified
Christ. The life of faith is therefore a matter of setting one's mind
where praise is the natural language (heaven), and allowing one's
whole life to be transformed accordingly. Paul contrasts this with
those who 'live as enemies of the cross of Christ' (3:18). This seems
to mean a life that refuses the transformation of sin and suffering
offered by Christ to those who glory in him. The mark of this
rejection is the orientation of their minds ('set on earthly things',
3:19), focusing the energy of their capacity to praise on the wrong
objects: 'their God is their belly and they glory in their shame'
(3:19).

The theme of praise and trust is gathered up in chapter 4 in a
series of exhortations and a promise. 'Rejoice' (4:4) is the keynote,

and the forbearance, lack of anxiety and prayer that Paul encourages, could be seen as being born in that rejoicing rather than its presupposition. The promise attached to this way of living is that the peace of God which passes understanding will keep their minds and hearts in Christ Jesus. The life of rejoicing in the Lord is here seen as resulting in a stable condition of the whole self in which hearts and minds have their proper environment for flourishing. It is not a condition that can be grasped or controlled by the mind, but one in which the mind is stretched to capacity in joyful exercise and still surpassed, because its object is God. The otherness of God is here stated absolutely, but not as a threat or discouragement in the use of the mind. Rather, rejoicing in the Lord and appreciating his glory is the only safe context for full and free intellectual and emotional life. The remarkable verse which follows is explicit about this. It describes the activity of the mind that lives by praise. It meditates on truth, goodness and beauty, with the emphasis on those things which embrace truth and goodness in the delight of beauty, and which help us to develop our capacity to appreciate, to honour and to praise:

> Whatever is pure, whatever is lovely, whatever is gracious, if there is any excellence, if there is anything worthy of praise, think about these things (4:8).

The action accompanying the thinking is imitation of and obedience to Paul, and the promise is again added: 'the God of peace will be with you' (4:9).

Paul goes on to show how life in Christ transforms his material existence. He has learnt to be content, whether he has much or little. 'Contentment' is a Stoic concept, and Paul's use of it in this Letter is a good example of the thorough 'baptism' of a term. To the Stoics it meant a contentment and self-sufficiency that expressed indifference (*apatheia*) in the face of the world and history. Even if this attitude can be more richly understood, it certainly could not accommodate the life of praise and rejoicing that Paul has been encouraging and living. Paul's contentment is possible because in a basic existence of praise he receives blessing and strength: 'I can do all things in him who strengthens me' (4:13). Praise, joy in the Lord, is the mediation through which he faces ordinary life and suffering. Paul is talking about what makes him a powerful person and it is something more basic than a human capacity or the energy that comes from food or even the love and fellowship of other Christians in his suffering. The latter point is important, because not even the best human relationship is sufficient. The language Paul uses here has many resonances with contemporary accounts of what was considered the ideal relationship: friendship. But Paul's

gratitude to the Philippians makes clear that, while he was touched
by their generosity, the secret of his mission is not their assistance.
This recognition of the sheer superfluity of their action lets him give
it its true meaning:

> Not that I seek the gift; but I seek the fruit which increases to
> your credit. . . The gifts you sent are a fragrant offering, a sacrifice
> acceptable and pleasing to God. And my God will supply every
> need of yours according to his riches in glory in Christ Jesus. To
> our God and Father be glory for ever and ever. Amen. (4:17–20)

The meaning of the gift is its place in the ecology of praise, honour
and blessing. There is a new level of exchange and coinherence
marked by the beauty of reciprocal pleasure and joy, always
overflowing in new expressions and gifts. This for Paul is real life,
the life of faith.

Some greetings and a blessing conclude the Letter, and we are
now in a better position to understand something of the implications
of 'the grace of the Lord Jesus Christ' being 'with your Spirit'
(4:23). What were suggested above as the two key acts of recognition
and respect have been worked out in terms of the knowledge of God
through Jesus Christ on the one hand, and, on the other, the joyful
movement of honouring, glorifying, obeying and trusting.

The Gospel of Mark

Philippians is mainly concerned with the practical working out of
the gospel in one situation in the early Church. It takes for granted
that the gospel has already been communicated, and that the initial
recognition and acceptance of Jesus as Lord has happened. Its focus
is more on the existence that springs from the recognition of faith
rather than on the content of recognition itself. As time went on,
the Church spread, the oral tradition became less reliable, and there
was an increasing need for generally accepted accounts identifying
who Jesus Christ was. The Gospels were written to meet this need,
among others. There is a complex history behind them, and each
is distinctive in many ways. We will take for granted much New
Testament scholarship in our approach, and examine what is probably the earliest Gospel, that of Mark, in order to give an example
of interpretation in the light of the praise of God. There are many
further questions that would need to be raised if this were a book
of scholarly interpretation, not least regarding the theory of
hermeneutics (interpretation) that informs our approach, but the
aim here is to practise interpretation with one limited aim rather
than develop the theoretical backing.

Mark's first sentence indicates how basic for his whole work are recognition and respect for Jesus:'This is the Gospel of Jesus Christ, the Son of God.' He goes on to make clear the dimensions of what he is treating: John the Baptist announces the fulfilment of the greatest expectations of the Old Testament, and the baptism of Jesus shows the recognition of him as Son of God, the focus of the Father and his Spirit. So the Gospel starts simultaneously from 'above' and 'below', the thrust of Israel's history and the present action of God meeting in this man's life. Evil is concentrated here too, in the temptation of Jesus, and so we have right at the start the main elements in the transformation that follows: God, Jesus, the history of Israel, and evil. One way of seeing what happens next is in terms of an information explosion, taking information in the broad sense of words, acts or experiences that are communicated and received. Mark is fascinated by the reactions to Jesus and describes the network of communication and misunderstanding. Jesus announces 'the Gospel of God'. 'The time is fulfilled and the Kingdom of God is at hand; repent, and believe the Gospel' (1:15). During the rest of his ministry Jesus does all he can to communicate his message in a combination of teaching, healing, controversy and various activities, but he fights a losing battle for the right sort of recognition.

The rest of the first chapter tells first of the call of some of the disciples, who will be key figures in the process of communication and misunderstanding, and then gives a series of stories of teaching and healing. The reactions to these show the force of the information explosion: 'astonished', 'amazed', 'a new teaching', 'everyone is searching for you'. But there is also a questioning of it by Jesus, who tries to restrain it: 'say nothing to anyone' (v. 44). There is need for a deeper level than miracles, and the next chapter gives it; the paralytic has his sins forgiven before being healed, and Jesus suggests that the forgiveness is more difficult. This not only deepens the message, it heightens speculation about Jesus himself: 'Who can forgive sins but God alone?' (2:7). The result is a new level of astonishment and this time 'they were all amazed and glorified God'. There is also a question of deeper levels in the new form of communication Jesus uses in chapter 4, parables: their imagery of seeds multiplying, light shining, mustard seed growing, is that of an information explosion, but the vital question is the quality of response (4:10–12).

The parables are followed by a series of astounding new events, with the responses evoked. There are the calming of a storm ('filled with awe', 'Who is this?', 4:4l), the wildest demoniac calmed and in his right mind ('and all men marvelled', 5:42), five thousand fed, walking on water ('utterly astounded', 6:5l), and healing after

healing on an ever vaster scale ('village, cities or country. . .', 6:56).
Parallel with this is astonishment at his teaching (6:2) and misunderstanding or hostility. At best, Jesus had elicited an uncom-
prehending amazement which occasionally led to praise of God.

Then comes the climax of the Gospel in chapters 8 and 9. The
two sides of amazed acknowledgement of Jesus and drastic misunderstanding are intensified at the centre of his closest circle by
Peter's 'You are the Christ', which is followed by his rejection of
Jesus' talk of the necessity of suffering, and Jesus' reply: 'Get thee
behind me, Satan! For you are not on the side of God, but of
men.' Mark makes it quite clear: suffering is the new element to be
embraced if Jesus is to be appreciated. This is the heart of the
transformation of recognition and respect which gives a new content
to praise. The discipleship that Mark goes on to describe is one in
which denial of self, taking up one's cross, following Jesus, losing
one's life and never being ashamed of Jesus and his words are
inseparable from a right relation to the glory of God (9:38). The
way to acknowledge God is that of the cross, and the very concept
of God's glory is thus transformed.

It is only after this that Mark tells of the transfiguration, the
climactic event of Jesus' ministry. As Jesus, isolated in his mission
even from the understanding of his closest friends, prepares to go
on with it, we are given, as in chapter 1, a reminder of his true
network of communication and support – the law and prophets of
the Old Testament, represented by Moses and Elijah, and God
himself. We also are told of his own glory in dazzling clothes and
face. This simultaneous affirmation by inspired witnesses of the
glory of Jesus and of the Father has remained at the heart of
Christian praise.

The rest of the Gospel shows the working-out of this glory through
suffering and death. The disciples go to Jerusalem caught up in
fearful amazement (10:32). The entry to Jerusalem has an outburst
of recognition and praise, ironic in view of what was to follow.
There is an intensifying of conflict and misunderstanding in chapter
12 and an ascesis of thought that invites us to think of things from
God's viewpoint. In chapter 13 there is a vision of discipleship that
faces up to the worst that is to come, and then in chapter 14 the
focus is on the person of Jesus himself. The woman who 'wasted'
her alabaster jar of ointment by breaking it open and pouring it
over Jesus' head is one of the archetypal images of the essence of
praise as recognition and sacrificial honouring. Jesus accepts it with
a reference to his death, which will justify it. The story of the Last
Supper takes the concentration on Jesus and his Body yet further
while also intensifying his representative reality ('poured out for
many', 14:24, cf. 'ransom for many', 10:45). This event centring on

this person is to be universalized by re-enactment, without losing its particularity.

The description of the Last Supper is flanked by two passages which stress the isolation of Jesus. The first is his prophecy of his betrayal by Judas, the second his prophecy of his denial by Peter. In these final days of his life, when the events happen through which Jesus is to be most decisively identified and recognized, Mark shows a process of isolation, which is completed in the Garden of Gethsemane. Gethsemane repeats the transfiguration, but now in the mode of suffering. There is the same concentration on Jesus and his Father simultaneously, which Mark now underlines by giving his only recorded words of Jesus in prayer, and using the intimate 'Abba'. After all the complexity of Jesus' ministry, the astonishing events, the confused and hostile reactions, and the disappointments, there is now the simplicity of one symbol, the cup of suffering, and one repeated prayer: 'Abba, Father, all things are possible to thee; remove this cup from me; yet not what I will, but what thou wilt' (14:36).

The final knot of suffering and glory is about to be tied by Jesus' own death. The 'above' and 'below' are also tied together in a piece of history that includes the worst that can happen 'below' – physical, social and spiritual suffering, and death. The unity of will between Jesus and his Father means that attention to these events is attention to the working-out of God's will. There is a new knowledge of God that is being enacted through Jesus. It breaks through the categories of 'Messiah', 'law', 'king', 'prophet'; it hinges on the necessity of suffering and death which has already scandalized Peter; but the strangeness of the suffering and death is equalled by the strangeness of its sequel. This double extraordinariness is highlighted in the crucifixion narrative by Jesus' cry from the cross, and in the sequel by the puzzle of the Gospel's ending.

And at the ninth hour Jesus cried with a loud voice, 'Eloi, Eloi, lama sabachthani?' which means, 'My God, my God, why hast thou forsaken me?' (15:34).

Jesus is quoting the opening verse of Psalm 22. Are we meant to take it by itself, or to assume the rest of the psalm, in which God acts to save the Psalmist and is thanked in powerful praise?

The afflicted shall eat and be satisfied;
those who seek him shall praise the Lord!
May your hearts live for ever! (Ps. 22:26).

Even in itself the cry is still to God, with the sort of agonized faith so often found in the Psalms. In faith it represents the maximum of tension within the unity of wills affirmed in Gethsemane, and it raises the sort of questions about the relation of God, Jesus and death that we follow up in chapters 4–8. Yet the content of the rest of Psalm 22 can hardly be irrelevant in view of the other echoes of it in the same chapter (15:24 from Ps. 22:18; 15:29 from Ps. 22:7) and the sequel of resurrection. In giving this as the only 'word from the cross' Mark is offering a context for interpreting the climax of his story: the context of praise of God in the face of suffering and death.

The ending of the Gospel is a perennial problem for scholars, as the best manuscripts close abruptly at 16:8. Yet that sudden ending could well be Mark's own, and we side with those scholars who think so. It is not the only puzzle in the Gospel, and the rather smooth account given above has deliberately not drawn attention to the awkward features. Gathering them together now, we see how enigmatic a story it is. The very sequence of Mark's narrative is jerky, discontinuous, with sudden, abrupt transitions of time and place. He inserts apparently superfluous details and incidents – as in the account of John the Baptist's death through Salome's dancing, or the second feeding of the crowd, or the youth who ran away naked after Jesus' arrest. He includes awkward details like Jesus' family thinking him mad, or Jesus not being able to do mighty works in his home town. Mark's interpreters since then, beginning with the authors of the other Synoptic Gospels, have often tried to soften such jagged edges.

More deeply, there is the theme of secrecy, with Jesus not wanting universal publicity and recognition, yet on the other hand telling the Gerasene demoniac to spread his news, and at his own trial identifying himself unambiguously as the Messiah (14:62). At the heart of his teaching in parables lies the offensive statement:

> To you has been given the secret of the kingdom of God, but for those outside everything is in parables; so that they may indeed see but not perceive, and may indeed hear but not understand, lest they should turn again and be forgiven (4:11f).

There is also the stark, unexplained, treachery of Judas, and the extreme emphasis throughout on the obtuseness and stupidity of the other disciples. Then, finally, there is the ending at 16:8:

> And they went out and fled from the tomb, for trembling and astonishment (*ekstasis*) had come upon them; and they said nothing to anyone, for they were afraid.

Three women had arrived at the tomb and met a young man dressed in white. 'They were amazed', and were told that the crucified Jesus is risen, and that he is going ahead into Galilee where Peter and the disciples are to meet him. Their response of scattering, astonishment, silence and fear underlines the transcendent strangeness of what had happened, crowning the accumulated enigmas of the Gospel.

In the context of praise, how can this ending be understood? Mark has written a Gospel which has continually shown Jesus as one who breaks out of categories in an amazing and puzzling way, Trocmé sees in Mark a 'Christology of awe', and this reaches its greatest intensity in the final verses. Mark knew how the resurrection had produced a colossal explosion of praise and evangelism, informing many new communities. In his ending he describes its initial trigger: there is the news of the resurrection of Jesus and the promise of a future meeting in which the disciples could recognize him; and there is the physical, mental and emotional response of the women in their amazement. Here is the nerve-centre of Christian praise and preaching: recognition and awe-filled wonder. In the way he has told his story, especially in the transfiguration sequence and in the events from the Last Supper through Gethsemane to Easter, Mark has portrayed a network of relations which he wants to imprint on all Christian praise, preaching and discipleship. Crucial to that network is appreciation of the glory of Jesus as suffering and resurrected Messiah. It is a story deeply disorienting to ordinary perspectives. Mark is acutely aware of the newness, the overflow of previous forms, the challenging discontinuity and sheer surprise. His style embodies this, and he does not pretend that the story is smooth and unpuzzling. Above all, his grasp of the dazzling event with which it ends is meant to encourage his readers to live from this new reality and never to accept its domestication or to dissociate it from *ekstasis*.

Old Testament Praise

The Psalms, which have already appeared at one crucial moment of Mark's Gospel (and are referred to there at other critical points too, as in Jesus' baptism and transfiguration), have played a remarkable role in Christianity. Perhaps no other book of the Bible, in the Old or the New Testament, has been used more by Christians down the centuries. The Psalms have been the main way in which the Old Testament has permeated the Church. This has shown a deep instinct for the most vital continuity of the tradition, in its praise of God. The New Testament itself is shot through with references to and echoes of the Psalms. The renewals of the Church have usually set new music to Psalms and patterned new songs on them. Most of the great Christian teachers have devoted much energy to expounding as well as singing the Psalms. Origen, Chrysostom, Augustine, Thomas Aquinas, Luther and Calvin are together in this. It is no accident that in each of them lifelong use and interpretation of the Psalms went together with passionate wrestling with key doctrines and the knowledge of God. Aquinas even said that the Psalms contain all theology in the mode of praise.

What is the secret of the Psalms? Partly it is that of great art and literature, the ability to express what is of deep and universal interest through particulars. The Psalms use fairly simple means with great effect: balancing of sense in a twofold parallel pattern; suspense, emphasis, tempo and contrast; and concentration on strong and clear traditional images with a wide resonance in experience. Stories are one of the most effective and universal ways of communicating across barriers of time and culture and the Psalms constantly tell or refer to the foundational stories of their tradition, such as creation, the covenant, the exodus from Egypt, the founding of Israel's worship and events of the Davidic kingship. This framework is united with a wide range of basic human concerns and feelings, individual as well as communal, so that most people most of the time can find something in the Psalms that reflects their condition. But beyond all that is the fact that the Psalms are classic expressions of the lively intensity of praise of God. They offer above all a vehicle for realistic but jubilant joy in God, taking up the good and the bad into a faith that always (even if it takes a struggle) results in praise of God.

The worship in which such praise first developed is worth investigation. Some of the most exciting Old Testament scholarly discoveries of this century have been about Israelite worship. We will take just two aspects which are both fascinating in themselves and also of relevance today.

FESTIVAL PRAISE

During the period in which the Old Testament was written, the main way in which worship of Yahweh shaped its life year after year was through what scholars call 'the cult', the complex of festivals, customs, sacrifices, prophecy and special personnel that made up the public performance of worship of Yahweh. As a more complete picture of the cult has been pieced together it has become clear that it was a far more pervasive influence on the Old Testament than was previously thought. The festivals were the most important times of the year, especially the three main ones (Passover, Festival of Weeks, and Tabernacles), and through them the central stories, laws, traditions and practices were brought to bear, often in dramatic form, on the formation of Israel's distinctive identity.

That identity was most deeply structured by the covenant of

Yahweh with Israel. A great deal of Israel's mode of worship was borrowed from or held in common with other religions and cultures. The crucial role of the covenant was as the dynamic pattern and content which transformed such material into worship of Yahweh alone. This process of creative transformation has been a major area of historical study in the past century, with the three main festivals themselves as prime examples of how largely agriculture and fertility celebrations were taken up into a new religious and cultural ecology informed by the covenant.

The covenant itself in its most influential form, as associated with Moses and the law given during the exodus from Egypt, was the basic relationship of mutual recognition and commitment between Yahweh and Israel. It is worth examining the ten commandments as given in Exodus 20 to see how intrinsic to the covenant were worship and its key acts.

The passage begins:

I am the Lord your God, who brought you out of the land of Egypt, out of the house of bondage.

Crucial information is concentrated in that sentence. The 'I am' points to a God who is personal and who introduces himself to people. The reference to the exodus shows a God who takes initiatives, acts in particular ways in history, and has a moral concern – Israel was constantly reminded by her prophets of Yahweh's concern for the oppressed. The sentence simultaneously expresses the identity of Yahweh and Israel; Yahweh is known through the events which formed Israel as a nation.

After this basic act of recognition in the form of a summarized story, the ten commandments give the archetypal pattern of respect for God and for other people. First there is the absolute priority of worshipping only Yahweh. This inclusive respect as God which is demanded by Yahweh is reinforced by the forbidding of images and the guarding of the name of Yahweh. Imageless religion was a revolutionary principle liberating worship towards a transcendent, active and moral God, always 'beyond' even while present. Next comes the law of the Sabbath, ordering the regularities of time around Yahweh and especially around appreciation of him as Creator. Finally, the complement of proper respect for Yahweh is presented as an ethic of respect for parents, for life, for marriage and for property. The rest of the chapter focuses on the awesomeness of Yahweh on the mountain where the commandments were given, and on regulating the central act of worship: sacrifice.

Exodus 20 gives the essence of the covenant, which could be expanded almost indefinitely as its implications were spelled out, as in the Book of Deuteronomy. It was not inflexible, and part of its power as a principle for worship was that it enabled confident adaptation of new material and response to new situations.

The emergence of the monarchy under Saul, David and Solomon was the occasion for important changes in the cult. The temple was built in Jerusalem, and the king became a major participant in the ceremonies and festivals. This was the most creative period in Israel's worship. It is now recognized that most of the Psalms were composed during the monarchy and had their settings in the major festivals. So the generative matrix of these powerful songs was structured by the covenant (as accommodated to the monarchy), and filled with energetic worship. At that festival there were acts of purification, dramas of God's victory over his enemies and his testing of and support for the king, recitals of important aspects of the covenant, and sacrifices (representing the costly giving that worship involves) which expressed key aspects of the covenant relationship such as praise and thanks, atonement and reconciliation. Worshippers were deeply involved physically, in washing, dancing, shouting, prostration, clapping, singing and feasting. It was an experience with many dimensions, rich and concentrated, and in the Psalms it was distilled yet further into poetry.

These origins give to the Psalms a vital element in their effectiveness through the centuries. Just because they sprang from such vivid, many-levelled worship, later in new situations they have constantly encouraged worshippers to take up their whole selves and communities into praise. Psalm 47, for example, had a precise setting in the festival at each new year. It is the ecstatically joyful acclamation of Yahweh coming among the worshippers with power and salvation. Yet it is easy to see how it can transcend that setting and lead generation after generation of Jews and Christians into fresh praise:

All peoples, clap their hands,
acclaim God with jubilant cries!
For Yahweh is manifest as the Most High, inspiring awe,
The supreme King over all the earth . . .
God has ascended with acclamation,
Yahweh with the noise of horns,
Play and sing to God, play and sing,
Play and sing to our King, play and sing!
To the King indeed of all the world,
to God triumphant play and sing!
God has become King over the nations,
God now sits on his holy throne.[1]

[1] Psalm 47, as translated by John Eaton in *Vision in Worship: The Relation of Prophecy and Liturgy in the Old Testament* (London 1981), p. 3.

In these ancient festivals was born a vision of exultation that takes up all of life and creation into the celebration of Yahweh:

Splendour and majesty shine before him,
Glory and beauty are in his sanctuary,
Attribute to Yahweh, clans of the peoples,
Attribute to Yahweh the glory of his name,
bear gifts and enter his courts,
fall down before Yahweh in his divine majesty!
Dance because of him, all the world,
declare among the nations, Yahweh reigns!
So the world is secured and will not totter,
he rules the peoples with justice.
Let heaven make merry and earth rejoice,
let the sea thunder and all that lives in it,
the fields exult and all that is in them,
let trees sing out, all the trees of the forest,
before Yahweh, for he has entered,
he has come to rule the earth.
He rules the world with right order,
the peoples in his faithfulness.[2]

Such hymns set a horizon of praise which has never been transcended. Within it, all worship and theology are stretched beyond their capacity.

PRAISE AND PROPHECY

The reconstruction of the festivals of Israel has not only let us more fully understand the Psalms through the worship they sprang from and inspired; there has also been a set of findings which show the extent to which dramatic, prophetic interaction between Yahweh and Israel was part of this worship. It makes sense that with Yahweh present in special power he should not be characterized only by past words and acts. The prophets were the charismatic men and women who had the gift of intimacy with Yahweh. Prophecy grew from within the liturgy, interpreting its message and relating it to the present situation. Prophets in the festivals spoke on behalf of Yahweh – warning, encouraging, instructing, inspiring – and also on behalf of the people in intercession and petition.

The Psalms are full of prophecies, the address of God to the people. In Psalm 50, for example, there is a statement of the ethical implications of worshipping Yahweh that sums up much of the teaching of the great prophets:

[2]   Psalm 96, ibid.

Hear, O my people, and I will speak,
  O Israel, I will testify against you,
  I am God, your God.
I do not reprove you for your sacrifices:
  your burnt offerings are continually before me.
I will accept no bull from your house
  nor he-goat from your folds.
For every beast of the forest is mine,
  the cattle on a thousand hills . . .
Offer to God a sacrifice of thanksgiving,
  and pay your vows to the Most High;
and call upon me in the day of trouble;
  I will deliver you, and you shall glorify me . . .
  What right have you to recite my statutes,
  or take my covenant on your lips?
For you hate discipline,
  and you cast my words behind you.
If you see a thief, you are a friend of his;
  and you keep company with adulterers . . .
Mark this, then, you who forget God,
  lest I rend, and there be none to deliver!
He who brings thanksgiving as his sacrifice honours me;
  to him who orders his way aright
  I will show the salvation of God! (Psalm 50:7–23).

That passage, which can be paralleled by many others in Psalms and prophets, shows how prophecy guarded the covenant and championed the holiness and sovereignty of Yahweh. Yet in the face of the common misunderstanding that prophets were in opposition to priests and the cult, the evidence points to a definite role for prophecy in the cult. The prophet is typically one who is so taken up into worship and the vision that is given by God in it that he acts as a spokesman for God to the people and for the people to God.[3] If the cult and its participants have gone wrong then there is of course a confrontation between them and the prophet, but the issue is about what is pleasing to God, not about the cult as such.

So one basic point about prophecy is its inseparability from the covenant and its worship, and we will take this up in a Christian context in chapters 4 and 9. Yet the truth in the misunderstanding of prophecy as being in opposition to the cult is that, given who Yahweh was, and the tendency of religion to try to tame its gods, there was almost bound to be frequent tension. The very nature of Yahweh as a great God who frees the oppressed, who cannot be identified with any image, and who created and rules everything,

[3] cf. John Eaton, op. cit.

placed him in tension with any attempt to domesticate him in the cult. The prophets, especially at times of national crisis when the people wanted comfort and encouragement more than anything, accentuated this tension by stressing the independence of Yahweh from the cult.

This was a crucial development. The prophets showed the consequences of what Psalm 96 stated so clearly, that Yahweh is both good and Creator of all. They enlarged the conception of Yahweh and his concerns, and laid the basis for a universal, spiritual and ethical religion which could survive the Jerusalem-centred cult. This new future without temple or sacrifices, for which they laid the foundation, was able to use the Psalms of the festivals even more widely and influentially than when they had been tied to the cult.

BEYOND THE CULT

How could praise of Yahweh survive the cult? This was a fundamental issue posed by the destruction of the temple and of Jerusalem by the Babylonians under Nebuchadrezzar in 587 B.C., and by the exile of many of the inhabitants in Babylon.

> By the waters of Babylon, there we sat down
>   and wept. . .
> How shall we sing the Lord's song in a foreign
>   land? (Ps. 137:1,4).

The future lay with those who could creatively come through the crisis. One result was Isaiah 40–55, the supreme literature of praise and hope in Yahweh. These chapters are usually called Second or Deutero-Isaiah. They are in the tradition begun by the original Isaiah who wrote most of chapters 1–39, and show that school of prophecy responding to the unprecedented challenge of national disaster and exile.

Deutero-Isaiah shows the inspired surpassing of itself by the tradition of Israel. He takes up the basic themes of creation, exodus, covenant and cult and reworks them all prophetically. The focus is firmly on Yahweh and what he says. Knowledge of God is proclaimed as the basic answer to the crisis. 'I am the Lord and there is no other' is repeated with many variations. The issue is proper recognition of Yahweh:

> My glory will I not give to another,
> Hearken to me, O Jacob,
>   and Israel, whom I called!
> I am he, I am the first,
>   and I am the last.
> My hand laid the foundation of the earth . . . (Isa. 48:11f).

It is a reaffirmation of Israel's life and identity centred on knowing God and listening to him. At the heart of the message is that this God does new things, he surpasses previous liberations. Using the imagery of the exodus, Deutero-Isaiah describes the Lord as one 'who makes a way in the sea, a path in the mighty waters', and continues:

> Remember not the former things,
>   nor consider the things of old.
> Behold, I am doing a new thing;
>   now it springs forth, do you not perceive it?
> I will make a way in the wilderness and
>   rivers in the desert . . . (Isa. 43:16, 18f.).

The purpose of this is

> that they may declare my praise (Isa. 43:21),

and Deutero-Isaiah in anticipation offers unparalleled praise.

The middle term between the knowledge and the praise of God is that of salvation:

> Turn to me and be saved,
>   all the ends of the earth!
>   For I am God, and there is no other . . .
> To me every knee shall bow,
>   every tongue shall swear (Isa. 45:22f; cf. Phil. 2:10f).

Salvation involves recognition of sin and going to the root of it. Deutero-Isaiah's praise is equalled by the sharpness of his insight into evil and sin. His hope and joy carry a call to repentance too, since otherwise it would not be this God who is acknowledged. The all-encompassing promise is of joy instead of shame (cf. chapter 6 below), and the breathtaking conception of Yahweh's forgiveness does not obscure the devastating reality of sin and evil.

This vision reaches its greatest intensity in chapter 53, which has been perhaps the most important single chapter of the Old Testament for Christians. It helped to shape Jesus' own conception of his mission, and from the start gave Christians the terms in which their strange, suffering Messiah could be recognized. It is about the 'suffering servant' who is rejected and afflicted physically, socially and spiritually. He is innocent, and yet somehow his being shamed and killed is for others, and within the will of God. The result is his vindication and the participation of many others in a right relationship with God and each other. Deutero-Isaiah has here laid out the elements of the ultimate riddle: how do God, sin, suffering, death and innocence belong in the same reality? And he has offered a pregnant vision of the solution.

Then the next chapter begins: 'Sing. . .!' The note of praise sounds again, taking up the message of hope that has faced the worst. All this is in poetry inspired by the worship of Israel which has had its temple destroyed. In fact scholars can trace much of the imagery and form of chapters 40–55 to parts of the festival worship in the Temple.[4] There are traditional patterns of dialogue that were used: echoes of acclamations, proclamations, jubilations, royal ceremonies, confessions of sin, and dramatic presentations of themes essential to Israel's faith and life. Even the 'suffering servant' is probably a prophetic variation on a drama in which the king is humiliated by enemies before being saved by Yahweh. In a situation where the tradition seemed to have disintegrated, this is a breakthrough in theology and praise together, and appropriately culminates by setting us within the same horizon as did Psalm 96 above:

> For you shall go out in joy,
>   and be led forth in peace;
> the mountains and the hills before you
>   shall break forth into singing,
>   and all the trees of the field shall clap their hands.
> Instead of the thorn shall come up the cypress;
>   instead of the brier shall come up the myrtle;
> and it shall be to the Lord for a memorial,
>   for an everlasting sign which shall not be cut off (Isa. 55:12f).

This cosmic scope of praise, which embraced all nations (Isa. 49:6; 52:10) opened a way for the further Christian transformation that invited all into the salvation and celebration.

RABBIS AND CHRISTIANS

When some of the exiled Jews returned to Jerusalem and began rebuilding the city, and later the temple, the place of the cult could never be the same again, and the Davidic monarchy was never restored. Turbulent centuries followed, which could make a fascinating study in our theme, but it is sufficient for our purpose now to note that when the temple was finally destroyed in A.D. 70 by the Romans, the two main carriers of the tradition during the centuries that followed were rabbinic Judaism and Christianity.

They both managed to overcome dependence on the Jerusalem cult by taking it up into very different transformations. The rabbis took the way of reinforcing the boundaries of Judaism and building a highly ordered way of life within this periphery. They capitalized on the covenant's ability to shape a strong and exclusive identity, and they focused most of their synagogue worship on the Pentateuch

4   See John Eaton, *Festal Drama in Deutero-Isaiah*, London 1979.

(the first five books of the Bible), with its complex of detailed regulations. The cult lived on as an imaginative resource and as material for new types of interpretation. There was no difficulty in spiritualizing or turning into symbols the elements of the cult, and the basic imperative of praising God was still obeyed. The performance that was most highly valued was study of the Pentateuch and obedience to its ethical demands and to those regulations which could be separated from the cult. God was conceived as one who had acted decisively in the past in making the covenant, and would act finally in the future: meanwhile, the way to honour him was to bless his name and faithfully obey *torah*.

For Christianity, the final and decisive action of God had already happened in Jesus, and so the praise appropriate to that welled up. The whole tradition was reinterpreted in this light. The law, the temple, festivals, prophecy, sacrifice, kingship, wisdom and much else were taken up and transformed through relating them to Jesus as Messiah. The firm boundaries of the covenant were also changed: the new condition for being included was simply faith in Jesus Christ. Crowning all this was the experience of the Holy Spirit. The rabbis believed the Holy Spirit to have been quenched with the death of the last Old Testament prophets (Haggai, Zechariah and Malachi). For Christians their new reality had a double aspect: it linked the crucified and resurrected Jesus inseparably with a new giving of the Holy Spirit.

The result was an explosion of Christ-centred praise of God, and the Old Testament was taken into this new ecology. It was a development with many problems and conflicts, as the split with Judaism and the history of the Christian tradition (see below, chapter 4) show. We have already examined the beginnings of this transformation in Paul's Letter to the Philippians and in the Gospel of Mark. A praise-centred perspective would have even more obvious material to draw on in other New Testament writings.

Luke (cf. below, chapter 3) and Matthew make the theme of praise more explicit than Mark, especially in their introductions and conclusions. John's Gospel has the glory of Jesus Christ and of his Father as a key feature and shows throughout the basic dynamic of praise as recognition and respect in relation to God (cf. below, chapter 8). A letter in the Pauline tradition, such as Ephesians, can be even more explicit than Paul (see especially Ephesians 1; cf. below, chapters 5, 7); and Hebrews, one of the most sophisticated theological statements in the New Testament, makes its main points by concentrating on the transformation of Jewish worship by Christianity (cf. below, chapter 8). Finally, there is the Book of Revelation, the only one to dare to picture the ultimate in praise, worship in heaven.

One obvious conclusion is that the theme of praise is more articulated as the tradition develops. This is to be expected. At the beginning the new content of praise is the major concern of the authors, but when that has been recorded the later writers can explore its riches, share their response to it and stretch their minds and imaginations to try to do justice to the glory of God.

This chapter has tried to interpret how the Bible shows praise of God to be the heart of Old and New Testament communities. The Bible both reflects the praise of many centuries and also constantly inspires fresh praise, and its unity is best seen in the God to whom this is directed. We now turn to some key parts of the uninterrupted stream of praise in Christianity between New Testament times and today, with a special focus on God through whom its unity is seen.

Past Praise Now: The Tradition

We have been using one key to understand the Bible. The engagement of Paul, Mark, the Psalmists and other biblical writers with God was continued by many others in the centuries of church life that followed. When the same key is used on this tradition a dynamic unity can be seen, embracing all of Christian life and theology.

This unity flows essentially from the continual relating of everything to God. The reality and nature of God is at its heart, so the most important question is: who is this God? The answer of the Christian tradition is a surprising one: God the Father, God the Son, and God the Holy Spirit. The focus and inspiration of all praising and living is God the Trinity. How did this happen and how can sense be made of it? That must be the primary question in a treatment of Christian praise down the centuries. We will discuss how it originated in the exhilaration of praise and in the clash of debate, up to its adoption officially by the Church. Then we will suggest that the early Church did not go far enough in Christianizing its understanding of God. In the area of the relation of God to the world, to suffering, evil and death and to the future, the contemporary Church needs to take further the earlier revolution. This diagnosis sets the agenda for future chapters where ordinary living, creation, evil, Jesus Christ, the Trinity and prophecy are treated. The present chapter concludes with a discussion of the contribution of the twentieth-century phenomenon of Pentecostalism to the understanding and practice of praise. We begin, however, not at the beginning of the story, but half-way through it, with a plunge into what is perhaps the most complete expression of Christian praise.

The 'Divine Comedy'

As Europe pivoted between the Middle Ages and modernity, Dante wrote his *Divine Comedy*. This book could have been written in the form of a commentary on it, because all our themes, and many

more, are drawn together by Dante. He offers inspiration and a
model for taking up the whole of reality into praise of God.

That is his great aim. The *Divine Comedy* has many levels – the
literal story of Dante's journey through hell, purgatory and heaven,
the love story of Dante and Beatrice that is woven into this, and
the allegorical meanings such as the journey of the soul to the vision
of God, the Christian way of living ethically and politically, and
the artist's way to truth, goodness and beauty. Yet each level has
its climax and is fulfilled and satisfied in the love and praise of God.
Dante manages to do this in a way that not only is not boring or
escapist or similar in each case, but is actually exciting and leads
to an intensification of our sense of the reality both of God and of
the activity or person that is fulfilled.

The final vision is in three connected parts. First he sees the unity
of the vast complexity of the universe:

> O grace abounding, whereby I presumed
> So deep the eternal light to search and sound
> That my whole vision was therein consumed!
>
> In the abyss I saw how love held bound
> Into one volume all the leaves whose flight
> Is scattered through the universe around;
>
> How substance, accident, and mode unite
> Fused, so to speak, together in such wise
> That this I tell of is one simple light.
>
> Yea, of this complex I believe mine eyes
> Beheld the universal form – in me,
> Even as I speak, I feel such joy arise.
>
> And so my mind, bedazzled and amazed,
> Stood fixed in wonder, motionless, intent,
> And still my wonder kindled as I gazed.
>
> That light doth so transform a man's whole bent
> That never to another sight or thought
> Would he surrender, with his own consent;
>
> For everything the will has ever sought
> Is gathered there, and there is every quest
> Made perfect, which apart from it falls short.[1]

Next he sees something of the unity and Trinity of God:

> But as my sight by seeing learned to see,
> The transformation which in me took place
> Transformed the single changeless form for me.

---

[1] *Paradiso*, xxxiii, 82–105. Trans. D. L. Sayers, London 1962.

That light supreme, within its fathomless
Clear substance, showed to me three spheres, which bare
Three hues distinct, and occupied one space;

The first mirrored the next, as though it were
Rainbow from rainbow, and the third seemed flame
Breathed equally from each of the first pair.

How weak are words, and how unfit to frame
My concept – which lags after what was shown
So far, I would flatter it to call it lame!

Eternal light, that in Thyself alone
Dwelling, alone dost know Thyself, and smile
On Thy self-love, so knowing and so known![2]

Then finally he sees something which explodes his understanding,
the mystery of the union of the two previous realities, the creation
and the Trinity, in the incarnation:

The sphering thus begot, perceptible
In thee like mirrored light, now to my view –
When I had looked on it a little while –

Seemed in itself, and in its own self-hue,
Limned with our image; for which cause mine eyes
Were altogether drawn and held thereto.

As the geometer his mind applies
To square the circle, nor for all his wit
Finds the right formula, howe'er he tries.

So strove I with that wonder – how to fit
The image to the sphere; so sought to see
How it maintained the point of rest in it.

Thither my own wings could not carry me,
But that a flash my understanding clove,
Whence its desire came to it suddenly.[3]

The final stanza then describes the result of that fulfilled desire:

High phantasy lost power and here broke off;
Yet, as a wheel moves smoothly, free from jars,
My will and my desire were turned by love,
The love that moves the sun and the other stars.[4]

The final two lines show the union of personal and cosmic vision

---

[2] *Paradiso*, XXXIII, 112–26, ibid.
[3] *Paradiso*, XXXIII, 127–41, ibid.
[4] *Paradiso*, XXXIII, 142–5, ibid.

that Dante offers. It is a combination that has become increasingly difficult, especially since the Enlightenment. Dante can set his own autobiography in a story which embraces the whole of the known universe. The modern predicament is typically that of a dichotomy between contemplating the universe and one's own life in it. Kierke-gaard, at one extreme, finds God meaningful only in relation to his subjective willing; whereas Einstein believes in a God who created a cosmos of great beauty and precision, but who is not involved with the source of human lives.

The modern predicament has many ancient parallels, especially in the attempts to marry Greek and Hebrew thought. Dante's synthesis was the outcome of centuries of Christian thought and practice, but there were medieval alternatives at least as hostile to it as are most modern positions. His solution was not an undisputed achievement possible only in that culture at that time; it was, rather, a delicately precise integration that challenged many others and represents a tradition of responding to the basic content of Chris-tianity and to the universe that has helped to inspire the one attempted in this book. He answered perennially fundamental ques-tions in a way that has not simply gone out of date with Ptolemaic cosmology and the details of Florentine power politics. We are trying to sketch a modern way of doing something similar, which will of course mean thinking afresh about cosmology, politics and much else, but which can be instructed by Dante in several vital ways.

Most important is the intrinsic logic of Christianity that he expresses. This sees praise and adoration of God, and, in approp-riate ways, of people, as the essence of every person's vocation, and constitutive of right relationships. Dante's own way of praise begins as a child in Florence meeting the child Beatrice. In the *Convivio* IV:xxv, Dante says that 'the young are subject to a "stupor" or astonishment of the mind which falls on them at the awareness of great and wonderful things. Such a stupor produces two results – a sense of reverence and a desire to know more. A noble awe and a noble curiosity come to life. This is what had happened to him at the sight of the Florentine girl, and all this work consists, one way or another, in the increase of that worship and that knowledge.'[5] There in that key formative experience is the interaction of praising and knowing that matures in the *Divine Comedy*.

Dante was in love with Beatrice; as a young man he wrote poetry about his love for her, and when she died the vision that he had seen through her inspired the *Divine Comedy*. The quite common experience of falling in love was taken up into the vision of the

---

[5] Charles Williams, *The Figure of Beatrice*, London 1943.

transformation of himself from someone 'in a dark wood where the right road was wholly lost and gone' (*Inferno* 1:2–3), to someone able to write the last canto of the *Paradiso*. The way there went through an experience of recognizing his own sin and being humbled that radically changed the tone of his later poetry. The *Purgatorio* shows Dante's insight into the process of penitence through which his knowledge of God matured. His praise is the other side of a humility in which he sees himself realistically in relation to Beatrice and to God. Then he is ready for the *Paradiso*'s unique achievement: 'The possibility of enduring delight is grasped and presented in a way that the adult intellect can accept.'[6] Dante's progress through heaven continually astonishes in its ability to describe ever greater expression of praise, wonder and amazement in correspondence with the growing revelation of God.

> Glory to the Father, to the Son, and to
> The Holy Ghost, all Paradise began;
> And the sweet song intoxicated me.
> What I saw was like a universe in smiles;
> So that intoxication came to me
> Through my vision as well as my hearing.
> O joy! O happiness ineffable!
> O life entirely of love and peace![7]

Yet it also embraces the most sophisticated science, philosophy and theology of his day, repeatedly refers to the struggles of local Italian city politics, and manages to underline again and again the sheer physicality of the human approach to God. In all this it preserves the human perspective of the face-to-face relationship, mainly through the growing beauty in Beatrice's face as the clarity of her vision of God increases, but finally in the face of Christ that breaks open Dante's understanding and leaves him at one with love's movement.

To reach heaven Dante had travelled through hell. There God was not praised, and even honour and courtesy among people die out as he and Virgil go deeper. The atmosphere builds up – claustrophobic, smelly, noisy, colourless and restless. The most deadly evil is seen in all forms of deception, fraud and malice. These pervert the network of communication and trust that are necessary for genuine praise and respect. The antithesis to the constant overflow of joy and mutual honour in heaven is the frozen agony of ice and Satan's chewing of the traitors in the last circle of hell.

---

[6] Dorothy L. Sayers '. . . and telling you a story,' in *Essays Presented to Charles Williams*, ed. C. S. Lewis (Grand Rapids, Michigan 1966), p. 32.
[7] *Paradiso*, XXXII, 1:1ff. Trans. Louis Biancolli, New York 1966.

Emerging from hell into purgatory, Dante shows the discipline that is necessary for those who 'train to leap up into joy celestial'. The discipline has pain but it is also full of singing and hope, and for Dante it includes instruction in philosophy and theology and, finally, the departure of Virgil and a momentous meeting with Beatrice. This scene unites the rekindling of Dante's 'old, old love in all its mastering might', with his final shame and penitence as Beatrice exposes in detail how unfaithful he has been to his love. As soon as he has confessed, the very memory of his guilt is washed away, and he joins the dance around Beatrice. Then he is taught by her and is finally prepared for heaven by drinking of the river Eunoë:

> I came back from the holiest of waters
> Thoroughly remade – like those new trees
> That with new foliage are new again –
> Pure and prepared to climb up to the stars.[8]

What Dante has done is to show how in hell the results of sin make praise impossible, how in purgatory the willingness to let the roots of sin be dealt with results in the transformation of suffering into praise, and how in heaven there is a community whose total life is an infinitely interesting rejoicing. So what, from this standpoint, is sin? It is the senseless use of freedom to spoil joy, and the incapacitating of oneself for anything except misery. Dante has managed to give a glimpse of real honouring and enjoyment of God and of each other (experienced especially in smiles, eyes, light, music and dance) so that this is really more attractive than anything else. His achievement is not unique, but is unparalleled in its inclusiveness and sustained sensitivity of touch and tone. As a source to be explored for theological insight, Charles Williams's verdict is probably correct: 'We have hardly yet begun.'[9]

So the *Divine Comedy* shows how right praise is not an optional extra in life but is the fundamental condition for happiness and for staying in harmony with reality. The claim is that the intrinsic logic of life and of Christianity are at one in this, and that only in this activity are truth, beauty, goodness and love appropriately blended and fulfilled. Further, by telling the story as a journey from despair to the vision of God, Dante can say a great deal about education into the many stages and levels of praise. There is an epistemology in which all faculties – senses, imagination, intellect, feeling, will and the unconscious – are developed in their receptive and active capacities, and the knowledge (whether cosmological or intimately

---

[8] *Purgatorio*, XXXIII, ibid.
[9] Op. cit., p. 232.

personal) that is gained is continually expressed and receives its most appropriate form in poetry and praise. After Beatrice introduces him to

> the heaven of pure light –
> Intellectual light that is full of love,
> Love of truth that is replete with happiness,
> Happiness transcending every sweetness,

Dante has a typical experience of expanded capacity for reality:

> I realized that I
> Was now transcending my own faculties,
> And was inflamed again with such new vision
> That there is no light, however bright, that
> My eyes would not have been able to withstand.[10]

This development of the self is integrated into a world of meaning that reaches through the utterly particular (Beatrice's face, Florentine culture and politics, vernacular Italian) to the universal, and in doing this demonstrates the interplay of all levels of reality in the best praise. In line with Thomas Aquinas' statement that in the Psalms there is the whole of theology in the mode of praise, Dante wrote his own psalms, and wove in Aquinas' theology and a great deal else besides.

The Trinitarian Revolution Begins

Dante was the culmination of a long tradition of theology and praise, a great deal of which deeply affects his work without being often mentioned. The chief example of this is his understanding of God, fed by the centuries of discussion and meditation that produced and developed the doctrine of the Trinity. The final canto reveals what in retrospect is very clear: the Trinitarian pattern for thinking of God pervades the *Divine Comedy*. It is the 'deep structure' of his understanding of reality, but one which (as in most good psalms) is presented in a wide variety of mediated ways. The same is true of the whole Christian tradition. Its distinctiveness is perhaps most comprehensively presented in this doctrine, and so the question of the Trinity must be faced if we are to explore Christian praise of God.

Put very crudely, there are two tendencies in interpreting the development of the doctrine of the Trinity. The first is to see it as intrinsic to the gospel, a deepening of insight into what it is about, expressing as appropriately as possible who the Christian God is

---

10 *Paradiso*, xxx, ibid.

and the logic of the Bible and Christian life. The second is to see it as a later addition to the faith, a philosophical speculation or mythologizing, at best a helpful way of drawing together some key insights but certainly not the indispensable statement of what is essential to Christianity. There is a major debate about these, and about other more nuanced options, among contemporary thinkers. We are firmly in line with the first position, and see the thrust of early Christian praise beginning a revolution in the concept of God. It is an unfinished revolution, as we shall discuss, with our own period struggling to continue it and in a very good position to do so.

The explosion of thanks and praise in the early Church unavoidably raised the question of God and especially of the relation of Jesus to God. As soon as thanks focuses on whom it is addressing it becomes praise and the overflow of appreciation searches for appropriate words and actions. These in turn either enhance the thanks in a 'virtuous circle' or fail to ring true. The assessment of what 'rings true' is a many-levelled process in the individual and the group, with an extreme sensitivity developing over the years. What often seems like exaggerated attention to doctrinal distinctions in the early Church is more sympathetically seen as a search for the right note in common worship.

This is rooted in the way Christian identity was sustained. Groups have many possible means of identifying themselves and their boundaries – by blood, geographical area, dress, lifestyle, rules and laws, language, belief system, programme of action, etc. All of these have played a part in Christianity, but none is as fundamental as the gathering for worship, especially the Eucharist. The word eucharist means thanks, and this celebration became the distinctive act of the Church. It has many advantages as the chief carrier of identity. It has a clear boundary in the requirement of commitment to Jesus Christ, but within that has the capacity (not always actual) to allow for great diversity. It is sociologically sound as an embodiment of community, and is well suited to enable a group to experience the mutual reinforcement of three key relationships: with each other, with God and with the world beyond the group. The Eucharist also has at its heart the remembering and presentation of the story of Jesus, and stories are perhaps the key element in our conscious identity. But above all there is the movement of thanks and praise, the rhythm of receiving and offering, in the course of which God is unavoidably identified as a particular, definite God.

What sort of God? The novelty of Christianity in relation to Judaism lay in two main features: Jesus, crucified and risen, as Messiah, and the outpouring of the Holy Spirit. These came together, as in the baptism of Jesus, the farewell discourses of John's

Gospel, and in Romans chapter 8, in relating to God as Father of
Jesus. The Trinitarian pattern was acted out in baptism and
worship long before it became a doctrine. As a doctrine, it was
partly worked out to correct unacceptable distinctions and
emphases. Perhaps the most helpful way of seeing its negative
function (vital both in worship and the whole Roman and Hellen-
istic religious context) is as a guard against various forms of idolatry.
The idol could be a transcendent God who is not really free to take
a personal part in history; or a divine human being who himself
receives all worship; or a God who is within human beings or in
some other way immanent in the world. Those three basic ways of
absolutizing one dimension of the Christian God roughly correspond
to the Father, Son, and Holy Spirit. Taken as a unity, the Trinity
continually dispels illusions and fantasies about God. It applies a
corrective to any one type of language, whether talk about the
transcendence of God in analogies, or sacramental and historical
accounts of God's character and presence, or subjective, experiential
witness to the immediacy of God. So the Trinity is a comprehensive
'negative way', refusing to let one rest in any image of God. It offers
a ground rule: never conceive the Father apart from the Son and
Holy Spirit, or the Son without Father and Spirit, or the Spirit
without Father and Son.

Yet it is also a positive way, as the record of its development
shows. It is the outcome of a passion for God that unites head,
heart and body. The polemics are the reverse side of this passionate
concern with mystery of God, not as a blur or darkness, but as a
depth of brightness and precision of wisdom. This can never be
completely comprehended by human beings, but can be enjoyed
more and more fully. God is honoured by the striving for greater
understanding, and he stretches our minds past their capacity.

This stretching is very clear in those most responsible for
formulating the doctrine of the Trinity, such as Tertullian, Basil
and Augustine. They are straining to do justice to the God they
worship, and often acknowledge this. It is easy in summarizing their
thoughts to leave out this context, and it is only by returning to the
texts of their writings that the overwhelming concern to honour
and praise God appropriately stands out. Modern scholarship and
theology has to be especially careful to make this explicit because
its own context is often divorced from interplay with worship, and
is pervaded by an ethos of suspicion that feels automatically superior
and hostile to something as affirmative as praise. So there has to
be a more deliberate effort of imagination than in previous ages.
The doctrine of the Trinity in particular is indebted to radical
movements of worship for its creative development. Tertullian was
open to the recovery of the importance of the Holy Spirit by the

Montanists; behind the Cappadocian Fathers is the single-minded devotion of monasteries and the charismatic movement of the Messalians; and in the Middle Ages the intensity of intellectual activity that worked out numerous doctrines of the Trinity and culminated with Aquinas was rooted in the spiritual revolution of the friars and the daily worship of the monasteries.

What was the positive contribution of the doctrine of the Trinity? Praise is, among other things, a form of thinking, and aims to 'think God' as adequately as possible. The Trinity gives the logic of Christian praise, the way one thought or concept follows from another and coheres with all the others. It is not just a string of implications, it is a whole 'ecology'. The revolution that it achieved in the early centuries had several aspects.

The most obvious was the Christianizing of the understanding of God by discovering what the basis and consequences were of the unique recognition and honouring of Jesus. It was not just a matter of the status of Jesus in relation to God; the nature of God was also at stake. 'God' could not be assumed as already known, whether through Judaism or Greek philosophy or a combination of these. Their authority was relative to that of the ultimate event that was believed to have happened in Jesus Christ. So previous definitions of God had to be opened up to this story and experience. Many of the pressures were for compromise or the strict control of the gospel and worship by traditional concepts of God, and it is not surprising that, like most revolutions, it was bitterly disputed. What was thought to characterize God alone – new creation, universal lordship, ultimate salvation, and the receiving of worship – was now identified also with the person and activity of Jesus Christ. The debate could not avoid the fundamental issues, and so there were clashes between whole 'ecologies' which drew out the consequences of the options. The histories of doctrine and the Church tell this story in their various ways. Many earlier accounts tend to make the thinking seem as if it is happening in a vacuum; more modern approaches often exhaustively describe the context and various levels (political, economic, biographical, history of religions) but fail to give substance to a God-centred understanding, the fact that, without the passion for God which this experience of salvation inspired, the most satisfactory perspective on it is missed.

The climactic crisis was a confrontation between the consistent and straightforward traditional 'one God' of Arius and the far less neat God who, according to Athanasius, had expressed his very being in Jesus Christ. The principle of Athanasius, vital for worship, was that Jesus Christ is utterly intrinsic to God. This cannot be captured in definitions, and if it is taken out of the soil of Christian praise it withers to a paradoxical formula; but likewise the praise lacks integrity if it is not informed by the rigorous intellectual debate that still continues. Our own way through this is different from Athanasius, as will appear in chapters 7 and 8, but leads to agreement on that fundamental principle: God is one whose relationship to humanity is intrinsic through Jesus Christ, and whose very identity is imprinted with this character. He gives himself frankly in this person, and thanks and praise are the energy of every response to him for it.

What about the Holy Spirit? The last sentence of the previous paragraph is a basic Trinitarian statement. Further, the Holy Spirit was experienced not just as the energy of worship but as the generative thrust of every act that honoured God. It was not an impersonal impulse but the presence of God himself. Yet the New Testament and the 'grammar' of the faith learnt since then did not allow this to be straightforwardly identical with the Father or with the historical and resurrected Jesus Christ. There was an interaction of mutual honouring here that lost its life and interest if relationship within God was denied. God could not himself be less than the dynamics of praise and adoration indicated, and being taken into this life of God became the vision of ultimate fulfilment. Its intimacy had the marks of the 'paradox of grace' – the recognition that the more completely one is oneself the more one delightfully acknowledges that it is all due to God. The presence of God, united with one's self, by the very fact that it inspires thanks and praise of the Father and the Son differentiates itself from them. This explodes previous thinking of God's unity. From now on that unity must be differentiated, and the two distinctive features of Christianity, Jesus Christ and the Holy Spirit, must be recognized as intrinsic to God.

The above might be seen as an attempt to reflect simultaneously from both ends of the Trinitarian development, from Paul, Luke and John in the New Testament, and from Basil's treatise 'On the Holy Spirit' and Augustine's 'On the Trinity' as two high points in the early Church's thought. There are, however, two serious problems with our account. One is that it is far too neat and does not do justice to the diversity even within the mainstream. The other is that it does not show how the revolution was inadequate in ways that have been extremely harmful.

Revelation and Debate

A certain pluralism goes well with being Trinitarian. It is a doctrine which, when understood in historical perspective, makes it far less easy to claim exclusive and dogmatic correctness for one position, or to hold it to the point of idolatry. One great movement after another that arises and seems to threaten or deny others can be seen as reasserting some neglected emphasis in the Trinity. Each has its own thrust – recognition of the Fatherhood or the proper transcendence of God, of the 'Christ alone', or of the scandal of the 'practical atheism' of the Holy Spirit (that is, neglect of the intimacy and activity of God in new ways in the present and for the future). The doctrine of the Trinity is big enough and open enough to wrestle with these contributions and be enriched by them.

This process of debate and conflict, made almost unbearably intense by the experience of the intimacy and greatness of God, is not just incidental to Christian revelation. As in the Old Testament and the New Testament, the process of revelation is itself utterly historical, inseparable from human relationships and their strengths and weaknesses. The Bible was born through such a process, and is safely authoritative only when this is recognized. Jesus' life, death and resurrection are the limit case of this, a complex event involved in all the ambiguities and equivocations of life, and giving rise to a community that is likewise involved. There was no attempt by Jesus to give a comprehensive system of belief, or to cater for a desire for abstract clarity, and he certainly did not touch the doctrine of the Trinity. Rather, he invited to a new relationship with God his Father, available through the gift of the Holy Spirit, and always under the sign of the cross. This inevitably led to a new engagement with God, and, with that, a fascination which was bound to produce debate. The later documents of the New Testament show the maturing astonishment of Christians expressing itself in a diversity of praise and thought whose thrust is to universality. So Ephesians penetrates and takes up a contemporary world-view and cosmology into a fuller understanding of Christ and the Church; Hebrews meditates on Jewish worship, Christian faith and suffering, and offers one of the most profound of New Testament theologies; and John in the opening of his Gospel sums up the new participation in the knowledge and glory of God that Jesus embodies and offers. It has been one of the great contributions of biblical scholarship to point out and try to reconstruct the process of struggle and debate in the early Church that produced the New Testament. More recently there has been renewed emphasis on how God-centred a book it is. These two characteristics, the struggle and the God-centredness, continued in the debate about God in the early Church. That debate and its fascination with God are part of the process of revelation.

What Jesus did can therefore be seen as initiating a new stage in the debate about God. To be involved with him as a Christian is to find that the question of God is inseparable both from the person of Jesus Christ, and from the active participation in that debate in the Spirit. Statements in the debate are not just in words, but in acts, celebrations and suffering. Revelation can therefore never be divorced from our responsibility to take part in this debate. It is part of the logic of incarnation: 'The word became flesh and dwelt among us' (John 1:14). Jesus' life was in debate, confrontation, action and suffering, and knowledge of his revelation demands following that way. All of this is embraced within what John calls glorifying God, and what in Luke and Matthew is the aim of the first petition of the Lord's prayer: 'Hallowed be thy name'.

The early Church's Trinitarian doctrine is in direct continuity with this debate and its thrust to glorify God appropriately. The diversity is part of the way this revelation works; the polemical concern for one truth is part of the respect for God. It is not possible here to discuss the early Church's debate in detail, but we will note one major divergence that is still important today.

This is the difference between the understanding of God that became dominant in the Western or Latin Church centred in Rome and that in the Eastern Orthodox Church that spread out from Asia Minor and Greece and for centuries was centred in Constantinople. In the simplest terms, the West tended to stress the unity of God rather than the Trinity, whereas the East had more to say about the Trinity as itself a community in threefold interaction. The official reason for the split between Eastern and Western Christianity in 1054, still unhealed today, lay in the understanding of the Trinity. There were many other factors besides this, but each side had developed very differently and it is significant that their differences were focused on the doctrine which embraces the whole ecology of Christianity. The oneness and threeness were of course affirmed by both sides, but in divergent ways which, in particular, gave worship and theology different roles in the ecology.

Our project could be seen in terms of this East–West debate, in which the East has been content to let its case be presented primarily through its liturgy and certain patristic texts, while the West has in comparison been much more concerned with the mind's role in responding to, exploring and teaching about God. The praising and the knowing have never been separate in either tradition, but their relationship has been very different. There is in the East an element of intellectual self-denial whose advantage is that it cuts off many ways of escaping from the slow immersion in disciplined and joyful worship. But once that worship is being done, and the process of 'taking the mind into the heart' is sustained in that way, then the Western adventurous questioning and rationality must be granted freedom. This book is one little result of what happens when this is tried, and in chapter 7 we offer some thoughts on the unity and Trinity of God.

God and the World

For all the wide range of the early Church debate, and the Fathers' working-out of an unprecedented understanding of God, the modern period has rightly had many reservations about their achievements. This is where the unfinished nature of their revolution appears. We will follow up three lines of positive criticism under the headings of 'God and the World', 'God and the Cross', and 'God and the Future', which together point to a transformation of the patristic position and set up the framework within which our own will be built.

The first is the understanding of how God and the universe interact. This includes the questions of creation, providence, the relation of science and theology, the nature of space and time, and many others. The inadequacy of the early Church's position here is ironically the other side of the thoroughness with which it did its job. It was part of a sophisticated civilization with centuries of systematic philosophical and scientific work behind it. If the educated were to be converted in depth, then the challenge of this tradition had to be met. The alternative was for Christianity to remain an enthusiastic sect in an educational and intellectual ghetto, unable to transform what it did not understand or take seriously. The mainstream of Christianity did face this, and tried to follow where its faith led in understanding the world in scientific terms. The relevance of this to praise of God is fundamental. Most praise is of God in interaction with the world. He is praised for his creation, his acts, his words, his loving presence and involvement. If the credibility of this interaction is weakened, then the very nerve of praise is numbed. The world of the early Church, like ours, was full of conceptions of God and of the world which ruled out such interaction or reinterpreted it so as to evacuate it of power. Their response is instructive.

One objection they met was the anthropomorphism of a God who did particular things within his own world. Did this not make God too much like a human person? Their reply to this was partly to accept it as true: such language does not say nearly enough, and needs qualification. But they also challenged the concept of a God who is not free to interact in this way. He is free, they said, and concerned enough to do so, and in this he allows himself to be described in human terms. Anthropomorphism has its good side because humans are in the image of God, and the humility of God in Jesus Christ was taken as the encouragement of praise in language that was in harmony with him and his human story.

That did not grapple with the tough problems of science and cosmology. There the response could not avoid thinking about the nature of the world. There were two main opposing cosmologies, in neither of which did praise of God make sense. The first was the stoic identification of cosmology and theology. In this, God was immanent in the universe, he was the life of the whole system and had no distinct existence of his own in interaction with it. The second was a Platonic dualism in which God was so transcendent, so remote from the world, as to be uninvolved in matter and history. The notion of God's action could not appear in either, and neither could radical newness. Even when all the pressures of the culture were towards one of these options, it was clear that they must contradict the Christian understanding that lived from celebrating a God of love who had done something new and decisive in history. This gave the impulse to think through an alternative cosmology, which was done with increasing thoroughness.

Key ideas in this were the rational unity of the universe as created by God, which encouraged investigation of the regularities of the world and grasping its laws; the openness of the universe to novelty, both materially and through the freedom of people; and the freedom of God within the universe to act in Trinitarian ways, from within the system and within people as well as by transcendent creativity. There were even attempts to follow through with a revolution in the ideas of space and time. For God to be this sort of God, the picture of space and time as a container of everything, in which he intervened from time to time, would not do. There could be no such container with clear boundaries – God was the one who defined boundaries, and by his mode of relating to the world made it clear that he was free in relation to the very basics of space and time. However, the exciting implications of this were not followed through. Christian cosmology became dominated by dualistic views of God and the world and by container concepts of space and time. The Middle Ages brought Christian cosmology to its peak, but for all the immense importance of its theorizing and its orientation of all reality to God, it generally (and conspicuously in Aquinas) failed to let the Trinitarian God break open its Aristotelian concept of space, time and the freedom of God with the world.

With the rise of modern science, Christian cosmology on the whole went along with a dualism it had helped to form. The view of the world as a mechanism of linked causes with no room for God's presence, dominated science. It led religion to see God either as a remote figure who merely set the system going, or as identified with history's meaning, or as a presence in the subjectivity of people – the God of feeling, intuition, regulative ideas or morality.

One way of seeing the effect of recent centuries on the way of understanding God is to trace the fragmentation of the Trinity. Some favoured a transcendent creator God who makes the universe but does not 'interfere' with it. This went well with a popular picture of God as distant and benign, but to be ignored in practice. The sophisticated development of this was Deism, which is still influential in the British tradition.

Others placed little or no stress on transcendence in that sense, and instead saw God completely involved with history and its meaning. The popular Christian version of this was a focus on Jesus as Saviour, Lord, Friend, Teacher and much else, to such an extent that in practice the Father and Holy Spirit tended to be forgotten and devotion became 'Jesuolatry'. Other, more secular versions saw the crucial meaning of existence in evolution, or human progress, or economic reality and its class conflicts, or the supremacy of a nation, race or system of government. Such ways of finding in historical process the key meaning of reality have had immense influence in the modern world and reflect, in religious or secular forms, an anti-Trinitarian absolutizing of the God of history and incarnation.

The third way in which the Trinitarian ecology fragmented was through the fascination with human subjectivity, consciousness and will. The popular Christian version of this is to make our own experience, feeling or judgement the criterion of everything because of the presence of God in us, whether as inner light, conscience or unique individuality. This God indwelling us has its secular counterparts in many variations on individualism, autonomy and self-fulfilment, and is often in tension with the more socially oriented absolutes of historical process.

This fragmentation was accompanied and influenced by an explosion of science in which disciplines developed in highly specialized ways, and their technical applications and implications proliferated with a momentum of their own. The recent growth of ecological awareness has recognized the high cost of the fragmentation of science. The cost has been both theoretical, because relations between fields were neglected and general theories deprecated; and practical, because each area 'doing its own thing' meant, when carried over into applied science, that there were unco-ordinated and often disastrous interactions with the environment of life. Today science has largely gone beyond its earlier mechanistic determinism, and there are many fresh attempts to cope theoretically and practically with problems of communication, co-ordination and the unity and application of scientific knowledge.

There has been a parallel labour in theology. This century has been more fruitful in doctrines of the Trinity than any since the Middle Ages. They are usually concerned to overcome the fragmentation analysed above, but unfortunately few grasp the nettle of science and cosmology. The lesson that we gather from the past is that this must be done. The early Church did do this but its very success in working out a relationship with ancient science makes it only indirectly relevant to us, while its flaws require the positive help of modern science to be overcome. In the following chapters, and especially chapters 5 and 7, we will put some positive suggestions about all this.

God and the Cross

Our second basic question about the early Church is: How far did it allow the centrality of the crucifixion of Jesus to influence its understanding and praise of God? The answer is that its praise, as well as its spirituality and activity, were affected far more than its explicit understanding of God. It failed to carry through the revolution, and as a result passed on a concept of God that has done much damage and misled millions.

This has been a specially acute problem in modern times. Modern atheism has often rejected God in the name of human freedom, because the God atheists they have heard about was one of transcendent power demanding subservience at the cost of human maturity. They saw him as an idol distracting people from responsible action in the world and easily used for many sorts of alienation and oppression. Christian theology has increasingly learnt from this: it has begun to recognize that the traditional concept of God was only partly Christian, especially in his expression of power. Bonhoeffer summed up the positive conclusion: 'Only a suffering God can help'. This hits at a great deal in the early Church's concept, but above all at the 'impassibility' of God: that God cannot himself suffer, change or be affected by his creation.

'Bringing the cross into the centre of the Trinity' has been a very slow process, and both the Eastern and Western Christian conceptions have been criticized by it. In the West there were deep streams of spirituality in the Middle Ages which pointed in this direction. When these were assimilated by Luther and mixed with various other elements, above all Paul's cross-centred preaching of justification, the result was an explosion that split Christendom apart. Luther is the seminal figure in modern theology of the cross, the mountain that there is no way round, and so must be climbed. It is no accident that it is in the Lutheran tradition that some of the most daring recent developments of this theology have happened, as in Bonhoeffer, Eberhard Jüngel and Jürgen Moltmann.

'True theology and recognition of God are in the crucified Christ,' said Luther. The key to the whole of existence is to live *coram Deo*, in the presence, before the face of God, and this God is identified through the cross. Luther's way of bringing together the cross and the *coram Deo* precisely defines the distinctiveness for him of Christian praise. Praise is simply faith being freely itself before God. 'Faith is a living, daring confidence in God's grace, so sure and certain that a man would stake his life on it a thousand times. This confidence in God's grace and knowledge of it makes men glad and bold and happy in dealing with God and with all his creatures; and this is the work of the Holy Ghost in faith. Hence a man is ready and glad, without compulsion, to do good to everyone, to serve everyone, to suffer everything, in love and praise of God, who has shown him this grace.'[11] 'This grace' is defined through the crucified Christ. The ethics and Christian living that flow from this are described again and again as a matter of gratitude before God, and Luther's passion for the Psalms lets the dynamics of thanks and praise move through and shape his whole theology.

The cross shows the absolute impotence of human praise without the activity of God. To identify with it as Luther did is to find sin and impotence before God agonizingly real and yet answered by God himself with acceptance and new life. For this the first response is simply thanks, addressed to a God now known through the crucified Jesus.

Yet while Luther gave a massive correction to the tradition, and a many-levelled insistence on the centrality of the cross, he too failed to carry through the revolution to the point of criticizing the traditional doctrine of the Trinity. He thus left his theology vulnerable to being domesticated within systems which used ideas of God uncriticized by his theology of the cross. This failure in relation to the reality of God has perhaps been Protestantism's basic flaw. Without following through the *coram Deo* of Luther it easily loses his focus on and freedom with God, and ends without the objectivity of praise.

In the past hundred years there has been a chorus of thinkers from many traditions who have been trying to carry out the task of conceiving the nature of God in relation to suffering and death. Jewish thinkers have reflected on the God who agonizes over Israel and the rest of his creation. Miguel de Unamuno's theme of the sorrow of God, Berdyaev's daring to talk of a 'tragedy in God', Simone Weil's meditations on affliction and the love of God, Donald Mackinnon's exploration of the self-emptying of God, Hans Urs von Balthasar's theology of Holy Saturday, and Rosemary Haughton's 'passionate God' are part of the explicitly theological side of a concern that finds some of its most powerful expressions in

[11] As quoted in *A History of Christian Doctrine*, ed. H. Cunliffe-Jones with Benjamin Drewery (Edinburgh 1978), p. 325.

biography, novels, drama, music and the other arts. All of this is the background to our own attempt in chapter 6 to follow the theme of the praise of God through the encounter with evil, suffering and death.

God and the Future

The third question we put to the early Church is about eschatology, its understanding of the future and goal of life. On the interaction of God with the world it had a firm grasp in worship, theory and practice, although, as discussed above, there were shortcomings, and its cosmology is inevitably dated. The crucifixion of Jesus played a vital role in its spirituality, liturgy and experience of suffering and asceticism, even though the consequences for the doctrine of God were not drawn. Yet both of these aspects, and most others, were deeply affected by the way the Church broke with the New Testament understanding of the future.

Perhaps the most influential contribution of modern biblical scholarship has been to show how eschatology and apocalyptic condition the whole New Testament and primitive Church. God's interaction with the world was above all his gift of the new age, the new creation, the Kingdom of God. This was already breaking in, the resurrection of Jesus was its reality, and the Holy Spirit was a taste of what life would be like when the risen Lord completed it. The appropriate response was an intense hope that put everything in a new light, with radical consequences for priorities in living. Worship was as much a passionate expectation of the coming Lord as it was thanks and praise for what had already happened. The top priority was sharing this news, inviting others to take part in this future now. The time between the resurrection and the end was already 'fulfilled time', the roots of evil and death had been cut, and in the conflict that continued there could be complete confidence in God's victory. The crucifixion of Jesus was the beginning of the birth-pangs of the new age, and Christians suffering for their faith was the way to take part in what was being born.

The end did not happen as soon as expected but (contrary to what some scholars have speculated) there are remarkably few signs of this causing any crisis. Among the New Testament authors there are various reactions to it, but the main effect is to focus faith and hope more on Jesus Christ as the bringer of the future. The sense of the Kingdom breaking in, the immediacy of the working of the Holy Spirit, and the confident resistance to evil are generally sustained. The ways in which the later Church transformed, domesticated and distorted these were various. The dominant concern in teaching the faith became a backward look at the New Testament events. The great doctrinal debates tried to be as clear as possible about the meaning of what happened then in relation to salvation and the person of Jesus, but their future perspective had changed drastically. On the whole eschatology was a matter of looking to the future beyond death, and within history the concern was for leading a moral life within the Church rather than for participation in the new things God promises and does. Heaven was distanced from earth, whereas the revolution of Pentecost had been to pour the Spirit of heaven out now. Worship maintained its thanks and praise, and its intoxication with the goodness of God, but it was God with a dimension ignored: he could be celebrated without an expectation of him working afresh through the whole congregation now, and without the future being intrinsic to him. The vital link between worship and the purpose and activity of God in the present age was weakened, and such changes as the linking of the Holy Spirit mainly with church offices, and the increasingly conservative content of liturgy, reinforced the division between sacred and secular.

There were of course many factors in these changes, not least the inevitable adaptation of an institution to the demands of continuity and stability; and the answer is not a romantic return to origins. But, if something powerful and true about the way God is to be hoped in was lost then it is necessary to see how it can be thought, prayed and lived through today. If God is the hope of the whole world, then both his nature and the world's need to be conceived in ways that take the strange reality of the future more seriously. If Christians follow a Lord who is the key to that future and also active in the present, then their praise of him will carry with it a prophetic call. Later chapters will take up these points.

Twentieth-century Praise: Pentecostalism

We conclude this selective examination of the tradition with a look at the main addition of this century, Pentecostalism. It began in 1906 with the 'Azusa Street outpouring' in Los Angeles, U.S.A. That happened when a group of black Christians experienced the gift of speaking in tongues, healing and much else, and at once became the centre of a new movement.

At Azusa Street worship at first went on almost uninterruptedly, with praise as its dominant note. Within weeks it had sent out missionaries to many countries, and people from many countries visited it. Racial tension was intense in America at the time, and most churches were racially segregated, but at Azusa Street, black, white and many other races came together, under the leadership of a black bishop, William J. Seymour. This has led a recent historian of the movement to suggest that its distinctive mark was not just speaking in tongues, but, as in the account of Pentecost in Acts, tongues as enabling and expressing reconciliation between the races.[12] There had been some speaking in tongues before Azusa Street, but the explosiveness of what happened there is plausibly attributed partly to this integration in the Spirit, and Seymour himself saw it this way.

Since 1906 the movement has grown to an estimated seventy-five million worldwide, and from the 1950s has had an increasing influence on other major Churches, notably the Anglican, Roman Catholic, Lutheran, Methodist and Baptist. Yet part of the price of its expansion was a serious compromise on the racial issue. Only a few years after it began in Los Angeles it split into black and white-led movements, submitting to the enormous pressures of white American society to segregate. Seymour himself persisted in leading an integrated church, but died in 1922 with only a handful of members in it. In Britain today the legacy can be seen too: the Pentecostal churches, with some fine exceptions, behaved like most other churches in response to incoming West Indian Christians. There was little welcome and less sharing of leadership, and the result has been a blossoming of independent black-led (usually Pentecostal) churches.

So we have twin symbols: the seventy-five million, plus millions more in other churches, often segregated; and Seymour dying with a tiny integrated church. They are the symbols of praise, for the supreme mark of the movement is its worship and all flows from it; and of prophecy, for the racial tragedy has been perhaps the most devastating of this century, claiming millions of lives, and still in progress. We see both huge joyful congregations and divisions that question the authenticity of the praise as Christian. 'The corruption of the best is the worst', and it is not surprising that the most powerful worship is also vulnerable in devastating ways – other forms of worship are often too dull to be so dangerous. The Pentecostal movement nevertheless is the most important source of world-wide renewal of Christianity, and we will now try to relate it to each key theme of this chapter, moving backwards.

PENTECOSTALISM AND THE FUTURE

Eschatology was central to Pentecostalism from the first: the end was expected any day, and this fired the joy of praise and the

[12] Douglas J. Nelson, *For Such a Time as This: The Story of Bishop William J. Seymour and the Azusa Street Revival*, dissertation submitted for Ph.D., Birmingham University, 1981.

urgency of mission. The end has not happened yet, and there has
been a range of reaction similar to that in the early Church, but
likewise no great crisis. The awkward question is: can such a movement only get going by encouraging in believers an expectation that
is proved wrong? A more practical question is: granted that,
however long the world lasts, all Christians agree on the need for
the Holy Spirit in the interim, what can be learnt from Pentecostalism's hectic re-run of much early Church experience? From the
previous paragraph one clear answer is that the imminent end
relativizes human divisions, and the Holy Spirit through tongues
and worship allows a prophetic glimpse of a united community.
This must then be followed through at all levels, and tongues and
the imminent expectation must not be idolized or trivialized by
separation from justice, love and community-building. Paul was
fighting a similar cause in Corinth. Another related answer is that,
as the early Church learnt, faith is not in a datable end but in the
one who brings it, and the focus on Jesus Christ ought to displace
speculation into praise without losing the prophetic ministry of
reconciliation.

PENTECOSTALISM AND THE CROSS

The place of the cross and suffering in Pentecostalism has aroused
questioning because of the temptation of all enthusiasm to bypass
it. A look at the origins shows that the opposite is true. There were
many roots of the new movement, notably Methodism (Britain's
greatest contribution to the praise of God and prophetic Christian
reform), the nineteenth-century American evangelical revivals and
the Holiness Movement; but the tap-root was the 'invisible institution' of slave religion. That could not avoid the reality of the cross,
and it faced suffering squarely, but also took it up into praise of
the crucified Jesus. The power of Pentecostal praise was probably
prepared by the Christian slaves in the south of the U.S.A. The
sort of praise that Pentecostalism offers needs such deep roots if it
is to maintain its balance. Part of the tragedy of the divisions in
the movement is that white American Pentecostalism has been cut
off from this root, and so is all the more open to triumphalism,
seduction by worldly success, and the many forms of ecclesiastical
pride that only the right grasp of the cross can guard against.

PENTECOSTALISM AND GOD'S ACTIVITY IN THE WORLD

The interaction of God and the world has no more been thought
through theoretically by Pentecostals than it was by the first Christians. It is their practice that poses sharply the traditional questions.
God's activity in healing, in communication, in giving gifts, in

answering prayer, is a more vivid and dramatic part of their religion than in most other Churches. There is a twofold challenge here, one for Pentecostals, the second for other Christians. For Pentecostals it is the same as that facing the early Church: a choice between conversion in depth, which inevitably means tackling the intellectual and scientific questions; or remaining an enthusiastic sect, however large. For other Christians the challenge is about their expectation of God, their willingness to risk having such things happen, and also their openness to conceiving God appropriately. Another aspect of this issue is that of 'natural religion'. Professor Walter Hollenweger suggests that the Pentecostal integration of dance, body movements of all sorts, embracing, shouting, popular music, oral tradition, communal solidarity, laughter and spontaneity within worship are a way of 'baptizing' the most basic elements of human nature, as embraced in primitive religion but often denied in later practice. If so, then Pentecostalism can stimulate fresh appreciation of creation and incarnation, especially as they can be actively enjoyed in worship.

PENTECOSTALISM AND THE TRINITY

Thought about the Trinity might seem remote from Pentecostalism, but in fact, just as between Eastern and Western Christianity, this doctrine has been the overt cause of the deepest split in the movement. We say 'overt' because the schism also went along colour lines: most whites stayed Trinitarian, while some of the blacks called themselves 'Oneness' or 'Apostolic' (sometimes labelled 'Jesus Only'). The Oneness Pentecostals spread especially in poor third-world countries, as well as among American blacks. They are one of the most lively and adaptable of modern Churches, and also growing in Britain. We have had conversations with them about the Trinitarian problem. It seemed clear that their reaction was mainly against a crude dogma of the Trinity which made it seem like three Gods, and that there was almost complete agreement on essentials; but clearest of all is the fact that their worship has the patterns and content that were present in the early Church long before they inspired Trinitarian doctrine.

The fact that doctrine and race went together in this split raises the question of the interplay of belief with other levels and factors. This chapter would look very different if written by a social, economic or political historian, or by a psychologist. Our aim has been not so much to try to give a complete account as to do justice to the subject from one perspective and leave it open to supplementing from others. To say the split was racial does not rule out taking the doctrine seriously, and vice versa. It is this sort of combination that shows how healthy praise cannot be separated from prophecy, discernment and knowledge. The union of these is the theme of our final chapter.

PENTECOSTALISM AND DANTE

'Laughter, indeed, does not vanish in the *Paradiso*: it is intensified there,' notes Dorothy Sayers.[13] In Dante's heaven there is delight, dancing, merriment, gentle comedy and dazzling smiles as well as laughter. If, in the unlikely encounter of Dante with good Pentecostal worship, one were to look for an obvious point of contact, it would be here in the lively awareness of heaven. One of the signs of it is the freedom of laughter in worship. In Pentecostal services it is often not laughter at a joke or at anything in particular; it is simply an overwhelming liberation in God's presence. The laughter rings out, spreads through the congregation, and faces beam to God. Then it stops and the service continues with a new tone. Laughter for no adequate earthly reason, as appreciation of the joy of God, is as good a sacrament of heaven as any. It is a foretaste of the complete praise of God in the infinitely good environment of his presence 'at home'. However one may conceive or shy away from conceiving what God's creativity can prepare in this way, Dante and the Pentecostals are part of a long tradition that has let its energy and imagination be stretched in praising God for promising the ultimate in fulfilment and allowing it to be anticipated now.

Conclusion

This chapter completes the gathering of the past into relationship with praising and knowing God. In chronological order, the subjects selected for attention in this and the previous chapter have been the Old Testament; the New Testament; the Church of the first four centuries in its worship and its development of the doctrine of the Trinity; Dante's poetry in the Middle Ages; Luther's theology of the cross at the Reformation; the major transformation and fragmentation of Western understanding and life since the seventeenth century and, finally, the rise of Pentecostalism in the twentieth century. Many of these themes will be developed in later chapters, including above all the master theme: God the Father, Son and Holy Spirit.

[13]   Op. cit., p. 33.

Basic Christian Existence as Praise

How can thinking and living go on in recognition of the abundance of God? How can God be allowed to be God in practice? Coping with God and his generosity is the central task of Christian faith, and what is given stretches all capacities. God is more than sufficient for all people and all situations, but he is so in particular ways which invite recognition and response. This chapter tries to work out something of what that involves.

This is the central chapter and in many ways the book pivots around it. It applies a God-centred realism to basic elements of existence: ordinary experience of life and nature; personal identity and dignity; space, time, causality and power; the nature of respect and blessing; and human maturity. It begins again with a poet, whose poems set the tone of the chapter.

Basic Christian Existence as 'a laugh'

'God must be allowed to surprise us,' said the Irish poet Patrick Kavanagh. He also wrote:

> A year ago I fell in love with the functional ward
> Of a chest hospital; square cubicles in a row,
> Plain concrete, wash basins – an art lover's woe,
> Not counting how the fellow in the next bed snored.
> But nothing whatever is by love debarred.
> The common and banal her heart can know.
> The corridor led to a stairway and below
> Was the inexhaustible adventure of a gravelled yard.
> This is what love does to things: the Rialto Bridge,
> The main gate that was bent by a heavy lorry,
> The seat at the back of a shed that was a suntrap.
> Naming these things is the love-act and its pledges:
> For we must record love's mystery without claptrap.
> Snatch out of time the passionate transitory.[1]

[1] 'The Hospital', *Collected Poems*, London 1972.

The ordinary is transfigured in Kavanagh's poetry, and nature is taken up into it too:

> Green, blue, yellow and red –
> God is down in the swamps and marshes
> Sensational as April and almost incredible
>   the flowering of our catharsis.
> A humble scene in a backward place
> Where no one important ever looked
> The raving flowers looked up in the face
> Of the One and the Endless, the Mind that has baulked
> The profoundest of mortals. A primrose, a violet,
> A violent wild iris – but mostly anonymous performers
> Yet an important occasion as the Muse at her toilet
> Prepared to inform the local farmers
> The beautiful, beautiful, beautiful God
> Was breathing his love by a cut-away bog.[2]

In one of his own favourite poems Kavanagh weaves together some of our key themes of God, love, newness, prayer, overflow and honouring and sets the right tone for a daily existence in which they are the leading realities:

> Leafy-with-love banks and the green waters of the canal
> Pouring redemption for me, that I do
> The will of God, wallow in the habitual, the banal,
> Grow with nature again as before I grew.
> The bright stick trapped, the breeze adding a third
> Party to the couple kissing on an old seat,
> And a bird gathering materials for the nest for the Word
> Eloquently new and abandoned to its delirious beat.
> O unworn world, enrapture me, encapture me in a web
> Of fabulous grass and eternal voices by a beech,
> Feed the gaping need of my senses, give me ad lib
> To pray unselfconsciously with overflowing speech
> For this soul needs to be honoured with a new dress woven
> From green and blue things and arguments that cannot be
>   proven.[3]

The tone is summed up in Kavanagh's remark that 'a good poem laughs inwardly'. But the laughter is not just a spectator's response, to be expressed by the poet's lyric perception of mundane reality. That is only a whetting of the appetite, pointing to the main course.

---

[2]   Ibid., 'The One'.
[3]   Ibid., 'Canal Bank Walk'.

A little too comical to suit me — the resurrection + laughter

Kavanagh calls the resurrection of Jesus.

> . . . a laugh freed
> for ever and ever.[4]

That is the supreme surprise, setting the tone for basic Christian existence – an astonishing, endlessly fresh and 'eloquently new and abandoned' life. There is almost an 'orthodoxy of laughter' here, if orthodoxy could permit itself to lose its usual rigidity and over-seriousness. It is the note of joy which we followed through Paul's Letter to the Philippians, which is there even in the title of Dante's *Divine Comedy*, which chuckles in the sense of humour that Martin Thornton sees as a chief mark of English spirituality, and which is illustrated later in this chapter by Dietrich Bonhoeffer's '*hilaritas*' in the face of death. In a faith which has the 'foolishness of the cross', a 'lamb on the throne' and the 'justification of the ungodly' there must be an appreciation of upside-downness, and many ways of joining in the laughter of the resurrection.

Joy may be a better word than laughter

Part of the logic of laughter, poetry and praise is that of intensification and overflow. The intense, pointed delight and the explosion of laughter go together; the poem's concentration and economy let it communicate more widely and with more power. The resurrection of the crucified Jesus Christ is this logic at the heart of Christianity. There is the intensity of concentration on this one man crucified and dead, followed by his universal availability through the resurrection. The basis of Christian existence is not just a basis. It is also an environment of abundance created through this overflow of life, and giving reason for praise in all situations. If this is basic reality then all of existence can be thought through in the light of it. True realism will take account of this first, and live from it. What will that life be like?

Identity through Praise

The main characteristic will be that it is a life given to that movement of recognition, honouring and delight which runs through the Bible and Christian history, and has been freshly evident in this century. To describe this, it is wrong to start from problems, or even problems solved. The beginning is with a basic reality which is good, attractive and generous. To begin to see this is to be drawn into appreciation and delight that leads into deeper understanding and relationship, and so on into the spiral of love that we have followed in Dante. The problems of evil, sin, suffering, ignorance and alienation are hindrances and often paralyse this movement,

4   Ibid., 'Lough Derg'.

but they are best tackled in its light, as we attempt in the next chapter. Now we will try to trace a pervasive pattern and possibility for ordinary life that the perspective of praise illuminates. We find from this perspective something essential to human identity, and a principle of human action that comes nearer than any other to being the master key.

It can be seen from infancy. Babies rely on adults to affirm them in life in practical ways with food and other material needs, and also with attention, encouragement, comfort and the many other forms of parental love. Each of us is shaped in this interaction in which pleasing and being pleased are basic. Only as we receive love, affirmation and security of various sorts do we begin to have a sense of our own worth and the confidence to develop.

A vital transition happens as we learn to talk and handle all the symbols and patterns of behaviour that make up society's world of meaning. Then our sense of our own identity and worth becomes inseparable from a complex network of attitudes of friends, peer group, workmates, heroes, media, the opposite sex, and so on. A large number of our most intense experiences as children and adults are related to events and people who have threatened or enhanced our sense of self-worth. Deep springs of motivation are here and they affect every aspect of life. The plea for recognition and affirmation is heard from the cradle to the tombstone, and beyond that in the various other ways in which people are concerned for the way they are remembered beyond death.

The world of work is pervaded by distinctions of worth and status. Money is the most common measurement of it in our economy, but recognition can come in many other ways: fame, authority, conditions of work, respect of fellow workers, appreciation of one's family and friends, or simply gratitude for services rendered. Whole economies turn on the balance of types of recognition and their distribution. In most organizations there is acute awareness of who has what status and of what carries the rewards of recognition.

The way in which status has been reconstituted in our century is one vital perspective on what is happening in contemporary British society. The Victorian status system has been largely dismantled, and its relative stability has not been replaced. Instead there are new forms of status linked to education, money, citizenship, race, and other kinds of group membership, while at the same time there has been an increase in resentment at status distinctions. Status is closely connected with class, but it is a more fundamental concept, and far more sensitive to the pluralism of society and the realities of human nature. Even a classless society (in Marxist terms of classes based on control of capital and labour) would have many differentiations of status of immense importance to its members.

The pervasive importance of the network of recognition, mutual affirmation and acceptance or rejection could be charted in education, sexual relations, social customs, the army, sport, literature, the media, the Churches, international relations and all other significant areas of our own and other civilizations. We do not have any choice about performing in this drama, but we are shaped by our participation, and the way we perform determines a great deal of our life. We are constantly trying to 'place' ourselves in the play, to interpret our past and present role and to imagine future possibilities. Ernest Becker even suggests that

Almost all (man's) time is devoted to the protection, maintenance and aggrandisement of his self-esteem. . . Almost all of one's inner life, when one is not absorbed in some active task, is a traffic in images of self-worth.[5]

That may be rather crude, but yet has an uncomfortable amount of truth in it, and it could be filled out with the endlessly varied and subtle nuances, whether in dress, speech, lifestyle or life's work, that we all employ in the quest for recognition and affirmation by others. Vital in all this is the scale of values we use, our assessment of what and who are significant and worth taking seriously into account. Our habitual pattern of recognizing and respecting is intrinsic to our identity, and drastic change in this will seem very like the death of ourself.

One key concept here is that of 'human dignity'. This embraces 'human rights' but is far wider. Whereas rights tend to be egalitarian and measured by a lowest common denominator, dignity is less quantifiable and not necessarily based on equality. There are aspects of human dignity which are violated by the comparison and correlation of one person with another.

At the heart of human dignity is the free respect given by one person to another, recognizing their otherness, their distinctive life, the irreducible pluralism of being persons in relation. The other must be allowed to speak, to act, to understand, to be free to respond or not. There is not a simple symmetrical relationship of equality, but an asymmetrical one of looking up to the other as transcending oneself. Preferably this should be mutual but, as our interpretation of Paul's Letter to the Philippians (ch. 3, above, especially on Phil. 2) showed, at the centre of his concept of Christian living is the determination, even in the absence of mutuality, to persevere in respecting others, and to take the role of a servant to the point of rejection and death.

Paul had experienced a transformation in his pattern of recogni-

5 *The Birth and Death of Meaning* (London 1972), pp. 76f.

tion and affirmation, and Philippians shows the intrinsic relation between his new praise of God and his respect for other people. The authenticity of the praise and the respect are inseparable, and at the centre of each is Jesus Christ. He embodies a revolution in conventional ideas of respect and praise. Mark's Gospel describes a shattering of images of God and of what human success and status are. The nerve-centre of our identity is aimed at by the call to follow Jesus on his way of the cross.

The reverberations of this 'dying to self' are bound to spread into all the areas mentioned above where status, recognition, prestige and mutual affirmation are so important. Paul's letters tell of his personal revolution as he lets go all he used to boast about, preaches only 'Christ crucified' and follows out the implications at all levels of existence, as concisely set out in Philippians. He also tackled head-on some of the most powerful aspects of group status and identity in his day. 'There is neither Jew nor Greek, slave nor free, male nor female; for you are all one in Christ Jesus' (Gal. 3:28). He concentrated mainly on the 'Jew nor Greek', which was a racial, religious and cultural division, and a lot of his suffering resulted from refusal to compromise on it.

That story of persistent and awkward challenging of individuals and groups in their self-esteem and attitudes to each other is repeated in the great saints, prophets and movements of renewal and mission throughout Christian history. The investment of people in their networks of recognition and respect is so large that the most stubborn resistance and retaliation is almost bound to follow. Above all, the effort is made to separate the praise of God from its social and practical consequences. Everything is tried to undo that knot, and in each Christian too there are powerful drives urging this. Keeping it tied is not primarily a matter of gripping it tight, but of recognizing that it has already been secured, as Mark's Gospel describes. Then the starting-point is not standing face to face with a difficult problem but standing in the presence of Jesus Christ, real and active in our situation. Because of who he is, the keynote is one of constantly astonished joy, with expectation of more than enough being given to meet our problems, even if they are not all solved. This is the life of faith, basic Christian existence, and it springs from our recognition, respect and honouring being focused through Jesus Christ and being allowed to transform our network of relationships. Our whole life is continually thrown into the air in praise in the trust that it will be caught, blessed and returned renewed.

The day-to-day working out of this in all the areas mentioned is a matter of particular discernment in each case. The social nature of our habits of honouring and approval means that corporate discernment and commitment are essential. So the community needs prophecy, as discussed in chapter 9 below. The tensions that ancient Israel experienced as prophets exposed injustice and violation of human dignity, and linked them with a wrong understanding and relationship with God, are inevitable. It is through persisting simultaneously both in wholehearted praise (with the universal invitation to share in it) and in the nurturing of human dignity that the most characteristic dynamics of Judaeo-Christian living are created and developed. In performing this the discernment of God, of each other and of ourselves, is given. God's glory and his liberating action meet with our delighted surrender in love to him and to each other:

> Then our mouth was filled with laughter
> and our tongue with shouts of joy;
> Then they said among the nations,
> 'The Lord has done great things for them.'
> The Lord has done great things for us:
> We are glad (Ps. 126:2–3).

> Mercy and truth are met together;
> Righteousness and peace have kissed each other.
> (Ps. 85:10, Authorized Version).

The Ecology of Praise

We have been given an insider's view of Christian living as praise, and it has led into a discussion of the most basic conditions of human identity and dignity. Yet if praise is not just an arbitrary human activity but is in harmony with the way reality is, then we cannot limit it to the interpersonal. We must be able to follow it through by looking at the rest of creation in this light:

> Praise him, sun and moon,
> praise him, shining stars,
> praise him, highest heavens,
> and waters above the heavens!

> Let them all praise the name of Yahweh,
> at whose command they were created. . .

> Let earth praise Yahweh:
> sea-monsters and all the deeps,
> fire and hail, snow and mist,
> gales that obey his decree,

> mountains and hills,
> orchards and forests,
> wild animals and farm animals,
> snakes and birds.

All kings on earth and nations,
princes, all rulers in the world,
young men and girls,
old people, and children too!

Let them all praise the name of Yahweh. . . (Ps. 148, Jerusalem
Bible)

Kavanagh, in 'The One', quoted above, sees the swamps and
marshes, with their 'raving flowers', 'anonymous performers', doing
something similar, and in 'Canal Bank Walk' there is

... a bird gathering materials for the nest for the Word
Eloquently new and abandoned to its delirious beat.

Is this all simply human projection, the 'pathetic fallacy' of
imagining that nature is human? Or is the imagination of the
psalmist and the poet discerning something about the way the world
is? Are people only one set of performers in a symphony of response
to the Creator in which flowers, sticks, birds and breezes also join
in appropriate ways? It would be odd if, granted the reality of this
God, there was nothing like this response.

The most adequate starting-point for understanding this is to see
God himself as one who recognizes and respects. This is a vital clue
to the sort of reality creation is. God lets it be itself, he respects its
integrity, and that is the most important, all-embracing fact about
it. He affirms it to be good, he knows it in countless ways, and how
he loves it shows respect to be intrinsic to his love. This respect is
not just an attitude, but is worked out in the structure of the cosmos
itself.

A basic expression of the way God respectfully lets creation be
itself is the operation of space and time. They are the fundamental
conditions of existence distinct from God. Without separateness,
'otherness', there can be no respect. Modern cosmology has
sharpened this by its understanding of the relativity of space and
time. They are always the space and time of particular things or
fields of force, and so it is not possible to treat even physical realities
on the same level, contained in a 'box' of invariant space and time.
Instead, spatio-temporality is made up of a rich diversity, with
new developments of many sorts being constantly generated. The
universe is developing and pluralist. Pervading it all is a sensitivity
to differences, boundaries and suitable modes of interaction that
can be taken up to enrich our key concepts of recognition and
respect. The evolutionary roots of these concepts are deep, and they
are not just optional extras but essential to the delicate ecology of
the cosmos.

The structure of space and time and the dynamics of evolution are

the environment in which there emerge the interpersonal patterns of
recognition and respect discussed earlier. An ethic of respect can
also be seen as the most appropriate approach by people to animals
and to other levels of existence, as in Albert Schweitzer's 'reverence
for life' and the ecological concerns of the Friends of the Earth.
These all help to point to the sort of cosmology that is suggested
by some recent developments and that is urgently needed, one
which does not divide 'facts' from 'values' but sees that both are
intertwined in the way the cosmos is, and that its complex network
is violated and distorted if cosmology fails to take account of this.

If all the co-ordinated diversity of the universe is to be traced to
God's way of letting it be itself, then what about God's own interaction with it? The question of God's power and action in the world
is one of the most important in theology. A great deal of theology
and daily existence is bedevilled by inappropriate ways of understanding God's power. One of the commonest pictures is of God's
power in competition with his creation's freedom, and people
needing protection against his overwhelming omnipotence. The
model of power in this picture is a crude one of the coercive use of
force, so a new starting-point is needed.

One way of putting the question is as one about the way in which
God is a cause in the world. If we look for the highest forms of
causality known by us, according to the standards of recognition
and respect, then a simple answer is found: speech. If we wish to
cause someone to do something while respecting their freedom and
integrity, we may speak and ask them. This is the form of causality
most characteristic of human beings. Speech may of course be
coercive or backed by the threat of force, but that is not necessarily
so, and at its best it works by invitation and information rather
than by manipulation.

If God wants to respect his creation he will interact with it
primarily in some such way as by speaking with it. According to
the Jewish, Christian, Islamic and some other traditions, this is
what he does. The word of God is seen not only as creating the
world but as in constant interaction with it through history. We
have already followed the centrality of praise and allied themes in
the Old Testament, showing how in response to God's communication a network of worship and of respect for people was formed.
The respect of God for his people goes to the length of pleading
and agonizing, and even his judgement is aimed at shocking them
into proper recognition of who he is and who they are.

The crucifixion of Jesus is the summary of God's respect for
creation. This is God's speech expressed in suffering. He lets people
be themselves, lets them have their freedom even to be wrong, to
ignore him and to show disrespect to the point of killing. This is

met not with counter-force but with a willingness to go through the
final destructive experience and so respect the power that has been
given to the world. The resurrection is not a simple reversal of this
or a way of giving in, a few days late, to the taunt: 'Come down
from the cross.' It is the overcoming of evil and death in a way that
utterly respects but also judges and shows the limits of the world.
This is embodied in what follows it: an explosion of evangelism and
praise offering this event and person in an invitation to the whole
creation. It is an outcome which relies, with a purity less common
in the Old Testament, on the appeal of speech and the free response
of listeners.

As Paul recognized most explicitly, the crucifixion and resurrection are a demonstration of power that revolutionize the concept of
power. Now God is identified through the foolishness and weakness
of the cross, and honour and praise have, as we showed in chapter
3, undergone a transformation. There is now a new criterion for
who God is and how he acts in the world, and it carries with it the
commitment of the early Church to a basic existence of praise and
respect such as Philippians describes. The cosmic scope of the
transformation is worked out in two major documents of praise, the
Letters to the Colossians and Ephesians:

Blessed be the God and Father of our Lord Jesus Christ, who
has blessed us in Christ with every spiritual blessing in the
heavenly places, even as he chose us in him before the foundation
of the world, that we should be holy and blameless before him.
He destined us in love to be his sons through Jesus Christ,
according to the purpose of his will, to the praise of his glorious
grace which he freely bestowed on us in the Beloved. In him
we have redemption through his blood, the forgiveness of our
trespasses, according to the riches of his grace which he lavished
upon us. For he has made known to us in all wisdom and insight
the mystery of his will, according to his purpose which he set
forth in Christ as a plan for the fullness of time, to unite all things
in him, things in heaven and things on earth. In him, according
to the purpose of him who accomplishes all things according to
the counsel of his will, we who first hoped in Christ have been
destined and appointed to live for the praise of his glory. In him
you also, who have heard the word of truth, the gospel of your
salvation, and have believed in him, were sealed with the promised Holy Spirit, which is the guarantee of our inheritance until
we acquire possession of it, to the praise of his glory (Eph.
1:3–14).

Fascination with these cosmic implications has run all through
Christian history. The interest is, as the New Testament shows,

very much a part of Christian response to God, and bound into the life of worship. The core of astonishment around which it all spirals is that God is free to be involved with his creation from the 'inside' as well as from the 'outside'. He is prepared to follow through to their limits the negative consequences of his genuine, respectful participation in history. The result of this is to change the very nature of the universe, to produce something new yet in harmony with the best possibilities of the old. The implications extend even to the way the basic conditions of the universe operate. If space and time are not separate from the events that happen in them, Jesus' crucifixion and resurrection mean a new patterning of the spatio-temporal environment and of its possibilities.

Poet of Creation

There is a comprehensive biblical term for the powerful yet respectful interaction between God and the world, in which the world is enhanced at all levels. It is that of 'blessing'. In being blessed a person, animal, plant, situation or thing is affirmed by God in the way most appropriate to its nature and future. There is no manipulation, but a combination of discernment and active enabling. 'God rules creation by blessing,' said the Jewish rabbis of the time of Jesus. There is in blessing the logic of overflow that we have already discussed as characterizing the mutual freedom of love between God and creation. Blessing is supremely a non-necessity, a gratuitous bestowal of something new.

The reality of blessing needs to be rescued from the magical and superstitious associations it has gathered, especially in its trivialized, token usage in some ordinary speech. Its rehabilitation is tied to our conception of God's activity in the world. Blessing is a form of causality that is effective but is in accordance with the respect God has for creation. The ending of Luke's Gospel economically sums up the ecology of blessing that the event of Jesus Christ consummated:

> Then he led them out as far as Bethany, and lifting up his hands he blessed them. While he blessed them, he parted from them. And they returned to Jerusalem with great joy, and were continually in the temple blessing God (Luke 24: 50–53).

Blessing is the comprehensive praise and thanks that returns all reality to God, and so lets all be taken up into the spiral of mutual appreciation and delight which is the fulfilment of creation. For the rabbis of Jesus' time, to use anything of creation without blessing God was to rob God. Only the person receiving with thanks really received from God, and if there is one summary expression of Jewish response to God it is in the blessing of his name, which represents his whole being. Jesus was in this tradition, and himself blessed God, food, children and disciples. His whole work is summed up in Acts as having been sent to bless, completing the history of the blessing of Israel through Abraham (Acts 3:25f). Jesus is seen as the concentration of the mutuality of blessing, God blessing man and man blessing God. This is the dynamic of both creation and reconciliation.

Praise is therefore best seen as part of an ecology of blessing. All creation is a part of this, and praises God. What meaning can be given to this? Two levels appear in it. The first is that, since God's blessing is given by letting each creature, animate or not, be itself, and by enabling it, with infinite respect for its nature, to participate in the drama of the universe, then creation's response is primarily in its very existence. Creation's praise is not an extra, an addition to what it is, but is the shining of its being, the overflowing significance it has in pointing to its Creator simply by being itself.

The second level is the way this being can overflow into many forms of expression. When the glory of creation is glimpsed it can inspire painting, psalms, music, science, literature and a vast variety of less formal recognition and appreciation. This is the role of human beings in creation, articulating its praise in fresh ways. 'Man as the poet and priest of creation' is an ancient concept, with parallels in most religions. As George Herbert wrote:

Of all thy creatures both in sea and land
Only to man thou hast made known thy ways
And put the penne alone into his hand
And made him Secretarie of thy praise.

The mediating, communicating role in relation to all creation is expressed in the Genesis stories through the blessing which gives stewardship of the world to man, the task of gardening in Eden, and above all, the naming of the creatures. This naming could be seen as symbolically containing all artistic and scientific activity. Ancient Jewish commentators saw the naming as the unique human privilege of sharing in God's creative act, and saw this creative process continued in every act of praise and blessing.

So right praise of God leads into the most thorough and discerning involvement with creation, in a way that takes the praise of creation itself on to a new level.

O unworn world, enrapture me, encapture me. . .

asks Kavanagh as he offers his poetry. He does not lose the distinctions between God, man and the world, but he lets each bless and be blessed, and produces poetry to 'perfect the perfection'.

Maturity in Praise

Another request Kavanagh makes is: *note: otherness/side of self in praise*

> . . . give me ad lib
> To pray unselfconsciously with overflowing speech
> For this soul needs to be honoured with a new dress woven
> From green and blue things and arguments that cannot be
>   proven.

The new dress is given to be worn at once. It is not given in pieces to be sewn together according to a pattern. God's honouring is complete. Astonishment at this honouring by God is one of the mainsprings of praise. It makes praise different from an achievement or work of one's own: it is thanks for what is given, and the logic is again that of overflow and non-necessity. The very completeness of the gift rules out any response that is not first of all a matter of recognizing the all-sufficiency of God and what he gives. This is in line with centuries of reflection on the experience of grace, sharpened by the Reformation's understanding of justification by grace alone. We start off our praise in Christ, with Christ, putting on Christ, baptized into Christ, and we never get beyond that. Not only is this new life a sheer gift, but so too is the capacity to celebrate it, to 'pray unselfconsciously with overflowing speech'.

The unselfconsciousness sets this apart from many other forms of maturity. Often maturity is seen as the result of trying to conform to a certain pattern of development. A norm is set up by which growth is measured. That can be oppressive, even if the norm only claims to be a description of how the average person develops. There is often comparison of oneself with the norm or with other people, and much feeling of inferiority and failure, with constant anxiety about achievement. It is a developed form of self-centredness and Kavanagh sums up the disease and its cure in his poem 'The Self-Slaved':

> Me I will throw away
> Me sufficient for the day
> The sticky self that clings
> Adhesions on the wings
> To love and adventure,
> To go on the grand tour
> A man must be free
> From self-necessity.
>
> See over there
> A created splendour
> Made by one individual

From things residual
With all the various
Qualities hilarious
Of what
Hitherto was not:

A November mood
As by one man understood;
Familiar, an old custom
Leaves falling, a white frosting
Bringing a sanguine dream
A new beginning with an old theme.

Throw away thy sloth
Self, carry off my wrath
With its self-righteous
Satirizing blotches,
No self, no self-exposure
The weakness of the proser
But undefeatable
By means of the beatable.

I will have love, have love
From anything made of
And a life with a shapely form
With gaiety and charm
And capable of receiving
With grace the grace of living
And wild moments too
Self, when freed from you.
Prometheus calls me on,
Prometheus calls me: Son
We'll both go off together
In this delightful weather.

A widespread religious form of this concentration on the self is in seeing the whole of life as a matter of 'soul-making' or 'spiritual development'. But if the self is seen as completely secure, 'saved', from the start, it is freed to concentrate on God and other people, and in particular to be taken up in thanks and praise of God. In that case, all sorts of growth and change happen, but they are by-products, not aims, and flourish in freedom and unselfconscious absorption in God, the object of praise, and in whatever vocation is given. Praise takes one out of oneself into enjoyment of God, and into appreciating and sharing his desires for the world. The focus is on God, his will, and other people, and there is a liberation from concern for self.

There are many other practical by-products once this focus is got right. In any situation, to face the reality of God, who always evokes praise, is to be opened up for God to speak and act more freely through us. Through habitual praise it is normal to find that there is both a deepening and a speeding-up of our discernment in relation to people and events. Often this comes first of all in the form of the right way to pray and intercede for them, and then many consequences follow for what we are to say and do. The principle is that all relationships are lived through God, and we see the truth and possibilities of each other most adequately when we are most fully taken up with God. There is no competition between love for God and for each other. There is, rather, the greatest danger in thinking that any way other than their union is shorter or more effective.

Much else is given when praise is right, and the vision of Christian maturity is of all enjoying God and being given the gifts that others need. The effects of this are especially clear in experiencing the encouragement and hope that flow through the praise of God. Praise strikes at the roots of despair and discouragement of all sorts, and it puts all problems in a perspective where they lose their ability to fill the whole horizon. The ultimate test of this comes in the face of suffering and death:

> Yes, and I shall rejoice. For I know that through your prayers and the help of the spirit of Jesus Christ this will turn out for my deliverance, as it is my eager expectation and hope that I shall not be at all ashamed, but that with full courage now as always Christ will be honoured in my body, whether by life or by death. For to me to live is Christ, and to die is gain . . . Even if I am to be poured out as a libation upon the sacrificial offering of your faith, I am glad and rejoice with you all. Likewise, you also should be glad and rejoice with me (Phil. 1:19–21; 2:17–18).

Death is the end of all maturing, it takes our development and perfecting definitively out of our own hands. It is a moment of truth for the thoroughness of our reliance on God, and Paul's joy in the face of it is inseparable from his confidence in the 'God who raises the dead'. Yet it is easy to see how even this confidence could be distorted into another oppressive model of perfection. In the early Church martyrdom sometimes became itself an ideal of Christian living. The concentration then was on the self, rather than on the overflow of praise and witness of which the martyrdom was a by-product. To maintain the right focus here is especially difficult in times of great pressure, but it is perhaps only more obvious when the circumstances are dramatic. The call to focus on God in praise even when one is oneself under threat of death is in fact a description of the vocation of all Christians. One modern martyr who seems to us to exemplify, under extreme circumstances, the right sort of spirituality for basic Christian existence, is Dietrich Bonhoeffer, who was executed by the Nazis in 1945.

Bonhoeffer's 'Letters and Papers from Prison'[6] have a similar tone to Paul's Letter (also from prison) to the Philippians. His remarks about '*hilaritas*' express it best:

> On the whole, all the newest productions seem to me to be lacking in *hilaritas* – 'cheerfulness' – which is to be found in any really great and free intellectual achievement. One has always the impression of a somewhat tortured and strained manufacture instead of creativity in the open air.[7]

> Now that's enough for today. When shall we be able to talk together again? Keep well, enjoy the beautiful country, spread *hilaritas* around you, and keep it yourself too![8]

Another recurrent theme is music. His thoughts on the baptism of his nephew include the advice:

> Music, as your parents understand and practise it, will help to dissolve your perplexities and purify your character and sensibility, and in times of care and sorrow will keep a ground-base of joy alive in you.[9]

The whole complex of life, death, joy and music come together in a remarkable letter of 27 March 1944 to his friend Bethge:

> I'm constantly reminded that it is mainly to you that I owe my enjoyment of the Easter hymns. It is a year now since I heard a hymn sung. But it's strange how the music that we hear inwardly can almost surpass, if we really concentrate on it, what we hear physically. It has a greater purity, the dross falls away, and in a way the music acquires a 'new body'. There are only a few pieces that I know well enough to hear them inwardly, but I get on particularly well with the Easter hymns. I'm getting a better existential appreciation of the music that Beethoven composed after he had gone deaf, in particular the great set of variations from Opus III, which we once heard played by Gieseking. . .

> Easter? We're paying more attention to dying than to death. We're more concerned to get over the act of dying than to overcome death. Socrates mastered the art of dying; Christ overcame death as 'the last enemy' (1 Cor. 15:26). There is a real difference

---

6   London 1971.
7   Ibid., p. 189.
8   Ibid., p. 232.
9   Ibid., p. 295.

between the two things; the one is within the scope of human possibilities, the other means resurrection. It's not from the *ars moriendi*, the art of dying, but from the resurrection of Christ, that a new and purifying wind can blow through our present world. *Here* is the answer to δός μοι ποῦ στῶ καὶ κινήσω τὴν γῆν. 'Give me somewhere to stand, and I will move the earth' – Archimedes. If a few people really believed that and acted on it in their daily lives, a great deal would be changed. To live in the light of the resurrection – that is what Easter means. Do you find, too, that most people don't know what they really live by?[10]

In the light of all this, what is Christian maturity? Bonhoeffer again precisely puts two basic options:

I remember a conversation that I had in America thirteen years ago with a young French pastor. We were asking ourselves quite simply what we wanted to do with our lives. He said he would like to become a saint (and I think it's quite likely that he did become one). At the time I was very impressed, but I disagreed with him, and said in effect, that I should like to learn to have faith. For a long time I didn't realize the depth of the contrast. . . I discovered later, and I'm still discovering right up to this moment, that it is only by living completely in this world that one learns to have faith. One must completely abandon any attempt to make something of oneself, whether it be a saint or a converted sinner, or a churchman (a so-called priestly type!), a righteous man or an unrighteous one, a sick man or a healthy one. By this-worldliness I mean living unreservedly in life's duties, problems, successes and failures, experiences and perplexities. In so doing we throw ourselves completely into the arms of God, taking seriously, not our own sufferings, but those of God in the world – watching with Christ in Gethsemane. That, I think, is faith. . .[11]

Bonhoeffer's way is of constantly renewed recognition of God in all the complexities and agonies of living, and an accompanying liberation from concern for oneself. Maturity is faithfulness according to one's situation and gifts, the willingness to focus afresh on the presence of God here and now. The death and resurrection of Jesus Christ is the ultimate standpoint for Christian praise, and there we find an event and person that relativizes all differences in maturity, achievement and capacity. What follows recognition of this is not a vain attempt to progress towards infinity, but the praise, *hilaritas* and solidarity inspired by the Holy Spirit.

10 Ibid., p. 240.
11 Ibid., pp. 369f.

All of this is in freedom. There is no 'rule of praise', and no quantifying of it. Nor should it be identified with articulateness, though that is often welcome. The severely handicapped can mature as Christians in their own way. They do not develop according to the norms, and may even deteriorate. They do not fit most ideas of maturity and human fulfilment, and many definitions of what it is to be basically human (in terms of capacities of mind, freedom, responsibility, speech) would exclude them. But the ultimate all-embracing handicap is death, and it is from that that Christian praise is born. God especially delights to evoke praise from surprising sources, and perhaps one of the most beautiful gifts is to be the 'secretary of his praise' as it appears in those who cannot articulate it. Mary Craig was even able to call her book about her experience as the mother of two severely handicapped children: *Blessings*.

6

Evil, Suffering and Death

Among its other attributes, absolute evil paralyses absolutely –
William Styron, *Sophie's Choice*[1]

Evil at its worst has a dynamic of its own which counterfeits the
movement of praise. There is a logic of overflow in evil too, magnifying itself in a widening spiral and sucking up whatever it can into
its destructiveness. Yet it is fundamentally inertial. It is parasitic
and uncreative and on its way towards death it emasculates and
paralyses. So, as Styron says, writing of Auschwitz, it is an activity
which leads to the negation of all activity and life. Essentially evil
is not even interesting: it is a dull, infinitely depressing vacuum
which needs the skill of deceit to seem otherwise. Simone Weil
wrote:

> Imaginary evil is romantic and varied; real evil is gloomy, monot-
> onous, barren, boring. Imaginary good is boring; real good is
> always new, marvellous, intoxicating.[2]

Shame

An experience of evil that is close to the heart of our theme is that
of shame. This is not often discussed in our culture, which means
that we have lost a term that helps us to understand some of our
deepest problems. Most of us have had childhood experiences of
intense shame when we felt negated because of the rejection or
condemnation of a parent or friend or ourselves. It is not just a
moral experience, and it is more comprehensive than guilt. It is
best understood as the perversion of the movement of respect that
was central to the previous chapter. In extreme shame we are
deprived of self-respect and of the recognition and affirmation of
others and of God. It can be seen as the implosion of respect, in
which those energies which should be taken up into that ecology of
praise and blessing, as respect finds its proper form and goal, are

[1] New York 1979, p. 392.
[2] *The Simone Weil Reader*, ed. George A. Panichas, New York 1977.

instead turned against oneself. This negates what one lives from, and so it is a state of living death. It is a picture of ultimate rejection and horror, with the joy and hope of life drained away, and the energies of living turned against themselves. The despair of such a situation can lead to the paralysis Styron describes, or it can externalize its agony by striking at others with an alienated, demonic hatred – what happened at Auschwitz was not unrelated to the shaming of Germany at Versailles and the grasping by Hitler and his followers for the respect that must be granted to strength and 'superiority'.

There is a proper shame too. Granted that we can really do wrong and also feel and think in all sorts of wrong ways, then shame is a healthy result. Even if we simply are in the wrong through no fault of our own, shame can objectively be the appropriate response. It can be a realistic recognition of our true situation. This is sharpened by reference to God. In living before God there is a criterion of right and wrong shame: right shame is measured by God's judgement on us; wrong shame is what is inflicted unjustifiably, whether by others or by oneself or by a wrong conception of God. The central question is the existence and nature of God, in whose light we are known as we are. We will now explore in turn the nature of right and wrong shame.

Right shame is quickly summarized. It is a recognition before God of being in some wrong relationship or false position. It admits that we are in a state of 'living death', in shame impotent to undo the past or enable a better future. Confession and repentance recognize this, and it is not just a matter of deliberate faults but of the need for a comprehensive transformation beyond all self-caused wrong. What is hoped for is simple: joy instead of shame. That this can be given is a constant Old Testament theme, especially in the great books of praise, the Psalms and Isaiah.

> Instead of your shame you shall have a double portion,
> instead of dishonour you shall rejoice in your lot (Isa. 61:7).

Sexuality, marriage and family life are areas where shame is most intimately and excruciatingly experienced, and Deutero-Isaiah uses these to express the nature of God:

> Fear not, for you will not be ashamed;
> be not confounded, for you will not be put to shame;
> for you will forget the shame of your youth,
> and the reproach of your widowhood you will remember no more.
> For your Maker is your husband,
> the Lord of hosts is his name;

and the Holy One of Israel is your Redeemer,
   the God of the whole earth he is called.
For the Lord has called you
   like a wife forsaken and grieved in spirit,
like a wife of youth when she is cast off,
   says your God.

For a brief moment I forsook you,
   but with great compassion I will gather you.
In overflowing wrath for a moment
   I hid my face from you,
but with everlasting love I will have compassion on you,
   says the Lord, your redeemer (Isa. 54:4–8).

The crucial question here is who God is, one whose love does not
allow shame to be final but has created for joy. Knowing this God
is both the ultimate intensification of right shame and the promise
of joy. On the other hand, orienting oneself to a false absolute,
which in Isaiah is called idolatry, is to cut oneself off from the
liberation of joy:

They shall be turned back and utterly put to shame,
   who trust in graven images,
who say to molten images,
   'you are our gods' (Isa. 42:17).

All of them are put to shame and confounded,
   the makers of idols go in confusion together.
But Israel is saved of the Lord with everlasting salvation;
   you shall not be put to shame or confounded to all eternity
      (Isa. 45:16–17).

This is a matter of the radical distortion of the ability to respect
and praise.
   Wrong shame is the result of the most powerful drives and
processes of self and society being used to destroy joy, dignity and
all that goes with them. It oppresses millions. It can drag down the
whole of life, every relationship can be distorted by it, and it generates its own downward spiral. We all participate in inflicting it as
well as suffering it.
   The Psalmist continually cries out against the 'enemies' who
thrive on slander, fear, violence, deceit and the perversion of goodness and trust. He often recognizes his own sin and need for repentance, but beyond that is in no doubt about the evil that shapes
the state of the world. Our century has seen the power and terror
of evil on an unprecedented scale. Auschwitz has already been
mentioned. Stalin's Soviet Union is a parallel.

Solzhenitsyn calls one of his novels, which is set in a comparatively mild prison camp, *The First Circle*, named after the topmost
and least rigorous of Dante's circles of hell. In *The Gulag Archipelago*
and other works Solzhenitsyn exposes the deeper circles of this hell.
He tells of the lengths to which Stalin's Terror went in depriving
its victims of human dignity and in intensifying their degradation.
At its heart he finds the alliance of violence and lies. Violence and
the domination it wins need to conceal or justify themselves in order
to survive. They do so by weaving a network of lies and half-truths,
and promoting behaviour, ideology and power structures that
support them and punish deviation. Dante's *Inferno* shows a similar
insight into the dynamics of evil. It progresses from violence to
deceit, hypocrisy and falsehood. As Solzhenitsyn tells and reflects
on the story of his country in the grip of the Terror, the extreme of
degradation is not that of the prisoners in the concentration camps.
They at least, he says, were freed from the constant demand to
approve of the system, to support vociferously every directive and
official attitude, and above all to praise Stalin continually. In the
camps pressures were intense, and many succumbed to the temptations to co-operate with evil and to betray fellow prisoners, but at
least there was some possibility of integrity. Outside, in Stalinist
society, it was far more difficult, with the cancer of lies, hypocrisy
and false adulation almost inescapable. The cult of Stalin and his
system aimed at being totalitarian, embracing all reality, and as
such was a demonic opposite of praise of God. Solzhenitsyn
describes how it reduced millions to a state similar to that of Dante
in his reaction to the furthest thing from the praise of God, the last
circle of hell:

> I did not die, and I was not alive;
> think for yourself, if you have any wit,
> What I became, deprived of life and death.[3]

Stalin and Hitler are public, dramatic examples of the pervasive
worship of false absolutes and the infliction of shame that accompanies them. Money, family, power and every other attraction for
hearts and minds have, as the counterpart of the devotion they
demand, powerful penalties for heresy or disloyalty. The most effective of these is the loss of recognition and affirmation that is concentrated in shame. Poverty, alienation from parents, or rejection by
the powers-that-be all have tangible and painful practical effects,
but they are at their most terrible when internalized in loss of
identity and the despising of oneself. The therapy for this has many

---

[3]   *Inferno*, XXXIX, 25f. Trans. Allen Mandelbaum, New York 1982.

levels and aspects, but part of it must be to face the question of what is to be ultimately valued and respected.

In line with this, the most insidious forms of wrong shame are religious or quasi-religious, for 'the corruption of the best is the worst'. The rhetoric of right shame, the manipulation of humility before God, is the most potent instrument for shutting the way to joy. That is why the only safe perspective in Christian communication is that of praising God (cf. below, chapter 9). Legalisms of all sorts are the most common way in which shame is maintained without hope of joy. Once one is caught on the treadmill of trying to live up to an ideal, law or norm one has to live with a constant sense of wrongness. The legalism can even be one that operates at the centre of worship (including that which prides itself on its 'freedom'), and paralyses joy with others before God.

Jesus, in the complex tangle of right and wrong shame present in his, as in every other environment, characteristically comes down hardest on the false religious versions, especially when they block healing and forgiveness. He is also the friend of those shamed by society, and teaches of a God who welcomes even those with good reason to be ashamed. Yet as striking as any of this is the focus on himself as the criterion of true shame:

> For whoever is ashamed of me and of my words in this adulterous and sinful generation, of him will the Son of Man also be ashamed, when he comes in the glory of his Father with the holy angels (Mark 8:38).

This is borne out by many other strands in the New Testament tradition, and in the passion narrative there are the stories of Peter's denial and Judas' betrayal. The crucifixion itself was the climax of shame, in which its many dimensions focused: public humiliation, condemnation by state and religious authorities, desertion of friends, failure of mission, and identification with those rejected by God. In Styron's terms, evil achieved its paralysis even of this man, and he died.

The New Testament pivots round the sequel to this. In the perspective of shame, the resurrection does what is most needed: it vindicates. The Old Testament faith was in vindication in face of evil and injustice:

> For the Lord God helps me;
>   therefore I have not been confounded;
> therefore I have set my face like a flint,
>   and I know I shall not be put to shame;
>   he who vindicates me is near (Isa. 50:7–8).

That is the hope of the Servant Songs in Isaiah, and it rings through the deepest experiences of other writers too, especially Job, the Psalmists, Jeremiah and Ezekiel:

> let me never be put to shame;
>> In thy righteousness deliver me! (Ps. 31:1).

The other side of that is:

> let the wicked be put to shame,
>> let them go dumbfounded to Sheol (Ps. 31:17).

In these terms, the crucifixion is Jesus going the way of the wicked, and the resurrection is a new way through shame. 'Justification of the ungodly' is what Paul called it: a vindication that offers a completely new beginning and source of self-respect. 'In Christ' it is possible not to be ashamed, but to rejoice. The cost is simple: Jesus Christ becomes the criterion of shame. Paul passionately asserts this:

> We preach Christ crucified, a stumbling block to Jews and folly to Gentiles, but to those who are called, both Jews and Greeks, Christ the power of God and the wisdom of God. For the foolishness of God is wiser than men, and the weakness of God is stronger than men.

> For consider your call, brethren; not many of you were powerful, not many were of noble birth; but God chose what is foolish in the world to shame the wise, God chose what is weak in the world to shame the strong, God chose what is low and despised in the world, even things that are not, to bring to nothing things that are, so that no human being might boast in the presence of God. He is the source of your life in Christ Jesus, whom God made our wisdom, our righteousness and sanctification and redemption; therefore, as it is written, 'Let him who boasts boast of the Lord.' (1 Cor. 1:23–31).

So shame is opposed from the inside by suffering it, embodying it, and going to the roots of it as the perversion of respect. The result is a new object of respect and boasting, Jesus Christ. This transforms the meaning of shame and liberates it for the two basic Christian activities of worship and witness. Not to be ashamed of Jesus Christ becomes the central mark of identity of the Christian Church (cf. Phil. 1:20; 1 Pet. 4:16; Rom 1:16; John 12:42f; Luke 9:26; 2 Tim. 1:8; Rev. 6:9ff; Acts *passim*).

Against the Stoics

There are many ways of dealing with shame besides the Christian. Other conceptions of God greatly affect the sort of response possible and appropriate. The denial of God leaves shame only in the sphere of relationship to other people and to oneself, with no ultimate criterion for it. It is common for shame to be seen as pathological in itself, something to be got rid of by therapy, and the prevalence of wrong shame in a multitude of forms makes this plausible. Strategies for handling it are as varied as people and cultures, but we want to deal with one typical response.

We call it the stoic response. Its main mark is that it endures evil, suffering and death with dignity. It refuses to be dragged down by them or to be escapist when faced with them. Stoicism is one of the most admirable ways of handling the negativities of life that has been developed. It is patient, courageous and ultimately resigned, and this gives a sober freedom in relation to shame, which is never allowed to get out of hand or lead to panic or desperation. There are theistic forms of stoicism in which God is the impassible, imperturbable orderer of the universe who demands conformity with his order, and atheistic forms that stress the immanent order of the world and the importance of harmony with the best one knows. If the stoic does fail, then he faces up to this, does what he can to set it right (even to the point of suicide) and if possible sets about trying to do better.

We have deliberately drawn a 'type' which is recognizable within Christianity as well as outside it. It is deeply in line with some Christian values, especially endurance in the face of suffering, evil and death, and it is often the ethical core left after living faith has gone. For 'good' people in our civilization it is perhaps the most attractive alternative to Christianity, especially in its realism about the negative side of life.

It is just its attractiveness that makes it so dangerous, always threatening to be an inoculation against full faith. The perspective of praise and shame brings out its inadequacies most clearly. The Stoic avoids the ravages and abyss of shame at the cost of the possibility of joy. His world is marked by order and imperturbability in face of disorder, but he misses what we have called the reality of overflow. A God of joy is inconceivable as ultimate reality, and the vision of feasting, dancing and endless praise seems dangerously escapist, threatening his equilibrium. He has attained an eminently sensible solution which is by no means easy, and all his energy is taken in keeping to it.

One vital key to the theme of our chapter is given by a critique of stoicism. We have identified one terrible characteristic of evil as its logic of overflow, its self-magnifying dynamic which both paralyses and embraces more and more in its negation of life. We have seen this as the corruption of the joyful movement of respectful goodness which alone can creatively oppose evil. The stoic opts out of both intensities. He is the archetypal 'Greek' mentioned by Paul as quoted above, to whom the crucifixion is foolishness. Jesus' option was for perturbability and shame, which when vindicated result in joy and good news. The stoic above all has no hope of decisive vindication, only of successful resignation. Stoic realism cannot accommodate the resurrection, an event beyond any equilibrium, and it cannot be free in the Spirit, for this is continually leading beyond boundaries into new suffering and joy.

Examination of the various forms of Christianity shows how insidious the sensible stoic spirit is. It gets exasperatingly close to the real thing but can never make the breakthrough into overflow, the new ecology of blessing, laughter, mutuality and praise. It leaves people on the edge of the promised land and builds them a house there instead of crossing the river. 'The river Jordan is deep and wide' says the song, but it adds, as the stoic does not, 'Alleluia!'

Non-order

What is lacking in stoicism shows the need for a new concept in the description of both good and evil. Evil has often been conceived as a 'lack of goodness', *privatio boni*. This lack has been seen mainly as the disordering of good reality, and goodness therefore as primarily good in its orderliness. This has been true even in the more relational definitions – 'alienation', for example, is a disorder in a good relationship. The dominance of order (or words such as harmony, integrity, justice, peace, reconciliation, etc.) allows little room for another dimension of goodness, which follows the logic of overflow.

There is an ancient definition of man as the 'rational animal who laughs'. The rationality covers our orderliness in how we are and ought to function; the laughter is a free overflow, not reducible to one meaning or truth, a sequence of odd sounds pouring out, often spreading from one person to another, creating a new atmosphere and producing all sorts of unpredictable results. Laughter is not order, nor is it disorder: our term for it is 'non-order'.

Those who lay great stress on order as good like to describe all that is not order as disorder. Within their own terms they are sensible, because non-order is indeed a threat to them. Dictators fear laughter and good jokes as much as guns. Non-order thrives in the arts too, particularly in our century. It has constantly been under attack there beceause of its threat to order – for example, abstract and other forms of modern art. Most creativity has an element of non-order, without which it is impossible to transcend the old ordering and produce something new. In playfulness too, order and non-order go together.

Non-order is not just a means of producing new order, but is to be valued in itself, whatever its practical consequences. It is good simply to laugh, to play, to enjoy. Praise likewise is a combination of order and non-order, and has always suffered from over-ordering. Many forces, psychological, social and spiritual, try their best to order the non-order out of existence, often labelling it disorder.

The result is dullness and boredom. This applies to worship, and also to goodness. If goodness is dull and boring, evil tends to seem attractive and interesting. This is because evil has been allowed to take over the most exciting thing in goodness, its dynamic non-order. This is also true of God. For most people God is not a very exciting reality, partly because he is seen as the embodiment of order on the grandest scale – in charge of everything, watching everyone. In Western Christian theology this takes the form of far more concern about God's *logos*, his word and rationality, than about his spirit.

If evil is defined as a lack of good it must therefore be seen as disordering order and also distorting or counterfeiting non-order. The latter is much more difficult to describe – what is it that betrays false laughter? The combination of order and non-order in the overflow of respect and praise has its negative counterpart, we suggest, in the experience and expression of shame. This means that shame can only be overcome by something that takes its distorted non-order seriously and meets it with a more powerful genuine non-order.

This is what happens in the crucifixion and resurrection of Jesus. The paralysing evil that attacks him is met by suffering shame. It is not simply right shame or wrong shame, but the concentration and overflow of both of them in suffering shame for the right and wrong shame of others. Most parents have experienced this in relation to their children, and vice versa. It is particularly characteristic of our closest relationships, an intense experience of being with someone in extreme humiliation and alienation. Enduring this solidarity to the point of being sucked completely into an evil situation in all its dimensions is almost unthinkable without giving in to the evil in some way. Simone Weil's description of the elements in what she calls 'affliction' (*malheur*) is a masterpiece of discernment:

All the three sides of our being are always exposed to it (affliction). Our flesh is fragile; it can be pierced or torn or crushed, or one of its internal mechanisms can be permanently deranged, by any piece of matter in motion. Our soul is vulnerable, being subject to fits of depression without cause and pitifully dependent

upon all sorts of objects, animate and inanimate, which are themselves fragile and capricious. Our social personality, upon which
our sense of existence almost depends, is always and entirely
exposed to every hazard. These three parts of us are linked with
the very centre of our being in such a way that it bleeds for any
wound of the slightest consequence which they suffer. Above all,
anything which diminishes or destroys our social prestige, our
right to consideration, seems to impair or abolish our very
essence. . .[4]

A person in affliction loses all significance in his own eyes and the
eyes of others:

There is something in him that would like to exist,
but it is continually pushed back into nothingness,
like a drowning man whose head is pushed under the water.[5]

In affliction the great temptation is to escape by giving in to evil
in some form:

It is always possible for an afflicted man to suffer less by
    consenting to become wicked.[6]

One of the greatest miracles is to be in genuine solidarity with
anyone in extreme affliction: all parts of our being scream out
against it, we take refuge in all sorts of evasions and lies, because
what is demanded is that we go through their affliction with them
past our own point of no return: we are engulfed by this horror,
and lose significance in our own eyes and those of others while also
suffering in body and soul. Yet this solidarity is the only way the
afflicted can be given new life.

Affliction itself is, in our terms, the worst perversion of good order
and of non-order together. Jesus meets it with a further dimension
of non-order, of overflow: he suffers it for others, identifies
completely and gets sucked in. 'My God, my God, why hast thou
forsaken me?' is the result. In the vindication of the resurrection
this becomes the essence of the new free order. The good news is
that the depths of affliction have been come through by this man
in such a way that everyone can rejoice in him and what he has
done. He is present as the new reality of order and non-order, word
and spirit together. Faith is letting this become our reality, and so
irresistibly rejoicing in freedom from shame before God, others and
ourselves. In Paul's categories, it is not the order of the old law nor
the disorder of no law, but Jesus Christ, the fulfilment and

[4]   Op.cit., p. 454.
[5]   Ibid., p. 460.
[6]   Ibid., p. 467.

overflowing of all law in suffering love that both accepts and inspires us.

This is very far from stoic dignity and resignation. The stoic is the great orderer and controller, above all of himself, but the Holy Spirit is the gift of trusting oneself to another Lord and finding a freedom and joy that let one live beyond oneself, sometimes without dignity and never with resignation.

Hatred and Historical Evil

Shame and affliction have so far mainly been seen from the side of the sufferer. They threaten the very self of their victims, destroying self-worth and hope, and immobilizing them in an agony symbolized by the crucifixion. What about those who inflict shame and suffering? What happens to them as they go on humiliating, oppressing, manipulating, torturing? They too are involved in a process that cumulatively affects who they are. This transformation has many stages and modes, and its complexity is increased by the impossibility of drawing a clean line between shamer and shamed: the same person or group can participate in both, with mutual reinforcements. Anyone, for example, caught in an unjust power structure is likely to find intense pressures simultaneously both to submit to and to inflict shame and suffering. One extreme development which is possible is hatred. There is a terrifying dynamic in hatred which energizes the most powerful relationships. It is especially devastating and persistent in the fundamental areas of religion, politics, race, work and family. In all of these long-term hatred flourishes. Full hatred is never just a matter of grievance over alleged wrongs, but goes deeper to negate and eliminate the value of the enemy. It overflows any particular causes and has its own momentum, whose characteristics are very like those of praise.

If shame heads towards paralysis of the capacity for joy and praise, hatred actively perverts that capacity and mobilizes energies on the same scale as praise and love. It often makes an appeal to another focus of praise and honour (the 'true God', the 'just society', the 'superior race'), but needs to portray its enemies in terms more distinctive than those of simple contrast with what is valued. So a major part in sustaining hatred is played by the ways in which enemies are given a bad identity. They have to be 'known' and, as in praise, the knowledge is part of an active relationship in which memory, imagination and projection play a major role. In this there is a continual reconstitution of both hater and hated, and a world of meaning is created in which new and terrible actions can be conceived. Hatred cannot stay 'hot' all the time. Its continuity is ensured, and the invention of 'cool' plans and strategies enabled, by the way in which myths, stereotypes, theories and symbols are used to inspire and legitimate it. So a world is constructed in which hater and hated have their roles defined, and the violence of the relationship is supported by a network of lies and half-truths.

Evil in this form tends to be all-consuming. Its dynamic, historical nature emerges the more it is opposed. It is never a matter of simply isolating it and dealing with it. Each such attempt provokes new developments of evil in oneself and the situation, and exposes new depths of it. The fact that our whole world of meaning is pervaded by lies and falsehood makes it impossible even to be honest about evil – and those most confident of having diagnosed it correctly are often most deluded, especially as regards their own innocence of it. Evil pollutes, fissiparates, and ramifies, and it endlessly disguises itself. Attempts to meet it head-on find themselves stabbed in the back. Attempts to contain it (the classic stoic and 'law and order' responses) find that the container itself leaks and disintegrates. Capitulation to it, in the hope of rest from the struggle, turns out to be only the first in a series of capitulations demanded, with increasingly appalling consequences. Neutrality is impossible, as hatred above all demonstrates: its actions and statements constantly pull and push at anyone sitting on the fence. The language of hatred too takes hold on the imagination and subconscious, and offers a fatally exciting fantasy life which can seduce even the hated into seeing themselves in its terms.

At the heart of hatred is the phenomenon of the curse. Cursing, like blessing in the previous chapter, needs to be freed from its trivial and magical associations. The curse is the meaning of hatred come to its point of greatest intensity. Blessing affirms and enhances, respects and liberates. Cursing negates, dominates, humiliates, binds and paralyses. The logic of the curse is that of shame and death together. In its intensity it concentrates the identity of both curser and accursed; for in the act of cursing there is a wholehearted other-directedness which commits the very self of the curser in the relationship of hatred.

What the Nazis did to the Jews was this sort of cursing, and both sides have been irrevocably marked and identified through it. Stalin periodically defined new enemies who were to be purged, with the help of the modern media for cursing and comprehensive condemnation. Racists of all sorts use cursing epithets of hatred as the focus and support of their violence. But these are just the most obvious, public tip of the iceberg of hatred. It is in family life that the power of hatred, and of its variants, jealousy, envy, anger and cruelty, is often first experienced. A major element in this is the projection on brothers, sisters, children or parents of identities that imprison and humiliate, with a dynamic of mutual 'cursing' spiralling into hot or cold warfare. Between families and nations, between workers and management, between political and religious groups the same cursing happens. The language of cursing may change, but not the reality of hatred's search for control and degradation of the enemy's very self.

What hope is there for the hater? There can be no general answer to that question. It is a matter of what the best possibility is that can be offered to the hater. Is there a blessing that can meet cursing? Can a self consumed with hatred be given a new identity? In the previous chapter we said that the network of recognition and respect is vital for human identity: is there a form of recognition and respect due to the hater too?

The terrible dilemma here is that to recognize hatred as what it is, to unmask it and bring it to light, itself provokes more hatred. Its lies and perversions are exposed at the risk of increased hostility and raw violence. A further intensification of the dilemma then emerges: the only security seems to lie in escape, in trying to move out of reach of the hostility and protect oneself. This self-protection in the face of evil and aggression characterizes most strategies for dealing with them. The world is full of individuals and groups whose identities are formed in reacting to threats, strengthening the walls which surround them. Is there any alternative?

The Sermon on the Mount suggests a radical one:

> But I say to you that hear, love your enemies, do good to those who hate you, bless those who curse you, pray for those who abuse you (Luke 6:27f.).

It is a way that involves staying within reach of the enemy, the hater, the curser and abuser, and exercising the active respect of loving, doing good, blessing and prayer. This is the way haters are offered a new possibility, unimaginable within their own horizon. They meet the demonstration of a vigorous alternative. The horizon of this new possibility is clear: the Father himself 'is kind to the ungrateful and the selfish' (v. 35). Without this assurance the whole Sermon on the Mount collapses: it lives from the recognition of who God is, what he wants and how he is actively present in the blessing of enemies. In the face of hatred and defamation the persecuted can 'rejoice and leap for joy' (v. 23) because their confidence is in this God.

The life of Jesus interpreted the Sermon on the Mount. He showed the new possibility that is offered to haters. He stayed within reach of his enemies, and even had one among his disciples. In the Last Supper he identified himself not by an exclusive, self-protective identity of his own but by the act of giving himself, body and blood, away for others; or, in the fourth Gospel, by washing the feet of others. In Gethsemane he agonized over the right orientation towards what was coming, and his horizon was set by the praise-word 'Abba!' (Mark 14:36). That praise was embodied in the union of will with his Father, which then went through its ultimate test in the crucifixion. The lethal enmity was met by the 'waste' (or, in the traditional interpretation, resonating with Old Testament worship, 'sacrifice') of a life, which brought him to the heart of hatred. Paul describes Jesus on the cross as 'having become a curse for us' (Gal. 3:13). He went beyond all limits, even beyond the final security of his relationship with his Father, to identify with cursing and hatred from the inside. They were offered a new possibility beyond their awareness: 'Father, forgive them; for they know not what they do' (Luke 23:34). The offer met hatred on its home ground, where it reached out to humiliate and annihilate the very self of the enemy, by accepting the annihilation without ceasing to bless. The resurrection of Jesus is the demonstration and celebration of a new identity over which cursing, hatred and death have lost their paralysing power. In that the hater has the possibility of recognizing an alternative, a new way out of hatred.

Paul took this way out when, for the best religious reasons, he was persecuting Christians. His transformation from hating to being hated because of Jesus Christ pivots around his grasp of the crucifixion and resurrection. They became intrinsic to his new identity:

> None of us lives to himself, and none of us dies to himself. If we live, we live to the Lord, and if we die, we die to the Lord; so then, whether we live or whether we die, we are to the Lord. For to this end Christ died and lived again, that he might be Lord both of the dead and of the living (Rom. 14:7ff).

Not only was death no longer final and definitive because of the death of Jesus; neither were sin, hatred, suffering and the law. Central to his new self is what Paul 'exults' or 'boasts' in. His language of exultation is taken from the Psalms but focused through Jesus Christ: now he exults in the death of Jesus, in his own weakness 'that the power of Christ may rest upon me' (2 Cor. 12:9), in the suffering for the gospel, and in the new possibility of transformation that he is communicating. In one of his few echoes of the words of Jesus, he draws the practical implications of this for confronting those who are like what he himself had been: 'Bless those who persecute you; bless and do not curse them' (Rom. 12:14).

Paul's greatest agony over hatred and enmity was about his own people's rejection of his message. 'I have great sorrow and unceasing anguish in my heart. For I could wish that I myself were accursed and cut off from Christ for the sake of my brethren, my kinsmen and my race' (Rom. 9:2f). His most thorough wrestling with this in Romans 9–11 comes to an extraordinary finale. He has followed the implications of the crucifixion as God's way of meeting rejection, and ends with a crescendo of praise of God's judgements as being beyond anything that can be imagined, even extending to 'having mercy on all' (Rom. 11:32). In this area above all, more recent centuries have shown how 'the corruption of the best is the worst', as the hatred of Jews in Christian countries denied and reversed Paul's vision.

Vindicating God

So far we have ignored the most awkward question of all about evil, suffering and death: is it not God himself who should be ashamed because of them? The presence of a good and almighty God is not an obvious conclusion to draw from the state of the world and the record of history. If God is so good and powerful, is he not in some sense responsible for the enormous amount of evil? If he is free to act in history, why does he not do so to prevent evil and suffering that any compassionate person would want to stop? This question of the vindication of God, technically called 'theodicy', has produced a vast literature, which is only the sophisticated token of the agonizing over it by ordinary people through the centuries.

Theodicy seems to be necessarily inconclusive. Some see the whole problem as a disproof of God's existence, others opt for a God of limited power, others for a God less than perfectly good. Most mainstream Christians defend God's goodness and power by blaming the misuse of created freedom. Among such positions the most plausible seems to us to be some version of the latter: if there is to be created freedom and the conditions for its genuine exercise, then evil, suffering and untimely death are rightly risked. We would develop this in terms of God's respect for creation and the understanding of the nature of his power which we stated in our previous chapter. We also agree with the mainstream tradition in seeing theodicy inseparable from eschatology: that is, that it is conceivable for God to be able to bring out of even the horrors of our history a quality of life, a salvation, that makes it all worthwhile even to those who have suffered most. All these are much disputed points, and would need the sort of discussion that only a separate work on the subject could give, but for now it is sufficient to state the broad lines of a position argued in detail by many others.

Yet there are major problems with most theodicy. One is that its aim is an ordered explanation of evil in relation to God. In our terms it is trying to give an ordered account of disorder. Yet in meeting the problem of freedom it always has to recognize the importance of what we call non-order, and therefore the limits of ordered explanation. Likewise with evil: some aspects of it are best understood as disruption of order and its relationships, but other aspects need appreciation of the ways in which the dynamics of non-order can go wrong. If it is granted that evil is a possibility in a world where freedom is valued, the answer to evil must be in the possibility of a free response to it that genuinely meets and over-comes it. Evil is both particular and dynamic, and the answer to it must be primarily in the language of action. So God will be justified if he does in fact respond to evil so that its distortion of order and non-order is overcome and taken up into something new. In other words, God is vindicated if he vindicates himself, and theodicy will depend on recognizing this justification.

This does seem to be the most satisfactory theodicy suggested by both Old and New Testaments. Vindication of God by God is the source of the Psalmists' hope and praise, appearing in nearly every Psalm, and especially in the depths of suffering:

> Save me, O God!
> The water is up to my neck;
> I am sinking in deep mud,
> and there is no solid ground. . .
>
> I am worn out from calling for help,
> and my throat is aching. . .
> Don't let me bring shame on those who trust in you,
> Sovereign Lord Almighty. . .
>
> But as for me, I will pray to you, Lord,
> answer me, God, at a time you choose.
> Answer me because of your great love,
> because you keep your promise to save. . .
>
> When the oppressed see this, they will be glad;
> those who worship God will be encouraged
> (Ps. 69, Good News Bible)

The theodicy of the Psalms is one of complaint, questioning and passionate protest, but all this is embraced by a faith in God as vindicator in spite of all appearances, resulting in a theodicy of praise. This is present in many of the prophets too, culminating in Deutero-Isaiah's vision of a new creation, meeting and going beyond all previous reality:

But the Lord says,
'Do not cling to the events of the past
or dwell on what happened long ago.
Watch for the new thing I am going to do.
It is happening already – you can see it now!
I will make a road through the wilderness
and give you streams of water there.
Even the wild animals will honour me;
jackals and ostriches will praise me
when I make rivers flow in the desert
to give water to my chosen people.
They are the people I made for myself,
and they will sing my praises!' (Isa. 43:19–21, Good News
    Bible).

He is clear that this is all essentially a matter of the vindication of
God:

I am the Lord; there is no other God.
I will give you the strength you need,
although you do not honour me.
I do this so that everyone
from one end of the world to the other
may know that I am the Lord
and that there is no other God (Isa. 45:5–6, Good News Bible).

The Wisdom literature too eventually faces this problem, classi-
ically in the Book of Job. There, all the traditional religious answers
to the problem of innocent suffering are found wanting. Job himself
simply clings to his confidence that God will vindicate both
himself and Job:

For I know that my redeemer lives,
    and at last he will stand upon the earth;
and after my skin has been thus destroyed,
    then from my flesh I shall see God,
whom I shall see on my side,
    and my eyes shall behold and not another (Job 19:25–7).

God's statement at the end of the story in chapters 38ff. can be
summed up as him asserting his freedom to do this in his own
mysterious ways, as illustrated by the mysteries of creation.

In the New Testament the theme of vindication is concentrated
in Jesus' crucifixion and resurrection. We have followed this in
relation to shame and hatred. The climactic events of Jesus' history
are themselves the Christian theodicy. They show God involved
with evil, suffering and death in such a way that their terrible reality

is recognized and more than adequately met. The resurrection is not a containment or a reversal or a denial of this reality; it is the revelation of the one person who goes through them in God's way and creates an alternative. Evil's historical particularity is met on the cross, and evil's dynamic, spreading overflow through history is met by the Spirit of the resurrected Lord. It is an answer to evil that is essentially practical, taking the form of a call to live in this Spirit and follow the way of the cross, trusting in the vindication of God by God.

Praise of God celebrates his identification of himself through the crucifixion and resurrection of Jesus. It goes to the heart of the most important question of all in the combat with evil: Who is God? It is in relation to this that we find the most insidious form of evil, hatred of God. Our century has seen more concerted hatred of God than any other. As with the other forms of hatred described earlier, its main strategy is to project a bad identity and to attempt to maintain it by all means. The denigration of God, the ridiculing of belief in him, the explaining away of anything that claims to reveal him, the association of God with oppression, neurosis, hypocrisy, immaturity and fantasy: all these have formed the atmosphere in which praise of God lives. Hatred of God, in hotter and cooler forms, has become a potent force in our civilization, and it often has the power to paralyse Christian vigour and praise even when it cannot kill faith in God. Hatred of God both dismissively identifies God as a non-existent fantasy and also explains how dangerous this is. The vehemence of this rejection of God and the energy put into creating alternatives to faith in him overflow and spread in ways that cannot be stemmed, except by a knowledge of God that is embodied in a way of life which comprehensively affirms him in the face of evil and hatred and is taken up into the free overflow of praise.

So the truth about evil, suffering and death leads into the heart of who God is, and it is only through praising and knowing him that their paralysing grip on thought as well as on the rest of living can be satisfactorily released. A theodicy of praise recognizes the vindication of God by God, but this by no means allows the problem of evil to be dismissed or forgotten. Rather, it places the cross and continuing discipleship at the centre of a faith which lives in a world of evil but fights it with confidence in a crucified and risen Lord.

7

Knowing God

The main lines of previous chapters converge on the central issue: Who is God? Knowing God has been going on all through them. They have, however, been concerned more with doing the knowing than with reflecting on the process of knowing. The present chapter, which is, perhaps inevitably, the most theoretical and complex in the book, examines how our experience and our capacities of mind and imagination come together in knowing God. This involves taking some account of knowing in the arts and, especially, in the sciences. The aim is to arrive at some definite idea of who God is, what the universe is, and how they interact and are given to be known by us.

Being Known

'Knowing is being knit into everything that is.' At its best, knowing recognizes and respects its object, tries to grasp it without manipulating it, but in such a way as to let it be itself for us. A lot depends on the nature of the object. Our way of going about knowing a stone differs from what is appropriate for an insect or an event of the past or a work of art or a friend. There will be diverse techniques and approaches, different capacities in use, varying degrees of self-involvement, and differing kinds of movement between knower and known. Few areas of thought have produced such a vast, subtle and difficult literature as this field called epistemology, the knowledge of knowing itself. This is partly due to the all-pervasiveness of the subject matter – all reality is the object of knowledge; and it is partly also because of the difficulty of turning our knowing to face itself and know itself.

We start with the main object of our knowing, God. Before asking the critical and sceptical questions we will explore for a while the implications of the existence of the sort of God who is indicated by the earlier chapters of this book. This God has been seen as one of abundance, of complete generosity. He both creates and respects what he creates. His knowledge of creation is for the good of creation; and he is 'knit into everything that is' without violating it. This means that God is open to all of its reality, including the distortions and agonies; he refuses to avoid the truth and so is involved in enjoying or suffering it. The crucifixion and resurrection of Jesus Christ are the main Christian criteria of what knowing the world means for God. They are the wisdom of God in its greatest concentration.

We are known by this God. That is a basic statement of faith. The first cognitive content of faith is the knowledge that we are known, and that this knowledge of us by God is not abstract or that of an omniscient spy, but passionately concerned to the point of identification with us. So any knowledge of God by us involves waking up to being surrounded already by his knowledge of us in a definite form. In other terms, to know God is to let him have the initiative as to the form of our knowledge of him, and therefore is first of all a matter of recognizing his initiative. If the object of our knowing is one who already knows us, then the main emphasis in our knowing will be on preparing for and receiving his communication with us. The disproportion between us and God is covered by his way of knowing us through Jesus Christ, through his respectful and vulnerable self-communication that allows our response really to matter. It is God's honouring of us in this way that creates the possibility of our knowing and honouring of him. His knowing is always respectful, and it enables our knowing to be always praising.

The interplay of knowing and praising God is the theme of this book. Their inseparability is simply stated: knowing this God is to know a glory and love that evokes all our astonishment, thanks and praise; praising this God is a matter of affirming truth as well as expressing adoration and love. Neither is instantaneous; praising and knowing develop together over time, a process which embraces the whole of life and is its true ecology.

Projection

But *is* God really known? Is it not all a matter of our imagination, of wish-fulfilment or fear-fulfilment? We have raised these questions already (chapter 2, above) and said that this way of thinking, and the way of living that goes with it, is the most serious challenge to praise of God. Modern atheism claims to have understood faith in God better than faith understands itself, and to be able to explain faith and the world without needing the hypothesis of God. Its simple centre is the claim that man creates God rather than vice versa. There are many modes and motives for this creation of God by man, and some may be comparatively healthy and beneficial. But in the last analysis God is an illusion who alienates us from ourselves and others, and he needs to be got rid of if we wish to be clear-sighted about the human situation and how to respond to it.

This position, as we said in chapter 2, can be neither proved nor falsified. It is by definition one which nobody can stand outside of and assess, because that very assessment could be accused of being the product of imagination. If it is always a human being who makes claims, then the fact that the projectionist position is radically suspicious of the human mind means that every claim by a human mind is invalidated. The logical end of this path is complete scepticism, but most projectionists stop short of that. So the first question to be asked of each projectionist is: why stop there in particular? It is clear that in the history of thought, what began as suspicion of God as a human projection spread out to engulf justice and ethics, the human self, all the arts, the objectivity of knowledge, and much else. Theology is not the only discipline challenged by projectionism, and the responses across the disciplines have had many family resemblances.

If projectionism stops short of complete scepticism, this means that it is defining projection according to some norm. The standard relative to which the claim to knowledge of God is seen as projection might be that of knowledge in the natural sciences, or in psychology, sociology, history, or a particular philosophy. All of these fields have their own criteria (sometimes conflicting sets of criteria) which can be used to set the limits of knowledge, beyond which everything is uncertain or unreal. Such criteria are of course necessary in every field; the critical issue is how widely they should be applied. In the case of knowledge of God, as with any other claimed object of knowledge, the question is whether the criteria and the way they are applied are appropriate to the object. If, for example, the only way to know God is to interact with him in particular ways, then criteria which demand a neutral, non-involved knowing will be inappropriate.

We find something in the whole mind-set of projectionism that sabotages the possibility of affirming God. Projectionism thrives on suspicion. It is, above all, afraid of affirming too much. It always prefers to err on the side of caution. Its maxims are prudential ones minimizing risk and heavily in favour of what can be repeatedly checked out. It aims at parsimony in description and explanation, taking as its guideline 'Occam's razor', according to which only the necessary minimum of entities should be affirmed. If God is anything like we have described in this book, it is clear how utterly inappropriate this approach is. If God is the very embodiment of 'too much', of overflowing abundance and generosity to the extent of risking himself in free acts of love, then a way of knowing which makes parsimony, necessity, caution and suspicion its guidelines is very unlikely to be open to his reality. This is not to say that those guidelines do not have their place in knowing, but it is to deny that they should be used blindly as principles without regard for the nature of what is being known. No method or criteria must be allowed to determine in advance what reality may be like. Projectionism tries to do this, and has no way of conceiving a God whose being is an example of the transcendence of its criteria.

Projectionism, therefore, is the result of a method that is intrinsically liable to fail in respectful knowing. It is least likely to allow the existence of the sort of God we have described, because it cannot cope with such a being. It is instructive to think what sort of God would satisfy the projectionist. It would have to be a God who is open to neutral inspection and verification, and satisfies other demands which, in the tradition of Judaism, Christianity and Islam, are only met by idols. Since, however, no sensible projectionist would accept an idol as a worthy God, the conclusion must be that no being worth worshipping exists.

Projectionism is not only inadequate to the nature of God; it also has a questionable view of the right use of human capacities, especially the imagination. Imagination is a part of all knowing. It is involved in remembering, conceiving, perceiving, comparing, hypothesizing, checking possibilities, and many other operations in knowing. Even the most neutral, analytical types of knowing require the imagination's capacity to remember, to perceive and compare patterns, and to combine data in various ways. When we come to the richer forms of knowing, in which thought and feeling need to be interwoven, then the role of imagination is even more important. To ignore the imagination is to impoverish all our knowing and living.

This insight becomes most urgent when we are dealing with what the previous chapter called non-order. As we have said, imagination is inseparable from the knowing of order. But to grasp non-order, the realm of free overflow and newness, we are especially dependent on imagination. We stretch our conceptual capacities through imagery, metaphors, projections and new connections. The more rich and dynamic the object of our knowing the more our imagination needs to leap and expand, create and project, in order to try to do justice to the reality. This happens in science, philosophy and other branches of knowledge, but the arts show the quintessence of it. When Patrick Kavanagh, in his poem 'Miss Universe', wants to describe learning the nature of God through an experience of blessing and overflow, he tries to do justice to it in daring, imaginative leaps and metaphors:

I learned, I learned – when one might be inclined
To think, too late, you cannot recover your losses –
I learned something of the nature of God's mind,
Not the abstract Creator but He who caresses
The daily and nightly earth; He who refuses
To take failure for an answer till again and again is worn.
Love is wating for you, waiting for the violence that she chooses
From the tepidity of the common round beyond exhaustion or
   scorn
What was once is still and there is no need for remorse;
There are no recriminations in Heaven. O the sensual throb
Of the explosive body, the tumultuous thighs!
Adown a summer lane comes Miss Universe
She whom no lecher's wit can rob
Though she is not the virgin who was wise.[1]

If our conception of God as supremely creative, abundant, generous and free is at all correct, then knowing him is likely continually to stretch our imagination in this way. Far from shunning projection we will exhaust our projective abilities in trying to do justice to God. Praise above all will be the endlessly fascinated attempt to let ourselves be knit into this reality, and will inspire psalms and theologies together. Being knit into it will mean participation in its creativity. Without this our knowing remains dull and static, and avoids the risk, the joy, and the expansion of heart and mind that come through meeting this God.

The Ecology of Knowing

If imaginative projection is a part of knowing, this still does not mean that it is always used well. It raises the further question as to whether any particular claim to knowledge of God is valid. It might well be projection in the bad sense, having little to do with God and much to do with human fantasies or ignorance. We are suspicious of wholesale suspicion, but particular suspicions may of course be correct. Is there any way of distinguishing the right answer? Can good and bad projection in relation to God be discriminated?

Our approach to this is 'ecological'. There is no simplistic 'one off' way of testing. Our knowing must be open to God as a reality who takes time to be comprehended, who involves all our capacities, and who is most likely to be known by loving and sacrificial involvement in a network of human relationships. In other words, the

[1] *Collected Poems*, London 1972.

knowing will be historical, holistic and corporate, and in all of these ways will resist the application of norms that are too constricting. Time, the whole self and community are indispensable for learning adequately who God is. The sort of testing that is appropriate will never be instantaneous, neutral, or individualistic, but will demand patient self-involvement and discernment at many levels. There will be a range of interlocking judgements to be made, and our own capacity to make them rightly will develop or diminish according to the quality of our way of life.

We have suggested that praising God, recognizing him as God in feeling, word and action, is a key to the ecology in which right knowledge of God grows, and we have seen how it fulfils the criteria of being long-term, self-involving and communal. Within all that there are rational processes and judgements which are our special concern in this chapter. They need to be treated from two sides. What does the accusaion of projection mean for the rationality of our claim to know God? And, how is the positive movement of our minds in relation to God best described?

Granted that imagination is part of all knowing, how do we tell whether our imagination is in touch with something beyond itself or not? Imagination is well able to project an infinite object, even one which is dynamic and infinitely receding so that imagination need never become static. This could be the ultimate in autonomous imagining, a useful self-made absolute with which to play and stretch our capacities and creativity. This is what, in the nineteenth century, the concept of the 'sublime' was in many romantic thinkers, and what the 'absolute' was for many idealists. How can it be shown that God is not merely the product of such a process?

The obvious reply is again that there is no knock-down argument – that is simply not appropriate to the subject. The whole ecology must be related to it, with the various forms of 'ringing true' that fit each level or aspect. At every point the projectionist can say: But you are inventing God. But at every point the projectionist too is trying to be rational, and the ultimate question is whether rationality itself is a brute fact, an arbitrary invention, or is given its proper character by what is beyond it: God. Many important modern arguments about the existence of God follow some such line, by arguing that God is best affirmed by reason as reason's own rational ground. We consider the result of these debates is at least to show the plausibility of God according to rational criteria, although they (and their concepts of rationality) often suffer from the obsession with order that we also noted in the previous chapter in most theodicy. We see knowing and praising God to be intrinsic to each other, and the God who is conceived as their real object to be the only sufficient enabler and inspirer of a rationality that delights in, respects and enhances its objects.

There is no way of standing outside this conclusion and proving it neutrally; but it is possible for both sides to continue to test it as thoroughly as they can, and this is rightly the source of a vast amount of dialogue in talk and print. Our conclusion about the rationality of knowing and praising God is that in this movement not only is God known (of which we have more to say later in this chapter), but also God enhances our rational powers. By knowing the reality of God we are changed by it, not only morally but also rationally. We are freed from the fixations and obsessions of reason (of which we believe that the projectionist's obsession with the non-existence of God is one of the most enslaving and impoverishing), and are gently opened to being knit into a reality that is delightful as well as true. Then we realize that our very capacity to know and enjoy God has only been kept alive by the respect of God. He suffers being misunderstood and dismissed as unreal rather than coerce our knowing: genuine thanks and praise could spring from nothing less than this freedom. The self-certainty that belongs to obsessions is not appropriate to God and does not respect him for what he is. But the demand for such tight security is likely to persist until the actual knowledge of God wins us over to a joyful, laughing rationality that recognizes that its main problem is coping with abundance of knowledge of God. Praise is the opening of knowing to this abundance which itself draws our minds into a true relationship with the rest of reality.

This brings us to the positive movement of our minds in relation to God. It is traditionally seen as the combination of affirmation and negation. The 'affirmative way', in which the stretching of our imaginative and other capacities is included (as in Dante's *Divine Comedy*), is balanced by the 'negative way' in which the concepts and images are criticized and if necessary broken in the interests of trying to do justice to a God who is always beyond their grasp. But 'balanced' is a dangerous word here. The secret of the movement is that it refuses to rest in any equilibrium. It is generated by the fact that its object and content, God, is always greater, always overflows our comprehension. So the 'negative way' is a guard against our projections becoming idols. In doing this it takes up many of the tools of suspicion used by those who understand God as merely a projection, but the tools are used in the interests of the logic of overflow. The negative way has endless subtleties, intellectually and spiritually.[2] These point to the double truth that

2   For a combination of the two, see Rowan Williams, *The Wound of Knowledge*, London 1979.

discernment here requires both sensitivity to a whole ecology and a rigorous self-criticism that is at least as searching and comprehensive as the projectionist critique.

There is a remarkable combination of the affirmative and the negative ways in what is known as the ontological argument for the existence of God. This approach to God's existence has fascinated many philosophers and theologians in this century again, after the previous century thought that it had been proved wrong. Its basic contention is that God, the being 'than which none greater can be conceived', cannot be conceived as not existing. This is because to conceive God as not existing is to have conceived a lesser being than a God who exists, and therefore this cannot be God. So if we can conceive God at all we must conceive him as existing. There are variations on this argument and a great deal of sophisticated discussion of all of them. We do not want to enter the debate, but we find that the central concept of God, as the one 'than which none greater can be conceived', expresses in formal terms the central truth of the intellectual aspect of praising God. It starts from God as the ultimate mind-stretcher and builds a negative critique into its positive movement.

The ontological argument is usually found in philosophical discussion where a rather bare notion of God operates. But what if it is linked to a more definite understanding of God as Trinitarian? Then it is possible to see it expressing not only the greatness of the Creator who transcends all other reality and is present in its order and non-order, but also the greatness of transcendence within history and within the self and its relationships. 'Greatness' can have its content suggested by the story of Jesus Christ and his revolution in the idea of power and glory. If his crucifixion and resurrection are taken as the event 'than which none greater can be conceived' this is another way of expressing what was central to the first Christians: the ultimate, eschatological nature of what had happened. It is an event embracing affirmative and negative, but not in equilibrium – the cross is taken up into the new life in overflow, while persisting in its critique of all escapism, idolatry and projection. The new event is recognized and responded to 'in the Spirit'. This is the ultimate in loving communication, than which none can be conceived which is more appropriate to and respectful of the recipient. This too does not result in equilibrium but in that basic Christian existence of praising the God who is always greater. The ecology of life is therefore Trinitarian. In it all the spiritual as well as intellectual gifts of the community can take part in the testing of truth, and when this happens with integrity there is the comprehensive 'ringing true' that can say: 'God dwells in the praises of his people.'

The Relevance of God

The projectionist critique has a companion which is also a mortal threat to praising God. This is an agnostic approach which says: 'I recognize the force of the projectionist suspicion, but I am content to say about both sides: not proven. What does interest me, however, is whether the issue has any practical consequences for other areas of knowledge. The God of much theology seems to be as disconnected from the world I know as is the illusory God of the projectionist. The challenge to theologians is to show how God might be significantly connected.'

The debate with the projectionist position was 'intensive'. It focused on our capacities at full stretch, on conceptions of God and the question of atheism. The ecology of knowing was seen in its relation to the central issue of God. The agnostic line, on the other hand, requires an 'extensive' discussion about the relevance of God to other areas of knowledge.

Both the praising and the knowing of God tend to be disconnected from the rest of living and knowing. Just relating them together might only increase their isolation in a religious ghetto. So far we have said more about the relationships of praise (to respect, prestige, affirmation, individual, social and historical identity, evil, suffering, death, and much else) than those of knowledge. The split between knowledge of God and other knowledge has widened in much modern thought until even those who want to affirm God often claim that this is a peculiar form of knowing, not comparable or vulnerable to other forms. But, if the God who is affirmed is seen as Creator, there can be no final division in the truth: there is a basic unity to which everything even now must be referred.

There are two main ways of trying to overcome this split between knowledge of God and other knowledge. The first is from the side of what we do when we know. Since all human knowledge is by definition known by us, if we examine our processes of knowing we will discover a unity through all fields. Since Kant, this is by far the most common way of trying to unify knowledge, focusing on the knower rather than the content known. In theology the most comprehensive attempt to do this in the English-speaking world in recent years has been that of Bernard Lonergan. He works out a 'critical realism' based on the operations of experiencing, understanding and judging, and demonstrates how it works in commonsense knowing as well as in disciplines across the sciences and humanities. Finally, he shows how the various areas of theology can be seen as coherent, disciplined ways of trying to know.[3] We

[3] See *Insight: A Study in Human Understanding*, New York 1970; and *Method in Theology*, London 1972.

find this the most impressive contemporary contribution to the subject, though in need of filling out with more consideration of imagination, the interpersonal, and the negativities of existence. Yet Lonergan's, for all its complexity and importance, is the easier of the two ways of bridging the gap we have described.

The other way is from the side of the content of knowledge. This involves taking a specific area (for example, a scientific account of some basic features of the physical world and how they develop in space and time), and asking how that relates to knowledge of God. There is no avoiding the demand for competence in both areas. Few theologians (though Lonergan is a notable exception) are much concerned about the actual content of the natural sciences – often they have an excuse in the form of some definition of respective areas that ensures neither need worry about the other. Few scientists bother much about theology – even the most interested tend to have a notion of God nowhere near the sophistication of their science. The solution is the slow and extended one of learning in dialogue. Each needs to test the other, while staying in communication. This is one of the major tasks for both the sciences and theology. In this chapter we cannot do it in detail, but will offer some outlines and conclusions.

We will now look briefly at how God relates to some features, first of the physical universe and then of human history.

God and the World

When Genesis 1 described the creation it used the best available understanding of the cosmos. This included quite a comprehensive grasp of what the basic elements in cosmic reality are – light, time, space, sun and stars, inorganic, organic and animate matter, species and reproduction, man, and an ecology of mutual dependence. A modern God-related picture of reality also needs to use the best current science and do today what Genesis did in its time. Genesis, in addition to appropriating contemporary world-views, also criticized them – there was no way the sun could be allowed to seem divine, for example, so light was created before the sun and moon. Besides, by ascribing responsibility for creation to God, Genesis pointed to the nature of God by way of what he did and the nature of the world as dependent upon God. We want to do something similar in this section: to take seriously some of the basic features of the world described by the sciences, to criticize some of the world-views that often claim scientific support, and to see what sort of God is suggested by the world as we know it.

After many years in which scientific knowledge seemed to become increasingly fragmented, and those who attempted to synthesize were an unpopular minority, contemporary science and philosophy of science have been producing fresh efforts to explore the basic characteristics of the world and unite them in coherent overall pictures. We will select just a few of the results in two broad areas, physics and biology.

In physics a major modern development has been a focus on energy and the randomness with which it changes and is distributed. The role of chance in the world has been stressed, greatly modifying previous views which were much more law-like, and which often identified scientific knowledge with what could be described in certain orderly forms. Now the random spread of energy, dispersing in arbitrary fashion, and also the random behaviour of sub-atomic particles, have exploded over-orderly theories. In biology there has been a similar development, seen mainly in the randomness of genetic variation. Biological populations are seen to be randomly derived. One can of course calculate statistically the probability of a particular outcome, but the old tight cause-and-effect systems have gone.

In theology this has often been seen as a threat. This is because the God of much theology has been the supreme orderer and controller, and to say that there is real randomness seems to reduce his scope. The result is that much theology, and most believers, have found themselves with a God who must be seen to be in tight control even when the discovered nature of his creation seems to rule out such totalitarianism. It is a mechanistic view of God and his mode of relationship with the world, and logically it is almost impossible to avoid determinism and its theological offshoots such as predestination. As a view of God it clearly matches the old over-ordered understanding of the world. The modern theme of randomness can therefore be liberating. It allows the richer concept of a God for whom there is non-order as well as order. In this light the randomness itself can be seen in a more positive way as the basic condition for overflow and abundance. This is not just a matter of some scientific data dictating the nature of God; it is allowing science to be connected with theology in order to contribute to conclusions which cohere with other lines of argument too, as chapter 6 has shown.

Complete randomness would, of course, be a denial of God. Some cosmologies do take chance as their fundamental fact. On this view there is no source of order, no purpose or patterning other than that produced by the randomly explorative dispersal of energy and by the fact that inefficient combinations do not survive. Yet the notion of 'efficiency' points to the fact that there are always constraints in operation. There is no such thing as complete, blind chance. In physics a fundamental constraint is the existence of three dimensions of space and one of time. Spatio-temporal dimensions order the random spread of energy, and whatever does not conform with them is cancelled out. In biology there are constraints such as the control exercised by the species as a reproductive community. In the complex set of exchanges that makes a species, randomness is severely limited.

Such constraints could be just temporary abatements in chaos, arresting energy for a while in its inevitable dispersal into random bits. This is a common cosmological option: the universe is steadily running down, the key process being that of entropy, the dissipation of energy. The 'goal' of this is a state of equilibrium with minimum density of energy. The universe is a brute fact governed by chance and by some temporary constraints – for even spatio-temporality as we know it need not be permanent.

Yet all the data that contribute to this picture can also fit another picture. The entropic one already given depends on a hypothesis about the long-term process of the cosmos. It sees the world moving to a state of exhausted entropy and takes as its base-line a condition of chaotic equilibrium. Departures from this equilibrium are oddities, temporary aberrations. But the base-line and the long-term process could be construed very differently. What if the fundamental state of the universe is non-equilibrial? What if all the randomness and the constraints point to an inexhaustible capacity for richness, complexity, and order continually transcending itself? There are developments in physical chemistry (associated notably with Ilya Prigogine) that show how stable systems can fluctuate in such a way as to produce more complex systems, new types of equilibrium. Change and constraint over time can evolve and maintain new order and structures. The cosmos has proved capable of actually producing such abundance, and it harmonizes with this fact to see its basic state as that of dynamic non-equilibrium. In other words, it seems more in accord with the overall picture of reality to see the universe as an abundant allowance of space, time and energy through which new abundance can happen. This view does more justice to all the aspects of reality that we know than do other views. It can accommodate the discoveries of physics and biology (in ways of which we have given only a small sample) and also other areas of knowledge. This is the conception of the universe within which many of our key, interrelated terms make sense: overflow, non-order, novelty, non-equilibrium, abundance.

If the universe is best seen in its basic character as unfolding abundance (which is not to rule out the possibility of its perversion or destruction, cf. chapter 6), the main choice is between this being a brute fact or being the responsibility of God and in relationship with him. As we have often said, there is no logically necessary proof either way, and it is important to note how hostile to the tyranny of logical necessity are the key terms listed above. But we do find that the whole picture makes more sense if God exists and is of a certain nature. The ultimate arbitrariness of the 'brute fact' position amounts to a complete randomness that does not accord with the way the cosmos is and changes, and it also sets an arbitrary limit to rationality. But what sort of God is more rational?

We have already seen that the extent of randomness shows many traditional conceptions of God to be inadequate. God must be at least as rich as his creation, and a rigid, over-ordered and over-ordering God is far too impoverished to be responsible for a universe such as ours. Likewise, a God who is conceived as an absolute equilibrium – beyond all change and exchange, unaffected and invulnerable – represents an idea of static completion and perfection which cannot embrace the life of creation in all its dynamic diversity. What would a non-equilibrial God be like? We see him as Trinitarian, involved in three modes of transcendence.

The first mode is as the source and ground of all abundance. God is the all-sufficient one, abundant in himself, and overflowing in creation, which itself bears his characteristic mark of generous abundance. His relationship is seen in the sustaining of this dynamic and life, and in its constant resistance to all the 'necessary' forces of disintegration and entropy.

The second mode of God's transcendence is in his respectful, creative ordering of the abundance. A key notion here is that of the proportioning and shaping of energy. God is not vague, indefinite and blurred either in himself or in his activity. He is specific without being totalitarian, and the Christian expression of this fact is that he creates and sustains by his word, or *logos*. The word respectfully addresses, shapes, and proportions reality, giving it its inner, non-equilibrial balance in movement. It is informed by the response and resistance of the world but not determined by them. It refuses all pigeon-holing, allows no self-sufficient closed systems, and, positively, it is the dynamic stability of reality, allowing freedom but also embodying constraints.

The third mode is best seen in God's transcendence of time. This does not mean that God is static and divorced from movement, but that he is 'always ahead'. He is not deterministic, but is there to enable new possibilities, to empower freedom to live in the abundance that is given, and to be intimately involved with all the joys and agonies that this entails. He is the God of new creation, new initiatives, and persevering patience in the beginnings that have been made; and all of this is taken up in the human enjoyment of personal relationship with him. The second mode sets the pattern and ideal, and this third mode is the inspiration and means of achieving and participating in it.

We have described some of the interrelated characteristics of God as a Trinity of Father, Son and Holy Spirit. This seems to be the most adequate and rational way of understanding the universe we live in, and it embodies the movement of praise. That movement is supremely non-equilibrial, always completing completion and perfecting perfection. It is taken up into the movement of God and celebrates his abundance while being shaped by his word and open to a new future. Praise and adoration are the new, spiritual abundance that are encouraged but not necessitated by all the other abundance of the world: they are the supreme ecstasy of inexhaustible knowledge and love in the enjoyment of God that is the true life of creation.

But what of God in himself? We have described God as Trinitarian in his relationship with creation, and this is usually called the 'economic Trinity'. We have not discussed God in himself, the 'immanent Trinity'. As much twentieth-century theology has argued, the two are inseparable to the point of being identical, but yet it does seem right at least to distinguish them. Praise above all raises the question of God in himself, and most ways to the immanent Trinity have stressed the importance of doxology. Our vision of God in himself would need much elaboration, but its outline is simply stated. God is in himself the source of all abundance: it is shaped and proportioned in himself by his word or *logos*, and its constant, joyful, fresh overflow is the energy of the Holy Spirit uniting God in dynamic life. That life is best conceived as the overflow of mutual delight, of mutual glorification in an infinity of interesting creativity. Yet when that includes the creating of free creatures, God's non-equilibrium risks being that of suffering as well as joy. The triumph of God is to transform even this into the content of realistic praise, and such an event is the heart of the gospel, revealing the heart of God.

Revelation

If God's knowing of the world knits him into everything that is as a respectful presence who wants to be known in return, then there should be no problem of scarcity of knowledge of God. The problem should be the abundance of knowledge of him. This is in fact the case. Everything can be seen as a sign pointing to God. The ordinary, as in much of Patrick Kavanagh's poetry, and the extraordinary, as in many accounts of 'religious experience', can both be eloquent of God, and we have seen how all creation can be understood to praise God. Some accounts make revelation seem like knowledge in a sea of ignorance, but that devalues God's creation and his resourcefulness, and leads to disastrous lack of respect for the riches of the world's religions and cultures, and for the vast amount of personal experience that fails to fit the categories of whatever is claimed as 'revelation'.

Yet the generosity of God in letting himself be known so widely can go along with his freedom to reveal himself definitively in particular ways. These can then be the criteria of knowledge of God, the points of greatest clarity which illuminate and discriminate between other points, proportioning and relating them. Christianity has sharpened this 'scandal of particularity' to its most acute form in the doctrines of the Trinity and Jesus Christ. It has dared to affirm the ultimate self-expression of God in Jesus Christ, the climax of history in his life, death and resurrection, and the overflow and communication of all this in the Holy Spirit available now. We will deal more with this content of Christian revelation in the next chapter, but will now prepare for that by exploring the logic of its scandalous particularity.

Our view of the world and God has already tried to show that particularity is not an oddity but is built into a universe that has non-order as well as order. The fact that events only happen once, and need not necessarily have happened the way they did, is quite normal. If the general account of reality allows for uniqueness and decisive contingency, then there can be no dichotomy between a general natural theology and a particular theology of revelation. It becomes a matter of accepting that revelation, the communication of God with the world, needs to be described in various frames of reference, the perspectives of cosmology, world history and theories of good, evil and human nature being a complement to the central stories of salvation. Every such story has its context in time, place and society; the basic dynamics of the world, such as we have discussed earlier in this chapter, operate there too; and there is a great deal in common between people of different periods and places. All of this warns against making any historical revelation seem too scandalously special, and this is accepted by the New Testament in a variety of ways – by claiming that all things were created through Jesus Christ (as Paul, John and the author of Hebrews say), or simply by the interweaving of nature and revelation in the parables of Jesus.

Yet while guarding against the wrong sort of revelling in the distinctiveness of Christian revelation, our approach does allow for a decisive particularity told in the central story of Jesus Christ. The crucial locus of love is the carrying on of ordinary life and history, with face-to-face relationships the central concern. This can never be adequately summarized or put in the form of principles or conclusions. The knowledge of what happens in such loving can only be told in its particularity by telling its story. The events only happen once, and are not reducible to truths or a meaning separable from the interaction of character, event and circumstance. If knowledge is to come out of this it must finally depend on the testimony of witnesses, because the events cannot be re-run.

So, if God wants respectfully to reveal himself as loving and enabling love, this will have to happen in a particular context and the knowledge spread by telling its story. This does not rule out exhaustive checking of the story and testing of the witnesses' reliability, and the story itself can be the result of a long process of debate, interpretation and conflict (cf. section 3 of chapter 4 for a statement on this aspect of revelation), but it does exclude attempts to bypass historical knowledge in knowing God. God is free to identify himself in this interpersonal way, and this is most in harmony with respect for human integrity and social nature. God shows his involvement in contingency at its most dangerous: in the free choices and responses of human beings, and in the power relations of society, religion and politics.

The way in which Christianity draws on its central story of Jesus Christ to identify God is itself a claim about the nature of God: that he is best known through the perspectives of ordinary social life. This pivotal perspective says a great deal about the distinctiveness of Christian revelation. It does not make the individual's interior relationship with God the main locus of revelation, nor does it give primacy to general principles for living or a pattern of spirituality. It also refuses to let the dominant perspective be an over-arching theory of world history (as in Marxism or some theories of progress or evolution). It needs to relate to such perspectives, but it pivots around its central story about people in Palestine.

In this chapter we have been mainly concerned with some of the wider perspectives, and the central story itself suffers if it is disconnected from them or is implausible in relation to them. But now we turn to Jesus himself.

8

Jesus is Our Praise

'Jesus is Lord' is a statement at the heart of Christian praise. 'Lord' means universality, and we have tried to point to the ramifications of praise through cosmic, historical and personal reality. 'Jesus' means a particular person, and we have rather neglected him, partly because we wanted to set up a context in which he is not understood in isolation or individualistically. The main guard against that has been the double thrust towards relating him both to an appropriate understanding of God and to the reality of the world and human life. But now it is time to contemplate him.

Our seminal definition of praise in chapter 3 was as the combination of recognition and respect. Later chapters have developed the meaning of those terms in several ways, but they all tended to come together again in relation to Jesus Christ. Jesus Christ acknowledged as crucified and risen is the central, dazzling fact for the tradition. There are two basic elements in this: the story of Jesus that culminated in his crucifixion; and the strange sequel called the resurrection. It is through these particular events that the essence of Christian praise was shaped in ways that deserve intensive exploration.

The Historical Jesus

The first Christians had their continuity with Jesus in the apostles and many other eyewitnesses. They were taken up with living from the central fact of the risen Jesus Christ, and with expecting his soon return, and they did not write Gospels. The Letters of Paul reflect this stage. But eventually the continuity with Jesus had to be embodied in narrative form. Jesus had not returned in the way first expected and this let the distinctiveness of the Christian hope emerge more clearly: what was unique to the Christian view of the consummation of all things was not that it would come soon (that was a part of the general culture, with its many apocalyptic expectations) but that it was inseparable from Jesus Christ, who had already overcome death. This made the importance of adequately identifying Jesus even greater, and the various oral and perhaps written traditions of his life and teaching were formed in complex ways into the four Gospels.

The Gospels offer plenty of material for identifying Jesus as a historical character, even if a very rigorous set of criteria is used and a minimal description of Jesus results. Historical judgements are always a matter of probability, but most scholars would agree about the authenticity of such elements as Jesus' baptism by John the Baptist, his message of the Kingdom of God, his accompaniment by a group of twelve close followers, his ministry of healing and exorcism, his use of parables, his conflict with the religious leaders especially over matters of law, his friendship with women and outsiders of society, his calling God 'Abba' (intimate form of 'Father'), and his eventual trial in Jerusalem followed by crucifixion.

That minimalism can, however, be a rather trivial exercise, leaving us with disconnected bits that happen to fit our most cautious criteria. A more satisfactory approach tries to embrace this, but goes beyond it in examining each major strand in the tradition and trying to discover what it might as a whole reflect of the historical Jesus. Different strands had very different 'interests' in Jesus, and these helped to shape their pictures without necessarily falsifying the facts. It then becomes a very subtle and complex exercise to try to reconstruct the history, but at least it is being recognized that no neutral account can ever exist, and that the best historical accounts, especially of people, require self-involvement and creativity if they are to do justice to their subject. In the last decade two of the best-known descriptions of the historical Jesus have followed this approach: Hans Küng in a more popular mode in *On Being a Christian*,[1] and Edward Schillebeeckx at much greater length in *Jesus: An Experiment in Christology*.[2] They show the sort of historical synthesis that is possible by drawing together and assessing the writings of many scholars, and their type of enterprise is necessary as part of a rational theology. They take seriously both the irreducibility of testimony and the need to subject it to many types of criticism before making some coherent assessment of the history.

We do not want to do that exhaustive work afresh, but to take it up into the theology of praising and knowing God. We take for granted such judicious reconstructions and their apparatus of critical scholarship, and try to move through and beyond them.

[1]   London 1977.
[2]   London 1979.

The Life of Jesus

How is the life of Jesus to be characterized? How are its content and movement to be identified? As Mark's Gospel makes clear, to refer adequately to Jesus is not a simple matter. Mark's mode of reference is by no means straightforward. He combines several levels and perspectives, uses Jesus' words and actions, responses to him, titles, silences, digressions, enigmas, backward and forward references, and a strange ending. Other Gospels add to this array, and for all of them there is the embracing perspective of the resurrection. The life of Jesus is described as many-faceted, and one of the strengths of narrative is that it insists on going through all the facets. There can be a false simplifying that concentrates on a few titles, or a key theme, or the later doctrinal statements, and is too quick to leave behind the less orderly richness of the narratives. Theology and Christian living have been impoverished by the abstraction and rigidity that have resulted from this. We have already gone through one of the narratives and have stressed their indispensability for identifying Jesus. But the complexity can also be clarified and made more powerful by an attempt to discern fundamental dynamics.

Jesus lived and died referring everything to God. His message was the Kingdom of God – letting God be God and orienting everything around this priority. This is the pearl worth selling all for, the yeast that leavens all the dough. The New Testament is God-centred throughout, and Jesus' life and death are the actualization of a person living for God. But for what sort of God? Jesus called him 'Abba', an intimate form of 'Father', and portrayed him as loving, generous, forgiving and blessing, as well as concerned for justice, judgement and truth. He is a God who is concerned for people and will go to great lengths for them. So Jesus refers everything to this Father who is completely for people. The result is that Jesus lives a life for others through his relationship with God.

This can be seen in terms of responsibility. On the one hand Jesus commits all responsibility for himself and others to God – God even cares for sparrows and lilies, so human beings can trust him too. On the other hand Jesus receives back responsibility in the form of a vocation and mission which lets him rejoice in the Holy Spirit (Luke 10:21ff.), but also leads him through Gethsemane to the cross. His responsibility for others before God overflows in teaching, healing, denouncing, forgiving, feeding and finally suffering. In all this his main concern is that others too should be free to refer everything to this God and receive back free responsibility for each other. This is the life of the Kingdom of God, the joyful exchange that Jesus pictures as a feast which can be begun now. But when the exchange is blocked or distorted, and the priority of God and his Kingdom is lost, the responsibility to God and others inevitably means conflict and suffering. 'Referring all to God' is the movement of praise: how does it happen with sin and evil? Chapter 6 has given one answer. It is possible to enter into evil and shame, and to experience it as one's own while still referring it to God, so that an exchange is set up which can contain even the negativities. Jesus' life is such an exchange, and the human circuit could not contain it: he died, but the very act of dying was his supreme act of reference to God.

The resurrection is God's way of referring back Jesus to the world. The life of Jesus, for God and for others, is affirmed and released for all. The previous affirmations at his baptism and transfiguration, and in many events of his ministry, are here summed up in the climactic union of God's glory and Jesus' life. It is not a neutral, amoral fact about what happened to a corpse. It climaxes the pattern of responsibility between man and God. God takes responsibility for everything, the resurrection is an initiative of God alone, but he gives back a new responsibility. For the disciples the resurrection was an experience of joy and vocation together. There is the joyful freedom of complete forgiveness and acceptance in the welcome of Jesus, and the limitless responsibility of mission to the whole world. We are in the realm of the classic paradoxes: everything is given, everything is demanded; there is justification by grace alone, yet faith requires obedience.

But paradoxes are too rigid, they are a tight balance of opposites, and the resurrection breaks out of paradox into doxology. Freedom and responsibility, non-order and order, grace and works, can come together non-competitively when both are focused in the free response of joy. The key is in the one who evokes the response, and who in his person embodies doxology beyond paradox, Jesus Christ.

Jesus beyond Dilemmas: The Life of New Responsibility

A double-bind is a dilemma in which it seems that, whatever you do, you lose. It is a paradox in life, a 'no-win' situation, as in the classic father–son relationship: the father demands that the son succeed in life, and punishes failure; but, if the son succeeds, the father feels threatened and, in more subtle ways, punishes success too.

Many of the Gospel stories show Jesus being placed in double-binds during his ministry. He is asked whether tax is to be paid to Caesar and it seems he must offend either the Jews or the Romans. He is asked for the basis of his authority and, it seems, must acknowledge established authorities or make a claim to direct authority from God which begs the question. He is asked to heal on the Sabbath and must either break the law or refuse compassion. That is also the issue when he is asked to condemn a woman caught in adultery. Some of the most important themes of his ministry run through such dilemmas: healing, forgiveness, the law, compassion, power and authority. How does Jesus meet them?

Sometimes he refuses the terms of the dilemma and passes beyond it; sometimes he firmly takes one option. But whichever he does, he refers the whole situation to God, the God who is greater than the law, and than Caesar, who forgives and has compassion, and uses his power to heal and help. Not only that, but Jesus often simultaneously refers the matter back to his audience: he asks a counter-question (Where did John the Baptist's authority come from? Would you pull your ox out of a well on the Sabbath?) or issues a challenge (Let whoever is without sin throw the first stone; pay to God what is due to God and to Caesar what is due to Caesar). In other words, he calls for the responsible participation of other people in breaking out of the double-bind.

Jesus' whole ministry is an acting-out and teaching of this new responsibility. Much of the Sermon on the Mount could be seen as instruction on how to handle the double-binds and vicious circles people get into when they follow the way of Jesus in the world as it is. The ways through such no-win situations as persecution, enmity, guilt, mutual recrimination, and demands for money or possessions vary. But they all presuppose a God who can be relied on to such an extent that one is freed for extravagant responses, for generosity beyond prudence, and for costly responsibility for other people. The persecuted are to rejoice and leap for joy, enemies are to be loved and prayed for, the guilty forgiven again and again, and the logic of overflow is experienced by taking part in a new non-equilibrial generosity:

> Give and it will be given to you; good measure, pressed down, shaken together, running over, will be put into your lap (Luke 6:38).

Who will give this? God alone can fulfil such promises, and faith in him frees us for a similar large-heartedness. 'He is kind to the ungrateful and selfish. Be merciful, even as your Father is merciful' (Luke 6:35f.).

This is a new reponsibility inseparable from faith in God and committed to finding the creative, life-giving way out of double-binds and vicious circles, whatever the cost. Faith itself combines taking responsibility for a situation and referring it to God. The two go together because this God shares responsibility – that is the life he offers. Jesus' ministry was one of sharing responsibility with

others, which is a fundamental form of respectful loving. He did it
by training disciples, giving calls and tasks, asking for faith and
responsible stewardship, expecting others to take the initiative
(parable of the talents) and encouraging the sort of active trust in
God that led the woman with a haemorrhage to break taboos by
touching Jesus, and the extravagant generosity that moved a
notorious woman to pour expensive perfume over his feet and wipe
them with her hair. He is not just wanting an orderly obedience to
commands and principles: there is something beyond that, an
overflow and daring that clearly delighted him and made him
picture the feast of the Kingdom full of such non-orderly people.

The cost of sustaining this vision was that he had to take the
responsibility to its limits. After years of trying to get the right
response to his message of the Kingdom of God, he faces his failure
to get others to participate in it with him. Even those closest to him
desert him. Just before that happens he prays in Gethsemane and
discovers that as he refers all to God ('Thy will be done') so God
refers it back to him in the form of suffering. His attempt to share
with others the new responsibility to God has met evil at many
levels, and as he unites his will with God's he finds that God's will
risks going right through the evil.

The crucifixion, seen as the will of God in the face of evil, shows
the double-bind that God himself is in when dealing with evil.
There is a classic Zen dilemma in which the master tells the pupil
that he will beat him with his stick if he does a certain action and
will also beat him if he does not. People put God in a similar
position. They say that if they cannot do wrong, but only what God
wills, then they are not really free and have no dignity as human
beings; but if they do wrong, and cause suffering and evil, they
blame God for creating a world in which such terrible things are
possible. The answer for the Zen pupil is to take the master's stick,
and so break out of the double-bind. This answer refuses to accept
the terms of the dilemma, and daringly has one taking the other's
role. The crucifixion can be seen as God's way of taking the stick
of the problem of evil, and also taking responsibility for all that it
involves. But unlike the Zen solution, which merely reverses the
master–pupil relationship and keeps the relationship of authority
(though Zen too can go beyond this), this exchange in the
crucifixion transforms the relationship itself. The resurrection shows
what this is. There is something beyond the double-binds and
paralysing vicious circles of evil. It brings a new shared responsibility between God and man, offering all and demanding all within
an ecology of freedom, blessing and praise. It is a new glory, as
described by John:

No longer do I call you servants, for the servant does not know what his master is doing; but I have called you friends, for all that I have heard from my Father I have made known to you (John 15:15).

The new sharing between man and God explodes from the resurrection, with its double focus on the glorified Jesus and his sending out others round the world. The energy and life of this sharing is the Holy Spirit, and the message it carries is 'Jesus is our praise'. The risen Jesus is beyond the dilemmas of disunity and the paradoxes of evil, and moves freely in the Spirit, liberating from the double-binds. Paul's experience of this was in terms of the law. His opponents continually tried to force him to choose between keeping the Jewish law or else being a law-breaker and condoning all sorts of moral and religious disorder. He refused the dilemma, and said that there is a third way: Jesus Christ is the fulfilment of the law, and living in the Spirit is the new way of life. This may seem like disorder but in fact it is an overflow of the order of God, with joy, freedom and needless generosity in loving as the fruits of the Spirit. It is responsibility in freedom, and its cost to Paul is extreme, but as our interpretation of Philippians in chapter 3 showed, he does not consider it at all heavy. It is neither a keeping nor a breaking of the law, but a different quality and power of life which shares in the glory of God as redefined through the cross of Jesus.

John's Gospel too shows this resolution in freedom of the paradoxes, ironies and oppositions that run through the earlier part of his story. His climax is the glorifying of Jesus in his death, and the resurrection is beyond all irony: 'Receive the Holy Spirit' (John 20:22); 'Follow me' (21:22). The framework for understanding this is set up by the massive affirmations earlier in the Gospel: 'I am the true vine, the good shepherd, the bread of life, the light of the world, the door, the water of life, the way, the truth, the life, the resurrection and the life.' These are entangled in a mesh of misunderstanding and ambiguity until the resurrection releases them into Thomas's direct 'My Lord and my God!'

Luke exemplifies the new responsibility at both ends of his Gospel. He opens with Mary accepting her motherhood of Jesus, and he has one song of praise after another in his first two chapters, above all the Magnificat of Mary. The foundation of his Gospel is this shared responsibility that gave birth to Jesus in an ecstasy of praise:

And suddenly there was with the angel a multitude of the heavenly host praising God and saying, Glory to God in the highest, and on earth peace among men with whom he is pleased (Luke 2:13ff.).

Then at the end, after the resurrection the disciples are told that

> repentance and forgiveness of sins should be preached in his
> name to all nations, beginning from Jerusalem. You are witnesses
> of these things. And behold I send the 'promise of my Father
> upon you; but stay in the city, until you are clothed with power
> from on high (Luke 24:47ff.).

There is then a pause for praise during which the Holy Spirit at
Pentecost comes to begin a fresh sharing of the call to repentance,
baptism and witness.

That first preaching of the Gospel was in the city where Jesus
had been condemned to death:

> This Jesus *you* crucified (Acts 2:23).

So the dead victim is offered as the hope of his oppressors. They
have to face up to guilty responsibility, but they are not held in a
vicious circle of despair or rejection:

> But God raised him up (Acts 2:24).

The resurrection is the liberation of life through forgiveness and
hope. This is acted out in baptism, which is the sacrament of
freedom, identifying with Jesus in his life beyond double-binds.

Perhaps the most comprehensive Christology of new responsibility is given in the Letter to the Hebrews. Jesus is seen in the
context of God and the whole cosmos:

> He reflects the glory of God and bears the very stamp of his
> nature, upholding the universe by his word of power (1:3).

But he is also seen as completely involved with the risks and contingency of the world. He suffered and was tempted (2:18), he had a
life which let him sympathize with our weakness through experience
of it (4:15), he prayed with loud cries and tears and learnt obedience
through his suffering. In all this Hebrews sees him in the priestly
role of representing others. He risks complete solidarity with and
for others (2:9, 14ff; 7:25), and the sheer agony and bloodiness of
this is central. Hebrews especially takes Jewish worship as the
context for understanding this life and death for others. Central to
that worship was the offering of sacrifice by priests. What Jesus
does is seen as breaking out of the cyclical repetition of sacrifice:
he offers himself as the sacrifice (7:27). It is the ultimate taking of
responsibility by one who can carry it through to the bloody end,
and his resurrection (or exaltation, as Hebrews prefers to call it)
makes it a permanent new relationship ('new covenant') between
God and man. There is a new economy of exchange, a breakthrough

from vicious circularity into a new communication, hope, blessing, forgiveness, service, ethics, confidence and joy (7–10).

Hebrews stresses Jesus' decisive taking of responsibility before his Father; but it is equally extreme in its demand for an answering responsibility. No other New Testament document has more stoic-sounding language than Hebrews, especially in its encouragement of endurance, struggle, faithfulness, holding fast to what has been given, running with perseverance, and discipline. Yet all of this is in context most un-stoic. Jesus endures the cross 'for the joy that was set before him' (12:2); and because of that decisive, lasting joy, even suffering can be joyfully accepted (10:34). The embracing vision is of celebration (12:22ff.), worship (12:28), and a union of praise with practical responsibility:

> Through him then let us continually offer up a sacrifice of praise to God, that is, the fruit of lips that acknowledge his name. Do not neglect to do good and to share what you have, for such sacrifices are pleasing to God (13:15ff.).

It is both ethical and joyful, pleasing all round.

The Resurrection is Knowledge and Praise

In the life of Jesus and its sharing, the resurrection has been seen as essential. The New Testament accounts clearly witness to an event of seismic proportions, but in themselves are just a collection of documents that invite us to believe them. Should the accounts of this key event, Jesus' resurrection, be trusted? Their historical worth has by no means been proved by showing how vividly they describe an extraordinary experience. Is resurrection possible? Did the resurrection of Jesus happen?

As regards its possibility, that depends on our view of reality as a whole (which may, of course, in turn be influenced by what we believe is the truth about the resurrection). We have offered an understanding of God and the universe within which the resurrection is quite conceivable: there is a God who is free to take initiatives; he has created a world in which new, surprising things can happen, so there is no tightly determined ordering which dictates that such a unique novelty as the resurrection cannot happen; and the character of God lets us imagine him creating an event through which people are offered, without coercion, possibilities that meet their deepest desires – for affirmation, a fresh start, purpose, community, life beyond death and much else.

But did it happen? By comparison with the evidence for many other ancient events, that for an extraordinary happening after the

death of Jesus is good. The echoes of it in a variety of documents
are too strong to deny that something remarkable generated the
faith and mission of the Christian Church. The main historical issue
is whether this was a subjective event in the disciples and others,
or whether it was also an event for the dead Jesus. In other words,
it is the familiar problem of projection again: was belief in the
resurrection of Jesus the result of something happening to Jesus or
only to the disciples? This is yet another of those debates in which
endless subtlety has been exercised. Of recent discussions we find
most convincing that of Rowan Williams in *Resurrection*[3] and, before
that, the arguments of Wolfhart Pannenberg in *Jesus, God and Man*[4]
and their refinements in his more sympathetic critics. We will not
try to rehearse the details, but the conclusions are important.

The strangeness and disorientation that come through all the
resurrection accounts do point to a faith generated independently
of the early community, and,

> . . . for all four Gospels, the story which identifies the ultimate
> source of this disorientation is that of the empty tomb. . . The
> apostles are drawn together by receiving the message that Jesus'
> body is not in its grave, and this helps them to understand what
> later happens as an encounter with a Jesus who is, now as
> hitherto, a partner in dialogue, a material other, still involved in
> the fabric of human living while also sovereignly free from its
> constraints. This leaves a good deal of latitude in dealing with
> the apparition stories: it certainly points us away from any simple
> view of individual or corporate 'self-authenticating' visions, and
> allows fully for their enigmatic and elusive nature.[5]

The key factor is the continuity of Jesus' living identity through
death, and not the exact mode of his presence. The otherness,
Lordship and aliveness of Jesus are intensified by whatever
happened. This is witnessed to, and the testimony can be either
believed or not; but it is not claimed as a brute fact, an isolated
event. The decisive 'proof' is always held to be an inextricable
combination of trust in the witnesses together with the presence of
Jesus himself in the community, all within the context of faith in
God. In other words, we would say that the structure of this knowledge is Trinitarian: a God who is able to do this, an historical
person who is the object of it, and a spiritual and social experience
of justified trust.

This underlines the unique logic of the resurrection stories. They

---

3   London 1982.
4   London 1968.
5   Williams, op. cit., pp. 105ff.

are stories about someone who, they claim, is still alive to confirm them. So the logic is circular, it includes the presence of the risen Lord. If he is still alive and in communication, the role of the stories is to point to him, and identify him, but there need be no legalistic precision about this, and there is no way of standing neutrally outside what happened in order to confirm or deny claims. This event is so big that it has no outside. There are 'hard data' associated with it which need assessment, but they are inevitably ambiguous. They need to be taken up into an ecology of factors and levels, including those in which we are most intimately involved, before we can affirm or deny that Jesus is risen.

The dimensions of this event have, as we explored them, taken on the dimensions of God. It has each of the three modes of God's transcendence which we discussed in chapter 7. There is the abundance of God in the new life beyond death and the universal implications of this. There is the new proportioning of life within this abundance, as the Lordship of Jesus is embraced, enjoyed and demonstrated in new responsibility. Third, there is the new future expressed in the calling and sending by the risen Jesus. In these ways the transformation of the concept of God begins in practice, long before it is conceptualized. To speak of the risen Jesus is also to speak of God and to have our ideas of God changed. It is 'to speak of creativity, finality, ultimate authority, inexhaustible living presence, universal significance'.[6] It is also to speak of the mutual relationship between God and believers in ways which demonstrate the essential structure of Christian praise.

The resurrection stories embody the dynamics of praise. They show the patterning and mutuality of recognition and respect among the participants. God decisively acknowledges Jesus by raising him from the dead. Jesus had been judged, shamed and killed, but is now vindicated. God acts, and Jesus appears as the content of his act. This means that his whole life is justified and honoured – 'glorified', as John says. The initiative of God focuses celebration and praise on a shamed victim.

Along with this recognition of Jesus by his Father goes the acceptance of the disciples by Jesus. They had deserted him, and Peter had denied he knew him, but this painful, shameful memory is healed by Jesus' initiative. He welcomes them back into community with himself, talks with them, eats with them and blesses them. Characteristic marks of his ministry are repeated, and these become a pattern for Christian worship. Jesus also pays his disciples the greatest mark of respect: he trusts them by calling them to do his work.

6   Williams, ibid., p. 95.

The third element in this network of recognition and respect is the disciples' response to the double initiative. Their recognition, like Jesus' self-presentation, draws on all their previous experience of him and so establishes the gospel story at the centre of praise.

But it is time to burst out of the rather tame terminology of 'recognition and respect'. The resurrection gives a content to this dynamic that transforms it into unprecedented amazement and joy. Matthew talks of 'fear and great joy' (28:8), and twice of worship (28:9, 17). Luke mentions 'while they still disbelieved for joy, and wondered. . .' (24:41), and he has an interlude between the resurrection and Pentecost which is filled with praise: 'And they returned to Jerusalem with great joy, and were continually in the temple blessing God' (24:52). John typically intensifies the theme. In the middle of his account of the key appearance of Jesus to breathe the Holy Spirit into the disciples, he writes: 'Then the disciples were glad when they saw the Lord' (20:20); and this is followed by the recognition of Jesus by Thomas, who says, 'My Lord and my God!' (20:28). The very diversity of the accounts shows the authors trying to grapple with something wildly, improbably new and exciting, news so gripping and powerful that it needs a circuit of God and the whole world to contain it. The resurrection is the genesis of Christian praise and mission together. It manifests the life of Jesus Christ as the presence of God, a resource for the whole world.

Chalcedon: Jesus, God and Man

In A.D. 451 a council of Christian bishops at Chalcedon summed up centuries of debate about the person of Jesus Christ in what became the classic definition. It affirmed him as

> . . . perfect in Godhead and perfect in manhood, truly God and truly man . . . made known in two natures without confusion, without change, without division, without separation, the difference of the natures being by no means removed because of the union. . .

It sounds paradoxical. It is quite definite about both natures and refuses any way out which reduces this definiteness. Many of the other proposals over the centuries had tried to resolve the dilemma by weakening one side of it (Jesus not fully divine or not fully human). The danger in maintaining both sides as strongly as Chalcedon did is that it will appear as a rigidly balanced paradox, with a permanent tension.

A tension-filled paradox would contradict all that we have said about Jesus beyond dilemmas. Chalcedon itself was, as we described in chapter 4 above, the outcome of centuries of praise, and that context refuses to let any interpretation rest in the balanced rigidity of paradox. The way beyond this is to refuse the conventional terms of the dilemma, which defined God and man in terms that made them contradictory and competitive. It is not a matter of us having satisfactory definitions of God and man and then applying them to Jesus Christ: he must be allowed to contribute to the definitions themselves, and this means great changes.

Chalcedon was open to the revolution in the concept of God that this meant. The doctrine of the Trinity, which conceived Jesus as intrinsic to the being and activity of God, had been developed. We have taken that up in chapters 4 and 7 and have pushed it further than the early Church did. What does it mean for the way the divinity of Jesus is conceived? It means that God is free to define himself in completely human terms. God's abundance, proportioning and movement are modes of transcendence which are expressed in this man who is and does for humanity what God is and does. God allows himself to be identified by reference to humanity in a particular way, and Jesus is divine by embodying this identity. This is all in line with Chalcedon.

Chalcedon was not so prepared, however, for a parallel revolution in the concept of humanity. The implications in terms of the astonishing dignity and shared responsibility of human beings were not encouraged. The source of these implications is the way God establishes the dignity of people by letting them be in freedom. The Council of Chalcedon was greatly influenced by the Roman emperor's demand for doctrinal unity in his empire. The agreed formula was meant to end divisions, and it was imposed later by force as well as persuasion. The overwhelming motive was to achieve 'good order' in Church and empire. So the Chalcedonian Definition came to be applied as a rule, a test of conformity, in the interests of political and religious unity. This compromised the essence of the humanity represented by Jesus. Jesus stood for shared responsibility, for asking others to think through who he was, for a dignity before God which liberated and enhanced human responsibility, and which ran the risks of freedom and *ekstasis* rather than submit to authoritarian discipline. Chalcedon (or at least the uses to which it was put) stoicized the person of Jesus Christ by the implied content of his humanity. It was the partial victory of the Roman Empire, which could not tolerate the non-order of a humanity allowed to have its full dignity and responsibility.

So whereas in relation to God Chalcedon encouraged the Trinitarian revolution, it failed to encourage the following-through of the consequences of the humanity of Jesus. The humanity of Jesus tended to be under-emphasized because the practical channels through which the emphasis could be fed were blocked in Church and society. This in turn had consequences for the understanding of God, some of which we have already discussed; for example, a false concept of transcendence which removes him from suffering and from time, and sees him exercising non-respectful, totalitarian power.

But what is the way beyond the apparent paradox of Chalcedon? Here the Council showed that it was not in fact suggesting a paradox. It stresses over and over again the unity of Jesus Christ. Beyond all dilemmas and paradox stands the person of Jesus Christ. He is not a problem but one who evokes amazement and praise, and addresses us from a unity with us and with God. This is the unity that culminates Dante's *Paradiso*, as we described in chapter 4.

Just as divinity and humanity are redefined in the light of Jesus Christ, so unity is too. There are many types of unity – those of a stone, a plant, a painting, a story, a community, a marriage, and so on. Some types are relatively self-contained, others are so woven into other realities that they can only be described in relation to a whole ecology. The unity of Jesus Christ, as we have developed it through this book, is woven into the reality of God, the cosmos and humanity. He is a new union of all these but yet respects the integrity of each. The union can be expressed as communication, action and being. One of the less inadequate expressions is in terms of the union that happens in the self-giving of love when it is mutual. That leads to an intensification of both the union and also of the differentiation of the lovers, and to constant amazement at each other and at the whole process. It is a union creative of deeper union, and it overflows with understanding, thanks, astonishment and fresh creativity. This is a pointer to the unity of Jesus Christ with his Father in the Holy Spirit. What he is of course goes beyond words and categories, but praise stretches all capacities in order to try to do some justice to him, and it is helped by itself embodying the inner dynamic of God's Trinitarian life of glory.

'Jesus is our praise' expresses the union and its two sides. He is our praise because he is himself to be praised and is identified with God in what he does and is; because he embodies the ultimate sacrifice of praise to God; and because he is ours, in solidarity and mutuality with us. And being for us, he constantly generates fresh initiatives and action, and his life is shared in particular ways which are the subject of our final chapter.

9

Praise and Prophecy

To praise and know God is itself prophetic. It affirms the most comprehensive truth of history and the future. It is an act of discernment and committed response that lets God be God, and so both criticizes and encourages in each situation. 'God is' is the supreme prophetic statement, the discernment which can illuminate all discernment and action. But it is not a statement about something static and fixed: it is about a God who is alive, active, listening and communicating. To recognize this God in each situation is always the most urgent priority.

It will nearly always seem that other matters are more important, and faith is continually tested in this conflict of priorities. It is a matter of 'remembering God' always. Remembering God, and letting him be God, is a habit which develops through years of faith. It is an experience with slower and faster movements, varied themes and instruments; it is sometimes solo and sometimes symphonic; and as in music the silences are as important as the sounds. But 'remembering' makes it seem too past-oriented, and spiritualities and Churches frequently get stuck with superb patterns of the past. They over-order God, get him taped and tamed, and miss the God of the present fresh situation who shares responsibility and is leading into a future where new things will happen and all is not ordered in advance.

In appreciating this God the nerve of constant astonishment and openness is kept active and sensitive through a life of praise. Recognizing God in each situation is not a matter of starting from scratch every day: it remembers the past and takes it up into today's praise, and that is the light in which the details of the present are clearly seen. But if there is any lesson that the past teaches, it is to be prepared for new events, because this God loves to create afresh and do surprising things. Prophecy is discerning this God and his ways, and following through their practical consequences. It is an unavoidable part of Christian existence because it recognizes that the life of faith is a vocation with a mission, which requires risky discernment about the way into the future. Prophecy is essential because God is the sort of God who has a relationship with us that involves communication and shared responsibility for the future. Amazingly, God shares his life with us, including his freedom, creativity and receptivity, and in every situation an alert attentiveness to him is the secret of appropriate response.

The God of Joy

If the great prophecy is 'God is', then it matters enormously who God is. Within this infinite theme it is itself an act of prophetic discernment to choose what truth about God to emphasize at a particular time. This whole book shows our perception of what most needs saying at present: that the balance and direction of Christian thought and living, both individually and in the Church, need to be corrected and energized by praising and knowing God. Further, this has implications for all areas of life, because if the Christian truth is not universally relevant it is not valid even as Christian truth.

So, within this perspective, who is God? Our most concentrated answer to that question has been a development of the understanding of God as Trinity – transcendent in three modes, the Creator of the universe, involved with it and its human history, and intimately involved with us in specific ways. We have tried to do justice to the God known in these ways, and have stressed his respect for creation and his way of going through and overcoming evil, suffering and death. In all this we have seen him as a God who is to be praised; maybe transforming our ideas of both God and praise in the process, but establishing the transformed knowledge and praise as the heart of reality and the spring of our ordinary life. It is a vision of God and the ecology of the universe together, with praise and respect uniting them in freedom. This God is in himself glorious, a play of mutually communicated delight and love always lively and fresh. The prophetic point of this is simple: it is the message of a life of joy with the God of joy.

'The God of joy' is a name of God which rings strangely in a century whose history and present situation seem to mock it. To rejoice in this God is a prophetic act which at once stings the habitual worldly wisdom fed on suspicion, bad news and equivocal or cynical judgements. It also stings the practical atheism of many 'believers'. Actually to carry through in practice belief in a good God to the extreme of making his goodness the spring of continual thanks and praise: that is to take God too seriously and therefore too joyfully.

To hold up in praise this God of joy lets light shine into some of the darkest and most corrupt parts of modern life. This applies not just to the obvious areas, but also to many which are all the more insidious by being so respectable, but which in fact are hostile to joy and will stop at nothing to discredit the good news of God. More intimately, it exposes the praisers to this penetrating light too, as a group and individually. The unavoidable cost of joy is the recognition of sin and evil, and turning from them to God. Yet, as the Bible and Christian tradition frequently emphasize, this turning, for all its pain and discipline, is itself a joy because it brings a fresh start with the God of joy. St Augustine's *Confessions* are a classic account of this phenomenon. He confesses his sin and confesses God. The result is a penitent praise which is doubly joyful, in thanks for forgiveness and in praise of God its source. This double recognition of God and of sin is Augustine's context and inspiration for comprehensive and particular prophecies to his Church and world.

We will not offer prophetic denunciations of the terrible evils of our century which are so easy to name at a distance and so difficult to confront where they can be dealt with effectively. War, racism, fanaticism in politics and religion; the corruption of power, sex and truth; poverty, starvation, torture: all of these could be analysed in terms already developed in previous chapters, such as dignity, respect, disorder, shame and responsibility. That would be valuable but is not appropriate here. What is relevant is to examine the corruption of 'the good' which makes it so impotent in the face of these and other evils. The evils are even made to seem the most interesting part of our century and they are given far more than their fair share of attention. The greatest blow that can be struck against them is to pay more attention to the God of joy. He is the supremely interesting reality, far more exciting than anything else, and from involvement with him comes the perspective in which the ultimate pointlessness, misery, and boring emptiness of evil are clear. As the joy of God is tasted and proclaimed, one both uncovers the strong and delightful liveliness of goodness, truth and beauty, and also comes up against the extent of the evil that opposes them. We will now take up one broad aspect of the threat that subtle forms of evil pose to the praise and joy of God.

Stoicism against Joy

A key idea in our treatment of evil has been that it is the corruption of the best that is the worst. In relation to praising and knowing God, that means that we will find the worst corruption in those places where God is known and praised most explicitly. The agony of the joylessness of many Christian communities, and of the oppressive forms of 'joy' in many of those which pride themselves on their praise, is that it is starvation in the midst of abundance. All is there to hand, freely available, and even sung about and proclaimed, but is somehow often frozen or not lived from or enjoyed. The agony of this is not only the deprivation of the believers but also the fact that they are not able to share the God of joy with others, and are actually off-putting. In each case the situation is complex and can be analysed at many levels, but all the threads lead to one central, perennial issue, the basic question of prophets century after century: who is really being worshipped, what is actually receiving our ultimate concern, our strength and love?

The answer is often that our concentration is divided, and all sorts of concerns are in disorderly competition for our attention and energy. So one of the main aims of religion is the ordering of concerns and desires, focusing them on the God who is to be worshipped above all. This is a long process, to be followed through in every area of life, and all spiritualities have their favourite methods and disciplines for it. No doubt a great deal that is wrong with Christian Churches is due to divided loyalties of groups and individuals, and the prophetic concern about idolatry could be brought up to date in relation to the idols of state, family, money, health, ideologies, race, sex, security, and all sorts of 'problems'.

Our concern, however, is nearer the centre than that, with those who do seem single-minded and single-hearted in their faith but still do not seem to rejoice in the God of joy. What is it that cuts or numbs the nerve of joy even in those who should be most free for it, and stifles at source the overflow of praise and good news that is the essence of Christian living? We are not talking about feelings or moods but about the blockage of the flow of the Spirit of God which is in every generation the target of reformation and renewal. There is a vast array of diagnoses, but the prophet must follow a 'journey of intensification' along one of them to make his point, and we see the need to take up again from previous chapters the theme of the threat of what we called stoicism.

Stoicism emerged in chapter 6 as an approach to life that is admirable in many ways. It is the most appealing alternative to Christianity for 'good' people in our civilization, and it is followed within as well as outside the Churches. It promotes patience, endurance, intelligence, bravery, justice and self-control, and it is above all concerned to be in harmony with the order of the world and, if God is believed in, with God and his order. It has a great concern for morality and the right ordering of self and society, and a very high view of the dignity of humanity. It also values scientific investigation, but sets it within a view of the organic wholeness of the world and so is sympathetic to the concerns of ecology.

We want to affirm all those things too, but as has already
emerged, we see stoicism as a whole in fatal conflict with praising
and knowing the Christian God. In chapter 6 we showed how it
cannot cope with the reality of 'overflow' in either suffering or joy.
It avoids the intensification of shame and of praise in the interests
of its sober equilibrium. It is only equipped to handle what is
ordered, and so when faced with what is good, but non-orderly, it
shuts it out or condemns it as disorder. In the last resort, when
faced with the tragedies of life in which order is engulfed, it can
only react with dignified endurance and resignation. It lacks the
vision of decisive transformation and vindication offered by the
Christian gospel, and its ultimate is never the God of joy. Only joy
can creatively oppose evil in all its perversion of both order and
non-order; stoicism at best contains it, resists it and maintains order
and dignity in the face of it.

Looking at the Churches of the West we see a dominant stoic
temper, criticized by protest or renewal movements that often
discredit themselves by rejecting instead of embracing and
transforming the stoic virtues. The Churches frequently see themselves engaged in a holding operation. This can take many forms.

There is a biblical form which takes the Bible and turns it into
a law, an invariant order and pattern which must be held on to
and defended. This typifies the stoic tendency to sum up everything
in ordering principles to be clung on to in the face of challenges.
Here certain 'fundamentals' are turned into a legalistic norm, a
stockade of resistance against liberalism, Catholicism and the freer
forms of Pentecostalism. It is the successor of the circumcision party
(Acts 11ff., cf. below) who opposed Peter's unbiblical innovation of
eating with and preaching to the Gentiles. Even the Letters of Paul,
who above all objected to the Scriptures being used as law rather
than in the spirit of the gospel, and who spent his ministry in
conflict with the legalists of his own day (as did Jesus), are taken
as law in their turn, and his expression of the living faith is mistaken
for the faith itself. This 'smother-love' for the Bible not only lends
itself to intellectual dishonesty in the face of modern scholarship; it
also tends to lose the freedom of the Spirit in relation to the Bible
and, like an over-protective parent, it discourages the risky adven-
tures of faith and vision (such as that of Peter and of Cornelius)
which are most in line with the Bible itself. So, as with the Genesis
account of creation (cf. chapter 7, above) or Paul's ruling on female
participation in worship, they end up repeating and trying to re-
enact what the biblical writers said rather than doing new things
in the spirit in which the biblical characters did their new things.

There is also an ecclesiastical form which bases its holding operation not only on Scripture but also on the tradition, past patterns

and decisions of the Church (or of one branch of the Church). This is often more sophisticated and more historically conscious than the biblical version, but it likewise kills the life of something in itself good by trying to use it beyond its competence as a principle for ordering the present and future. It is of course always open to debate whether it might be right to retain and defend a past form or structure. But as one reads some Anglo-Catholic contributions to debates in the General Synod of the Church of England, or some Vatican statements on church authority or on the priesthood or on the errors of controversial modern theologians, or some Eastern Orthodox theological arguments using the early Church fathers as authority, then one often senses that the ecclesiastical past is being used legalistically and defensively, as an unchangeable order of reality. In a community governed by such principles one casualty is bound to be the joy which flourishes where order gives play to non-order, and where the 'jazz factor' can inspire a newly improvised future. Of course the 'jazz' is irrepressible (like the slave Christianity from which it sprang) and we find Pope John XXIII or Dietrich Bonhoeffer or William J. Seymour (of Azuza Street, the birthplace of modern Pentecostalism). Yet the joylessness to which the Churches' concern with their own security condemns their members (and whole societies that they influence) not only deprives the world of fresh life and colour but adds more strands to the net that prevents flight in the light. Again, such oppression can be analysed in many ways (for example, in terms of the vested interest in the *status quo* that any institution develops if it survives a long time), but to begin to overcome it in the right way, nothing less than wholehearted commitment to the God of joy could be sufficient.

The stoicizing of Christianity happens in many other ways too. It is there in worship, in obvious ways in the more liturgical Churches, but also in the 'freer' worship of newer groups. Both classical Pentecostal Churches and the other Churches influenced by the Pentecostal and charismatic movements easily turn their freedom into a law. The height of irony is reached when speaking in tongues, the very embodiment of non-order in relation to God, and a fruitful catalyst of surprises is made into an expected badge of Pentecostal orthodoxy, the legalistic proof that one has been 'baptized in the Spirit'. There are also highly intellectual forms of stoicizing which insist on all doctrine and practice being in conformity with certain rationally defensible first principles, or which will only allow God to act in conformity with their patterns and proofs (whether conservative, as in 'covenant theology', or liberal, as in the tyranny of an epistemology or an historical method or some modern criterion of authenticity).

Above all, there is the moralizing aspect of this pervasive spirit.

This constantly reduces Christianity to a morality, to regulative principles and models. To live in harmony with these is said to be the goal of life, and religion is identified with good, ethical living. This is perhaps the most devastating perversion of all (as Jesus and Paul in the conflicts of their ministries made clear). Christianity of course has an ethic, but it is so all-involving and extraordinary that it can never be followed by setting it up as a duty to be carried out. The only way is to be filled with the Spirit, to be so taken up with the love of God that one can live with joyful discipline, extravagantly drawing on his grace and risking the shame of constant failure and repentance.

The irony of the moralizing of Christianity is that it does not even let us live in accordance with the morality. The tragedy of it is that it takes the joy out of goodness. Generations of 'good' people in the West have had their Christianity made dull and impotent by moralism. How many have even suspected that the God of joy is at the heart of it all? This has taken much of the life out of their goodness, and the power out of their encounter with evil. There is nothing more conducive to evil than the lie that goodness is dull. A goodness that does not know the intense excitement and confidence of the victory that is the meaning of the crucifixion and resurrection of Jesus is going to lack both the nerve to go to the depths of problems and also the attractiveness which can combine people in the strongest form of goodness, a community of love.

So the essential factors in Christianity – God himself, the Bible, the Church, tradition, worship and the practice of goodness – are all vulnerable to this attractive perversion. It can be seen operating in the three main streams of world Christianity, the Catholic (East and West), the Protestant and the Pentecostal. But there is a fourth stream too which is not so much an independent entity as a presence in each of the other three. This is the liberal tradition. At its best, liberalism stands prophetically for a passionate commitment to truth, justice and personal integrity, and for resolving disputes and ordering communities in ways which respect these values. As a Christian tradition it has continually exposed the ways in which doctrine can turn into oppressive ideology, in which legitimate authority can lose its compassion and justice, and in which legalism of many sorts can stifle Christian freedom. Intellectually, liberals have often courageously made sure that Christians take seriously new areas of knowledge. It is a tradition which has contributed a great deal to this book, and we see it as both an essential ingredient in the Catholic, Protestant and Pentecostal streams and also a vital part of their openness to each other.

Yet the only safe forms of Christian liberalism are those which live a basic existence of praising and knowing God within the other three streams of Christianity. Without this praise and knowledge liberals lose Christian credibility, and distort the very content of the freedom which they champion. As soon as freedom is seen as not primarily something given by God to be fulfilled in free praise and love of God, then the whole ecology of life is polluted. When liberalism of this sort refers to God it tends to become agnostic and vague, and loses the ability to know or proclaim much that is definite about him. When it studies the Bible and shows by historical and other criticism the errors of literalism and fundamentalism, it fails to go beyond its critique to find out what God may now be saying through the Scriptures understood in this new way. When it exposes the deadening effects of dogma which has become ideology, it fails to create a new order where beliefs avoid rigidity through their openness to the Holy Spirit.

When a liberalism that does not praise and know God attacks legalism or authoritarianism, it fails to affirm that laws and authority are necessary forms of order within a system in which they are relativized by attention to the new initiatives, freedom and direction of the Holy Spirit. When such liberalism recognizes the truth of much contemporary history, science and other knowledge, it easily takes over an atheist world-view as well. By their acceptance of the dominant ideas of our culture, these liberals often find it particularly hard to conceive of a God who really acts and communicates in the world. So they cut or numb the central nerve of Christian praise.

One irony in this perversion of liberalism is that, in the absence of a living, free God, freedom becomes a principle that acts rather like a law. Freedom itself is moralized, and stoically maintained in all areas. It loses the content of God as its ultimate source and orientation, and ends by being another form of stoicism, battling for its principles without knowledge of the God of joy. Liberal moralism is even more disappointing and impotent than other types because it tends to lack strong nourishing content, and its individualism leaves its followers isolated in their hunger.

It is easy to see how many allies in our culture a stoicized Christianity can count on. The nation state is delighted to welcome a religion that is so timid and orderly, leaving the passions free for economics, war and collective sport. In Britain today the civic religion might be described as a stoicism with Christian influence. It is full of rectitude, good patterns and principles, but it is being challenged by more exciting and extreme creeds to which it seems at present to have neither the daring nor the moral, intellectual and political creativity to respond.

The vacuum which is felt by so many individuals and groups is hardly likely to remain unfilled, and this is perhaps the most comprehensive challenge facing Christians, comparable in scale to the crises in the times of Augustine, Luther or the English Civil War. The prophetic importance of knowing the God of joy in this situation cannot be estimated, but it is worth following through at every level, in every area of life, and watching for the blessings God gives to those who let him have his way. As Mícheál Ó'Siadhail writes of 'A Late Beethoven Quartet', it is

> A poise not a posture; no truculent stance
>   Toys here with despair. The word is praise,
> The theme a scale of infinite permutation.[1]

The God of Hope

Joy in God transposed into a vision of the future becomes hope in God. In the face of problems, miseries and stubborn evils, knowing God entails trusting him for the future and being open to his decisive encouragement. The encourager is the Holy Spirit. The Holy Spirit is the greatest realist about evil, sin and all problems, exposing them to their depths. But, even deeper than all of these, the Spirit reveals Jesus Christ, crucified and risen. He is the demonstration of a hope that gives us the heart to tackle the problems.

This is not an optimism. It does not claim that the world is necessarily improving or that the freedom to do evil will not wreak havoc. It recognizes the possibility of an appalling fate for both individuals and the world if they resist God and his goodness. Christian apocalyptic sees the fate of the world as an analogy with the fate of Jesus Christ in crucifixion and resurrection, culminating in an unprecedented intensity of evil before the new creation of God. The final Christian historical perspective is a hope which, like resurrection of the dead, relies on God alone. Yet the Holy Spirit is the presence of this God in history and the cosmos now, inviting to shared responsibility. The scope of the Spirit's work is as wide as the cosmos and is concerned for every aspect of history, institutional as well as individual. For every area there is a message of hope. It is not simply to be identified with the great hope in Jesus Christ, but, before him, it embraces innumerable lesser hopes inside and outside the Christian Church. The Spirit brings the taste of a better future into the present and creates a thirst for more.

There is the universal hope for justice, which we have already approached from the angles of dignity (chapter 5) and responsibility (chapter 8). In itself it can be grim and stoic, but a look at movements of liberation shows how essential they find the overflow

---

[1] *Springnight* (Dublin 1983), p. 17.

of songs, sacrifices and ideals. There are also hopes for love, for beauty, for meaning and for knowledge, and all are notoriously ambiguous, the most powerful as usual being the most vulnerable to going wrong. In relation to all of them the experience of praising and knowing God gives rise to prophetic insights. We take as an example just one area, that of meaning and knowledge.

Most of the pressures in our educational system are towards gaining knowledge for practical reasons, especially finding employment. This is a proper role of education, but when it is idolized there is a corruption of motivation which poisons the deepest spring of learning. The capacity simply to wonder, to ask questions from a desire to know and to have the joy of discovery, is one of the fundamental human orientations. It is practically very useful, but it also opens the way beyond immediate needs and beyond what can be justified functionally.

The dynamic of wonder follows the same logic of overflow that we have seen in praise. Wonder continually questions, explores, compares, and delights in the use of all faculties in order to invent and discover. It is a realm of freedom yet definiteness, and it unites heart and mind in a movement of transcendence. The act of questioning has been described as our basic mode of transcendence, because it leads us beyond brute experience into understanding. An education which fails to nourish non-utilitarian wonder deadens one of the roots of human dignity and freedom. Ironically, it may also even fail practically, because it does not make the mind adaptable enough for rapid developments or changes of career. Worst of all is the betrayal of the increasing numbers who can find no employment. For them an education whose chief motivation is towards finding a job is a training for despair. The right education for the mind is a condition for hope.

Embracing all this is the question of the meaning of the life for which education is a preparation. The utilitarian tendency is to equate one's role in society, especially the economy, with one's vocation. This is always a fraud, but it is more obvious when the economy is in trouble and offers less attractive roles, or none at all. Then the despair of a useless life can grip millions, in quiet or violent forms. The good news that vocation does not depend on the state of the economy but on the call of God, which is for every single person, needs to be acted out prophetically by those who proclaim it. The massive assurance is: you do have a vocation, you are respected and called by God to very definite tasks, and to joy in doing them. Ironically, again, this can be the liberation which frees for a more effective role in society. The lesser hopes tend to be fulfilled as one risks living for the larger hopes.

Hope for the Church

The largest hope of all is at the heart of praising and knowing God. Paul expresses it:

> We rejoice in our hope of sharing the glory of God. More than that, we rejoice in our sufferings, knowing that suffering produces endurance, and endurance produces character, and character produces hope, and hope does not disappoint us, because God's love has been poured into our hearts through the Holy Spirit which has been given to us (Rom. 5:2–5).

The Holy Spirit in the Church produces that mature, tested hope which Paul describes, oriented towards the ultimate hope of sharing God's glory. It is a lively movement with three basic dynamics which have also emerged in the previous chapters: the overflow of praise to God, offering him everything; the overflow of love in a community that shares in the Holy Spirit; and the overflow in mission to the world. As those three interweave, the Church becomes what it is meant to be, a prophetic community whose vocation is to witness to the love of God in Jesus Christ. The prototypical church described by Luke in Acts (especially Acts 2: 43–7) shows all three in action, and they have been there at the origins of every major tradition in church history.

The prophetic signs of our times are that Christian praise, community and mission are being integrated in new ways.

The explosion in praise which has happened in this century has, as we have shown, had its prophetic dimension. It has held up the God of joy as the truth of life, and so confronted all that negates joy. Yet there is a further, more explicitly prophetic element in this praise. All over the world Christian communities have been rediscovering what was the experience of both the Old and New Testament communities: that prophecies can be given in worship. Wholehearted engagement with God in praise is the ideal context for clearly receiving his communication. He reveals both who he is and what he wants.

The recovery of this gift on a large scale is a revolutionary innovation. As the Bible and church tradition are acutely aware, prophecy's importance is matched by its dangers. It is only reliable in an ecology that includes openness to correction by Scripture, tradition and contemporaries. But the New Testament rightly saw the gift of the Holy Spirit as the fulfilment of the Old Testament hope that all receivers of the Spirit should be able to prophesy (cf. Acts 2:17). Paul tells the Corinthians to 'make love your aim, and earnestly desire the spiritual gifts, especially that you may prophesy' (1 Cor. 14:1). It is an expectation of receiving communication from

God as part of normal Christian experience. As Paul's discussion shows, it both springs out of worship and can lead even unbelievers to worship (1 Cor. 14:24f.).

Prophecy in worship can act as a critical check on the community. It discerns complacency or hypocrisy in praise. It sharpens moral awareness, as hearts and minds are opened in worship of the God of peace, goodness and justice. Self-protective narrowness of concern is dissolved in the expansion of appreciation of the God who loves the whole of creation. Prophecy that lives in praise can also give a vision of the proper shape of life in the Kingdom of God, and can offer inspiration, encouragement and direction to realize it. All of this is a sign of the presence of the God who speaks, and is intrinsically linked to the three dynamics of praise, upbuilding the community and mission.

This century has also seen new developments in Christian community. There have been periods in which inherited forms of the Church proved more or less satisfactory, but today that is not so. We are in a period of disintegration and fresh creativity. Every level of church life, from international and ecumenical organization to congregational and family life, is in transformation. The demonstration of Christian community has become a form of prophecy for which there is a deep desire and hope. The first Christians, numerous religious orders, the parish system, several Churches springing from the Reformation, the early Quakers and the Methodists, and many other movements and societies have in the past been such prophetic signs. It is not hard to find parallels today, mostly new variations on old themes. Friendship, family, and the idea of 'covenanting' together in communities are continually taking fresh forms and finding new prophetic directions. Without such environments, praise of God and Christian mission lose their depth and power. The God of joy gives the Holy Spirit in order to be loved by a community of joy, and praise of God is the strongest and most objective of bonds between people.

Finally, there is the third dynamic, the Christian mission, which has at its heart the respectful invitation to share in praise and community. We conclude with a consideration of this.

3 The Spread of Praise and Knowledge of God

In Thomas Mann's novel, *Joseph and his Brothers*, Jacob at the end of his life talks about his wife Rachel:

Anyhow, he simply loved to speak of her, even when there was no point at all – just as he loved to speak of God.[2]

This overflow of appreciation and delight is the master-spring of Christian mission and evangelism.

The Song of Songs has perhaps more to teach about the right spirit in this than any other book of the Bible. The Song has all the urgency, joy, agony and mutuality of love, but the main note is the pure praise of the beloved:

> your name is oil poured out. . .
> We will exult and rejoice in you;
>   we will extol your love more than wine. . .
> Behold, you are beautiful, my love;
>   behold, you are beautiful. . .
> Your lips distil nectar, my bride;
>   honey and milk are under your tongue;
>   the scent of your garments is like the scent of Lebanon.
> A garden locked is my sister, my bride,
>   a garden locked, a fountain sealed (1–4).

Then the right sort of communication to others can happen:

> Awake, O north wind,
>   and come, O south wind!
> Blow upon my garden,
>   let its fragrance be wafted abroad (4:16).

Praise is the primary form of the communication of the gospel, the sheer enjoyment and appreciation of it before God 'even when there is no point at all'. All other communication is an overflow of this, the spread of its scent, affirming in appropriate ways, in various situations, the content and delight of praising God.

It is of the greatest importance to the whole of Christian communication that it be praise-centred. This is in contrast with the problem-centred approach that has often been dominant. One popular image of evangelism is of it sniffing out sin and misery, making people feel guilty and inadequate, and then offering the gospel as the answer. Instead, the essence of mission and evangelism is in the intrinsic worth, beauty and love of God, and the joy of knowing and trusting him. This of course brings to light all sorts of things that are wrong, but it is not to be reduced to the solution of problems. Problem-solving lacks the logic of overflow, and easily lets the problem be the centre of attention, whereas praise puts what is wrong in a wider perspective from the start. Praise recognizes the

---

2 London 1978, p. 1181.

primacy and reality of the love of God, and in its desire to share delight in this it becomes evangelical and missionary.

This approach is in line with a transformation in the understanding of mission by many Christian Churches in the twentieth century. There has been a change in the dominant perspective. Beginning as the mission of the Western Church to the rest of the world, it shifted to the mission of the worldwide Church, and finally to the 'mission of God' in both Church and world. This can be traced in the great missionary conferences (starting with Edinburgh in 1910) and on into the World Council of Churches, the Second Vatican Council and some representative Evangelical statements. The God-centred understanding has many versions, in which the old problems inevitably recur in new forms, but the energetic discussion and experiment of this century have begun to produce a convergence of the main traditions, and in this the perspective of the mission of God is vital. Its emphasis on who God is and what he is doing means that praise and thanks become the starting-point for mission. As a by-product, the words 'evangelism' and 'mission' can begin to be liberated from exclusive association with their more shallow and manipulative forms.

The reasons why evangelism and mission have a range of bad connotations for many people are not just because they have often been carried on badly, insensitively or from doubtful motives. That is true, but to leave the criticism at that might imply that it was a matter of the perversion of something basically sound. Yet the very conception of much Christian communication has been questionable. It has often presented the good news in functional terms: it is useful for meeting needs, crises, limitations or other problems. It has been a gospel that fills gaps in one's life, or repairs things that have gone wrong, or is essentially practical in a host of ways. The seductiveness of this is that there is indeed good news for every problematic situation and person. The flaw lies in its missing the free praise of God, the generosity, the foolish abundance far beyond all need and practicality. The gospel is that all sin, evil and suffering, all need and want, can now be seen in the perspective of the resurrection of Jesus Christ in which God acts in such a way that the realistic response is joy. Even beyond this, it is the joy of love between us and God, the ultimate mutuality and intimacy. That is why the Song of Songs is the best expression of the communication that flows from it.

Recognizing and responding to this God inevitably leads to evangelism and mission as acts of love and celebration, longing for others to share in something whose delight increases by being shared. Yet expressions of praise easily become overbearing and triumphalist, and so does evangelism. When this happens, there is a contradiction

of the message. The history of evangelism is extremely painful, full
of examples of the message being falsified by the way it is spread.
The crucifixion of Jesus is the only essential guard against this. It
contradicts all glib praise and preaching. It continually demands
the repentance, reconversion, suffering and even death of the evan-
gelist. This is not just a matter of method, but a fundamental
truth about the unity of message and method, as Paul passionately
maintained throughout his Second Letter to the Corinthians. The
temptations of Jesus show the classic traps of evangelism – use of
worldly incentives, spectacular events and manipulative power. The
alternative is the way of the cross, from which the true ethic of
evangelism springs: an ethic of radical respect which refuses any
coercive communication, preferring to suffer and die, but which also
refuses to compromise on what is communicated.

The classic New Testament case of the ethic of respect in evangelism is in the story of the spread of Christianity beyond Judaism,
as told in Acts 10–11. This was the most revolutionary event in the
history of the early Church, and it meant a conversion for those
who were evangelizing as well as for those who were listening to
them. Peter, the story says, had a vision in which he was told to
go against his Bible, his upbringing and his whole Jewish culture
and religious practice: to break the law by eating food forbidden as
unclean. This prepares him to respond to the request of Cornelius,
who has also had a vision, to visit him and accept his hospitality
even though he is a Gentile. It is when both men follow their visions
and meet in this atmosphere of respect that Peter can share 'the
good news of peace by Jesus Christ' (Acts 10:36), and there is an
explosive event as faith comes alive in praise of God and in speaking
in tongues.

God is already ahead of all evangelism, carrying on his mission
in the world, and this adds further dimensions to the ethic of respect.
It means that the abundance of God is poured out way beyond the
boundaries of the Church, and a vital task is in discerning this
abundance and accepting it with joy. There is no Christian triumphalism in a theology of the all-sufficiency and abundance of God.
More often than not, respectful discernment will demand drastic
changes of heart and mind, as for Peter with his own traditions.
Christians are only beginning to glimpse the comprehensive reper-
cussions of this in relation to the various sciences, other religions,
philosophies and ways of living. It would take many books (for
many of which the experience is not yet available for them to be
written) to describe those implications. But without the right
content and mode of affirmation of God the horizon is lacking within
which all that can take place.

The crucified and resurrected Jesus Christ is therefore at the

heart of the method as well as the content of Christian mission. He
is also at the heart of Christian community and of Christian praise
and knowledge of God. Jesus is our praise, and through him the
God of living perfection invites others deeper into his life, dealing
with everything that spoils it, and promising in prophecy that

> he will rejoice over you with gladness,
>   he will renew you in his love;
> he will exult over you with loud singing
>   as on a day of festival (Zeph 3:17f.).

A chapter of the Bible that has had an extraordinary influence
through the centuries, including giving the terms in which Jesus
announced his mission, expresses both the hope and joy of praise.
It begins by setting the problems of life, such as poverty, broken
hearts, imprisonment, bereavement, lack of confidence, and the
destruction of cities and social fabric over generations, in the context
of good news and praise, and the glory of God. There is then a
repeated promise of joy and justice, and the culmination is a vision
of the 'new dress' and the universal network of praise and respect
which is the hope of faith:

> I will greatly rejoice in the Lord,
>   my soul shall exult in my God:
> for he has clothed me with the garments of salvation,
>   he has covered me with the robe of righteousness,
> as a bridegroom decks himself with a garland,
>   and as a bride adorns herself with her jewels.
> For as the earth brings forth its shoots,
>   and as a garden causes what is sown in it to spring up,
> so the Lord God will cause righteousness and praise
>   to spring forth before all the nations (Isa. 61:10–11).

Appendix A

The Systematics of Praise

The text of the book has shown how widespread in the tradition of Christianity is praise, and of what fundamental importance it has been, and should be, for the Christian. Nor, as has been seen, does it enter only into the worship of the Christian, as if that were distinct from other activities: it is fundamental to the knowledge, purposeful action and social relationships by which his or her life in the world with others is made possible. So integral is it to the whole range of human life with God that the material which could have been discussed is inexhaustible.

It may assist further reflection on our subject to provide a more systematic exposition of the nature of praise in relation to knowledge, action and social life. In doing so, we shall see not only the dynamics of praise in these areas, but also the interaction of these dynamics with those of relationship with God. This inevitably leads to consideration of the basic topics of systematic theology; and we shall explore some of the remarkable implications of the theme of praise for the nature of man, the nature of God, the Trinity, creation, providence, sin and redemption. We can only touch on these things very briefly, but all of them merit much more extensive treatment.

The Activity of the One who Praises

PRAISE AS HUMAN ACTION

Let us begin with an attempt to fasten on the phenomenon of praise in general, viewing it from the standpoint of the one who praises. As thus seen, it seems to be comprised of attention, determination or affirmation, and praise itself. Each of these varies in quality itself, and is present and productive in the others. Attention is the act of directing oneself with force or interest to an other, to an object or objects (and can in human beings be directed to oneself); it is as necessary to subhuman behaviour as to human, as necessary to eating as to thought and prayer. It originates from desire and has its own discipline, that which arises from concentration, contemplation and correction; it also produces what is sometimes called knowledge 'by acquaintance'. It is the necessary basis for understanding and action, and praise. Determination or affirmation is the 'positing' or 'putting' of the other by knowledge or valuation, as itself, whether as object of knowledge or as goal of action, without seizing an idea of it prematurely, and thus being blocked to the truth of it. Again, this has its own disciplines, especially intuitive, imaginative and rational ones, among them those which arise from suspension of understanding and valuation through fresh attention to the other whose true understanding and valuation is sought. Praise consists in attention and determination (through knowledge and valuation) appropriately directed and intensified, according to the excellence of that which is attended to. This excellence always exceeds what can be accomplished in attention and determination; so praise always 'overflows' attention, knowledge and valuation. Thus the appropriate direction and quality (or intensity) which arises in praise is that which makes determination appropriate to its object (that is, accommodates subject to object), and yet makes it inadequate to it in such a way that determination must always be subject to improvement.

THE QUALITY OF KNOWING IN PRAISE

We have seen that attention, determination and praise are intimately linked, and that each is reliant on the others. But the three are not simply to be seen as human activities generated by the human subject, and thus liable to the criticism that they are all human projections. They are to be judged by their 'nearness' to the other to whom they are directed, and this normally involves a self-emptying to receive the other in all his truth, a 'being found' or being drawn to the other. There is an asymmetry in the relationship of subject and object, in which the subject does not generate the relationship, except by creating the precondition for it by attending to the other; thereafter the relationship arises in so far as the subject is drawn into the truth of the other, or when there is an exchange between subject and object.

SELF-REFINEMENT THROUGH PRAISE

Each of the three – attention, determination and praise – varies remarkably in quality according to the way in which it is actually exercised. Attention requires constancy or tenacity in order to achieve the highest quality. Determination requires 'vision', or the capacity to find the truth of another and act by it, even where it is still only a potentiality; thus vision involves kindness, humility and joy in righteousness (cf. 1 Cor. 13:4–7). Here again, each requires the others, as the practice of any one of them readily shows. Constancy and vision are implied in praise and love; constancy and love are implied in determining vision; and vision and love are required for the fullest constancy.

It can be seen, then, that praise is a comprehensive activity which 'composes the spirit to love' (Coleridge), and does so by integrating man's capacities and his being by bringing them into a right relation with its object. It is not, however, accomplished fully in an instant. It is better seen as a self-refining activity or passion. Attention and determination give this activity its content, and are thus part of the activity of praise. But praise drives them to ever-closer discrimination of the truth of the object which is attended to and determined; praise brings their refinement through its satisfaction with, or enjoyment of, the object with which they are concerned. This is most easily seen by contrasting praise with blame (or anger or complaint, which are closely similar). Blame also requires attention and determination to provide its content, but instead of bringing their refinement through satisfaction with the object with which they are concerned, the dissatisfaction which is intrinsic to blame brings a selective attention to, or determination of, those features of the object which support the blaming which is desired. The self-refining activity of praise is radically distorted by an activity which is destructive of both the subject and the object. Praise, of course, does not disallow attending to and determining the object, 'warts and all'; it is what brings ever-closer discrimination of the truth of the object by refining attention and determination. But blame does something different, bringing a selectivity which supports a particular point of view by distorting attention and determination, in effect using selective attention and determination to perpetuate a stereotype. It is easy to switch from the one to the other because the temptation to cling to a particular viewpoint is so strong.

DEPENDENCE ON THE QUALITY OF THE OBJECT

Plainly, if praise is to bring about the fullest integration of the capacities of the one who praises, the quality of the object of praise is of crucial importance. To praise a leaf may refine one's capacities of attention and determination, but doing so is not sufficient to bring about that 'composition of the spirit' of which human beings are, at their best, capable. That will depend on a more excellent object of attention and determination. What will suffice for this? The usual practice is to make up for the insufficiency of particular objects by distributing attention among many 'interesting' ones. Furthermore, various ideologies suggest that praiseworthy objects are to be found by being 'realistic' or 'idealistic' or by interpreting correctly. (a) Many are inclined to say that it is the 'reality' of a thing, or the way it behaves or functions, which comprises its excellence, so far as it is excellent. That performance-orientated view confines the interest of an object or thing to what it is or can yield; and if 'it doesn't have it in it', so much the worse. (b) An alternative to this view is the more 'idealist' one which suggests that an object has in it an intrinsic ideality or value, which may or may not be reflected in its reality or behaviour. This view allows excellence to whatever can be identified as having this intrinsic value; anyone is interesting if everyone is lovable, for example. (c) An associated view is that which places the excellence of a thing in its interpretation-by-someone as excellent, whether by agreed criteria or by a particular tradition of interpretation. This view accords excellence to whatever 'fits' the notion of excellence held by particular people or groups, and thus makes instances of excellence relative to their notion. All of these ways of establishing excellence make it intrinsic, either as a characteristic or as a capability, to an object or a subject. They make the praiseworthiness of things dependent on what they are or are interpreted to be. In effect, this confines their value to their possession of this characteristic, or to their interpretation as having it. Their value, therefore, must always be a finite one, and the self-refining activity of praise can therefore have a definite terminal point – praise can at some point be finished, as can the attention and determination which are necessary to it.

Is the excellence of objects so confined that the activities of attention and determination, or the self-refining passion of praise, can ever be complete? It seems not. Are we therefore justified in employing such limited notions of excellence for these objects? Again, it seems not. But if excellence is not constituted by inherent characteristics or interpretations which are given, it can only be constituted by some excellence which comes to, and is presented in, particular objects, but which has its own excellence in itself. This true excellence, which realizes itself through presenting itself in lesser objects, will be worthy of all the self-refining activity of praise which we can devote to it, and will make any object in which it is present worthy of every effort of attention, determination and praise. One would not expect such excellence to be immediately apparent, either in itself or in its presentation in particular objects. Not even the curiosity which might drive attention, or the quest for understanding which might spur determination, would reveal this excellence. It would appear only through that self-refining activity of praise, and then only in the course of time, as this became the condition of the life of the one who praises.

What, then, in an object or a person merits praise? As we have seen, it is not their intrinsic or recognized (interpreted) quality, and any attempt to improve on this, by being or act, does not materially alter the situation. To be sure, these may stir interest, but this is not ongoing or self-improving. What does merit praise is the presence of that excellence-in-itself in the object or person; this is the sole source of the excellence which justifies praise. Imagine the freedom from anxiety which would follow if this were taken seriously! If life is the process of the self-refinement which occurs in praise, and if the condition for this occurs when the excellent-in-itself is present, it can be said that the praise of God actually constitutes the life which we live.

The Communication of Praise

COMMUNICATION

Praise, however, is also communicative: it expresses. In the most fundamental sense, communication consists in the transmission of energy in a form; and this is what occurs in all communicative activity, for example in speech, music and symbolic behaviour. For some of this, reasoned speech particularly, communication can be made exact through the use of logic, though with dubious results for the application of language to particular entities or events. For other communication, whether tactile, auditory or visual, there has been smaller progress in agreeing what should occur in such communication.

PRAISE AS A SPECIAL FORM

Is praise a special form of communication? Admittedly, there has been a consistent tendency for it to be treated as such. It is no accident that, in the earlier expressions of praise, we find that praise was often rendered in the form of poetry. It was, in fact, the case that poetry was considered the most appropriate form of praise. But, despite the frequent assignment of praise and celebration to the province of poetry which we find historically, this did not mean that poetry (and hence praise) was not also closely related to the rational sciences, logic, philosophy (including moral philosophy) and theology; poetry was not so sharply distinguished from these others as it later came to be.

Praise was not so much a special form of communication as the raising of something/someone to their true status. Thus, for example, when used for praise, poetry had certain characteristics: it was to recognize excellence, in heroes for example, and was thought to be successful in so far as it aroused emulation or imitation. In doing this, it drew on the life of the one who was praised,

particularly on his noble deeds, and employed techniques of comparison and 'amplification' to point up the virtues of the one praised
as compared with others in the past.

PRAISE AS RAISING TO TRUTH

If this characteristic of praise as communication is considered in
relation to the phenomenon of praise in general, as discussed above,
the purpose of the communication of praise is seen to be the raising
of the object of attention, affirmation or determination, or praise to
its true status – in such a way as to arouse in others the emulation
of this. Thus, at the level of attention, communication would call
the attention of others to the object; this would avoid what has
been a typical problem with poetic praise – exaggeration, with
correspondingly casual treatment of the reality of the object being
considered. Again, at the level of affirmation or determination,
communication would employ one of the traditional systems to
distinguish the object as itself, and establish its significance, whether
factually or as a goal of action. Praise, in the sense of raising
something/someone to their true excellence, is present both in attention and in affirmation or determination. But the communication
of praise also does more: it elicits a respect for the excellence of the
object as beyond what can be 'captured' by means of attention and
affirmation or determination, or a recognition of the excellence of
the object as overflowing what we know.

It should also be understood that the communication of praise is
not intended only for the benefit of others. If praise is the raising
of something/someone to their true status, and this is accomplished
by the transmission of energy in a form (the basic characteristic of
communication), this 'double activity' is appropriate regardless of
whether others emulate it. In the case of the Trinitarian God,
furthermore, as we shall see later, it is implicit in the Christian
understanding of God: to 'raise' God to his true excellence is accomplished by the movement of God's own spirit in us. But this 'double
activity', based in human activity and in divine grace, can never
be severed from the task of sharing it with others.

Praise Received

OPENING SPACE FOR THE ONE PRAISED

Now let us attempt to grasp praise from the standpoint not of the
one who praises, but from that of the one who is praised, the one
who is the recipient of the activity of attention, determination and
praise, and of the communication of praise. Perhaps the central

effect of praise here is that of opening. Very simply seen, the effect of praise is to open 'space' for the recipient to be himself, and thus to allow him to be himself without confinement or coercion; and this brings about an enlargement, both of him and of his sphere of relevance and relationships.

The demands of realism, idealism and interpretation, with their suggestion that the 'true' nature of a thing is intrinsic to it or to the interpreter, militate against such expansiveness. They suggest implicitly that the best which can happen to anything is to 'keep its place', to enlarge only by staying what its 'truth' allows it to be. Thus, for them, a thing is constituted by its limitations, that it is this, and here, not that over there; and a person is constituted by self-concern, his desire to be himself, or by the concern of others. By contrast, the effect of praise is to engender a different kind of self-realization, that which comes through opening to what is beyond, through sympathetic and loving relationship, for example.

Why does it not authorize an ever-expanding 'egotism' of the one praised instead? This is precisely the problem: it may do that, and even allow a cancerous expansion of the praised into surrounding 'tissues'. That, perhaps, is the underlying reason for the restrictions placed by realism, idealism and interpretation; they legislate against the 'takeover' of one thing by another, and do so by legal means, through a kind of moralism. They were, and are, a natural means of combating a basic fault in nature, recognized in Genesis 1–3, that of 'doing what you can get away with', or refusing to recognize imposed limitations. Praise, which authorizes expansiveness, is in this sense a risk: a misuse of freedom may result.

But, as we saw before, there is nothing undiscriminating about praise; it is active attention, determination and raising to truth. Thus, when it opens 'space' for the other to be himself, it does not continue when the other expands at the expense of others. At that point, it affords 'space' for the other to be his true self, not a false, aggrandizing one. It offers support for a true expansiveness, not a false one. The cost of offering such support may be very great. Praise, then, is the means of establishing a truly expansive identity, as distinct from a false one. Such an identity will be one involving appropriate relationships in all directions – 'doing all things well'.

MAINTAINING RELATIONSHIP

The implications of having 'space' opened are very great. It does not, as commonly supposed, provide the other with 'room of his own', despite the persistent tendency to think in these terms; that would be to alienate him in a privatized independence, and to legitimize the very thing just denied, the loss of relationships.

Rather, opening space is something done by those who maintain their relationship, and who remain actively with the one to whom they provide this space, supporting in and through their praise, with the constancy, vision and love which we have seen to be characteristic of praise. It is instructive to remember that the origins of racism and ethnicism, and indeed of all movements of hate, are in separatism, or the 'innocuous' form of it, leaving someone alone; such separation easily turns into the stereotyping blame already discussed.

So praise for the recipient gives space for expansion, but also supports expansion to his true self through the continuing constancy, vision and love of the one who gives praise, discriminating though they must be. The expansion is a dynamic process of self-realization through appropriate relationships, which are themselves those of praise. Thus, the dynamic of this self-realization is like a circumference which continually expands, rather than an exclusive centre concerned with establishing and maintaining its own individuality and uniqueness. This does not threaten this self with dissolution into its manifold relationships, despite the popular mythology that the self is a limited quantity which must not be squandered in overmany relationships lest it be destroyed in the process. For what is conserved is a 'style' or 'economy' of the self which is evident in its growth as it repeatedly achieves the expression of praise, thus repeating itself in its relationships. The 'self' which is conserved is not a possessed self but a 'given' self, one which is constituted by the praise given to others. The life which is achieved is the gift of praise which is given. Granted, some of the relationships and situations in which this must be achieved may be extremely testing ones, threatening the 'self' with self-loss; but even these may bring the expression of praise if they can be endured.

THE DYNAMIC OF SELF-REALIZATION

What is truly threatening is not the possible loss of the self, but the loss of praise as the proprium of (what is proper to) the self in its relationships, and in its place the growth of self-protectiveness and exclusiveness. For this has the double effect of destroying the possibility of a truly constituted self and of its supportive relationships with others, and thereby destroying the most natural foundation of human personality and society.

What is the basis for this which is most proper to the self in its relationships, by reason of which this can be called the 'most natural'? By what is this sustained in the presence of the threats which undermine it? Both rest on a further dynamic, not one which they intrinsically manifest, which is theirs 'by right', but one in which they can participate. This is the dynamic of their relationship with their 'ground', God, into which they enter by virtue of their praise of him. The use of words like 'basis' or 'ground' of him may be somewhat misleading, however, if they suggest that he is in himself static, 'absolute' in the sense discussed earlier, as though he is the only 'thing in itself' on which every other thing rests.

GOD AS KNOWN IN PRAISE

The praise which is offered to God, on which that which is proper to the human self in its relationships rests, offers to God the same 'opening' or 'space' to be himself which praise directed to others offers, and thus as for them engenders an expansion by which he may be most truly himself. Unlike others, however, for whom the benefits of praise are always restricted to a remedial function because of the damage which has been done through the loss of what is proper to them in their relationships, praise of God serves to recognize the expansion which is God's nature. For with him, 'space' and 'time' and 'energy' are actually expanding, something like that expanding circumference which we saw before. It is not, of course, a matter of expanding to places which were there but he had not reached before, though human imagination seems always to operate in these terms; in this case, God is expanding the very notions of space, time and place, and even energy. So when, in what is perhaps the most characteristic feature of Christian praise, God is in praise found to be ever more totally present, this is a profound intuition of the way he actually is.

This expanding nature, which is recognized in praise, is also permitted in praise. That is to say, it is not simply recognized as a 'fact' about God, which is true for him, apart from those who praise, it is also recognized as true for them. So, as they praise him, his expanding nature becomes the means by which they expand to become themselves in their relationships. What is proper to him becomes proper to them, though in a much more restricted sense because of the limitations of their praise. It is this, undoubtedly, which conveys to Christian people their awareness of the unrestricted milieu which is theirs as Christians in their praise – the sort of milieu which is pointed to by such notions as eternal life and the communion of saints.

It is not surprising that this recognition of God in praise requires a significant modification in terms conventionally applied to him, for example those which attempt to indicate his existence (being) and activity. Some approximation to these modifications may be found by saying that the emphasis in traditional terms like 'perfect being' or 'pure act' is changed, so that 'perfection' is not simply adjectival to 'being' or 'act' but that they (if anything) are adjectival to it. But even this is not enough, for perfection is too easily treated as the terminal point in a sequence leading from less to more to most perfect. The understanding of God which seems to be required by praise requires that even perfection be without a terminal point but capable of indefinite expansion. Likewise, the notions of 'being' and 'act' which are required are ones which do not confine these to simple instances of them – as in 'an existent being' or 'a definite act'; God's 'being' is the being of an expanding perfection of existence, and the act by which he constitutes himself an expandingly originative act. Their absoluteness is always that of a dynamic perfection.

THE ECONOMY OF PRAISE IN GOD

As it is sometimes claimed that the self may disappear in its relations, so it might also seem that the expanding perfection of God may dissolve in a vacuity. But this ignores the presence in God of a particular economy which forms that which is most proper to him in his relationships (his proprium). The economy of God in his expansive movement, however, is not to be seen as a quasi-mechanical outward thrust, somewhat like an explosion which moves outward in all directions with uniform thrust; that would provide a confining logical determination for the expansive movement, and at the same time indicate a progressive loss of momentum and an eventual terminus for the expansion. The economy is one which keeps the expanding space–time–energy God's own, rather thansubmitting it to a relatively static determination.

How does it keep this expansion God's own? It seems to do so by directing it to a further perfection and actually originating that further perfection from the perfection which has already come to be. This is somewhat, though remotely, similar to what occurs as one person praises another, where we saw that praise opens 'space' for the other to expand to his true self; in this case, the dynamics are not restricted in the way that they are in interhuman relationships. Thus, the economy which is in God is that of an inner distinction in God which posits a direction for his expanding perfection, and it can be characterized as an economy of praise, one which establishes the character of God as praise.

Since this economy 'conserves' the character of God in his expansion, it is natural to speak of it in a way which emphasizes this conservation. What more fundamental way is there than to speak of it as 'word', for words do 'fix' what is thought in a form of expression, securing the direction of the thought through expression? Likewise, since the economy also constitutes a further 'opening' or movement of God, it is natural to speak of this in a way which emphasizes its movement. What more fundamental way is there to do so than to speak of it as 'spirit', for 'spirit' always seems to connote the essence of the life-movement? So the begetting of the word through the spirit is an apt way of speaking of the economy of the expanding character of God. But what these ways of speaking do not properly emphasize is the central 'thrust' of the economy of God's being, which we have now identified as praise. For this, it is important to introduce considerations of the direction and movement of God's expanding perfection, rather than to rest content with the relatively more static and formal notions of word and spirit.

The Economy of Praise for Man

CREATION AND PROVIDENCE

It is this economy of praise which forms the basis for that which is most proper to the various elements of the natural world, and to human beings. Much discussion of creation has treated it simply as an event, one which occurred through an originative act of the Creator God; and this discussion has made it appear that the act and the event were uniform, more or less the same for all elements of the created order and at more or less the same place and time. But if what is proper to God is an expanding perfection whose 'nature' is conserved as an economy of praise, we would expect creation, both in its origination and its speciation, to be a history, and moreover a history with a thrust constituted by the expanding economy which this God provided through the praise which he lavished upon it. So our habitual understanding of creation has to undergo alteration in the light of what we have seen about God, and it is an alteration as relevant to eschatology as to protology.

SIN: BLAMING AND RESTRICTING

If creation is properly a history of praise, resting on its relationship with God, and if what is proper to human beings in their relationships rests on what is made possible for them by God's praise, there is nothing necessary about their response to this by praise offered to God. Indeed, they seem to make a habit of blaming God, confining him through this stereotype or that, even as he continues to make 'space' for them to expand to their true selves by the praise which he offers; and the natural correlative of this is a life spent in the ever-greater restriction of blaming others through restrictively stereotyping them. The consequences of this go very deep in each human self and in the society of selves, so deep that the damage done is virtually impossible to eradicate. So most people adopt a 'survival course', both for themselves and for their society, which will minimize the damage and secure what remains. And part of the support which is provided for this 'survival course' is to believe that nothing more is even possible.

THE NECESSITY OF RECONSTITUTION

Nor is anything more possible unless there can be a restoration of the dynamic with God whereby his economy of praise can begin again, and then continue, to open 'space' for us, in our relations with ourselves and others, to expand to our true selves – which, as we saw before, are selves given, not selves possessed. Of course, there is no law against the occurrence of such a restoration; if creation and speciation are products of a history of expansive originative activity arising from the economy of praise in God, there is no reason why there should not also be a crucial reconstitutive or reoriginative act, and one which – as an act – can continue to expand in history. Such an act would indeed constitute 'new man' (and since manhood is always such in its relationships, new society), and would continue to enlarge in history. To be sure, the possibility of such an act is unfamiliar, conditioned as we are to think that acts are singular and confined, and can only expand in significance or by causation; but, as we have seen, the economy of praise is to be self-same in expansion, and an act through which praise operates may surely itself expand while remaining itself.

THE PROVIDENCE OF GOD

The actual occurrence of such an act arises from the nature of the activity of God, that which we found was properly seen as an economy of praise. As we concluded earlier, God is self-same in his expansion, and is so (a) by positing a direction for his expanding perfection and (b) by originating that from his perfection which has already come to be; this is what establishes the activity of God in an economy of praise. Now, the nature of such praise is not to be distant, alienated from that which it has originated. Therefore, even as God expands, as an 'expanding circumference', he remains close to all that he has previously originated in the history of creation, retaining its direction and movement by continuing to establish the 'space' for it to be itself and 'moving' it to its true being. So a reconstitutive act is founded in this, which often goes under the name of providence in Christian theology.

CLOSENESS IN MATERIAL HUMANITY

This closeness demands more than simply a general 'nearness' of God for this direction and movement to be effective, for two reasons. If it is fully to open 'space' for human beings to be truly themselves, it must affect the material conditions of humanity; it cannot simply be an abstract 'spiritual' affirmation present only for those who have the appropriate means of access; that would make the whole process of praise into a gnosticism, with all the élitism and agony which that brings. Secondly, if it is to provide the possibility for the sort of expansion in relationship which in the greatest degree mirrors the economy of God's own nature, it must actually occur in a human being, where praise can become active, expanding and directed, as it is for God himself. So the closeness which is inherent in God's praise seems to require its concretion in the materiality of a human being.

Notwithstanding the fact that such a reconstitutive act in the materiality of a human being is required by the economy of praise in God, did it actually occur? There has to be evidence that this reconstitutive act took place in a particular historical person, and in quite a different way than could be claimed for others. What evidence could suffice for this? If the act is of the sort which we have been considering, one which re-establishes what is proper to the human self in relationship, expansion to its truth through praise, evidence will have to show that what was essential to this had in fact been accomplished, and that it did actually bring about the needed regeneration. What is centrally necessary to this reconstitution is the presence of the economy of God's praise made effective through its closeness and through its supplantation of that which in man renders it ineffective. And for this to regenerate humanity, God's economy of praise would actually have to become operative in man, displacing that which undermines it. Evidence for this would therefore have to be drawn both from what occurred in Jesus and from what thereafter occurred for those who believed in and followed him; evidence of one sort alone, from history or from faith, would not suffice.

THE NATURE AND EVIDENCE OF SALVATION

The principal deficiency in man which arises through his sin is his reducing self mirrored in his reducing relationships with others; his expansion to his true self through giving praise to others, thereby making space for them to expand to their truth, has been replaced by a contrary movement. What is seen in Jesus, however, is completely consistent praise for God and man, its direction and movement incorporated in his teaching and his life, in remarkable contrast to the limited and spasmodic praise characteristic of others around him. Consistently, he expands to his true self by giving praise, both to God and to all who surround him, and thus making it possible for them to expand to their true selves through their praise (which, of course, is very different). This leads to the conclusion that in him there has been a full closeness of God's economy of praise. But from the earliest stages of his life, severe restrictions are placed on his effectiveness by the reactions of those around him, though there is no reason to suppose that they apply also to the expansion of his self (and his relationships) as this is occurring by virtue of his praise of God. Limited attention and uncertain determination give way to the stereotypes of blame, and with them severe restrictions imposed on the operation of that economy of praise which was fully close in him. What obviously builds up is a collision of the expanding economy of praise with the restrictive, reducing conditions of life around him, and this culminates in his crucifixion – the collision of two dynamics, that of expansion with that of reduction. And, so far as the world is concerned, the power of the latter is there seen to be greater than that of the former, so pervasive is the dynamic of this reduction in the world.

The problem throughout was how one who so praised God that he was enabled always to praise others, even as they blamed him, was to sustain this – and indeed expand it in accordance with the economy of praise – as the blame increased to its maximum. But the fact was that he not only sustained but increased it to and in his death. His death was, it seems, an act of praise supplanting the blaming by those who put him to death; they showed that they had the power to put him to death, but not to make him blameworthy. As those nearby at his death recognized, Jesus' actions reversed that blame. That is not to say, however, that this death could have been other than offensive to God, for it still ended the life of the one in whom the economy of God's praise reached its fullest closeness to man.

What is it then which reverses the offence, and completes the reconstitutive act in Jesus? It is the persistent presence of the expanding perfection of God, now shown to expand even through its own defeat and to remain closer than ever to man, even in his materiality, in doing so. As the life and death of Jesus were the expanding closeness to man of the economy of God's praise, despite the restrictions placed on this by man, so the resurrection was the supervening of the economy of praise over its contradictions. If the death of Jesus had been offensive to God, notwithstanding the fact that Jesus had reversed the blaming by which he was crucified, this offensiveness was itself taken away by God's own praise given material form in the resurrection of Jesus, and those who crucified

him were returned praise in place of the blame which was due
them.

It is therefore not at all surprising to find the post-resurrection
presence of Jesus discovered by his followers as he attended to them,
determined their new identity and blessed them; these were the
means by which they found the new expansive power of the economy
of praise among them. Beyond this, the post-resurrection presence
of Jesus is found in the reconstitution of all who blame, and in that
of the various structures by which they have institutionalized their
blaming. These were the implications of the life, death and resurrection of Jesus as they came gradually to be understood by his
followers – such as Paul, for example.

But, as we saw, there must be evidence, not only that what was
necessary for the reconstitution of mankind was accomplished in
Jesus, but also from the lives of those who followed him, that it was
effective in regenerating life. Can we say that it was effective in this
way? Fundamentally, the answer will depend on whether those who
followed him were incorporated into the economy of God's praise,
and whether the expanding perfection of God is present in them
and in the world which they 'make'. That is to say, the closeness
of the economy of God's praise in the incarnation, God's collision
with blame, and the supervening of praise, are known as people
live in God's blessing. The test of such things is simple: do they
return praise for blame, or only return blame; and if so, do they
continue in praise, bringing others to their truth in doing so? If
they do praise, and continue in praise, it can only be by the presence
in them of the economy of God's praise, as that was fully manifest
in the life, death and resurrection of Jesus Christ and has become
the moving force of their lives by God's Holy Spirit in them.

Appendix B

A Review of Relevant Literature

Introduction

A line of argument and inquiry has been followed during the course of the book which is largely, if not altogether, without parallel in theological literature. It might easily be mistaken for a consideration of worship and its implications. There are already many books, some of them very good ones, which address themselves to the theology, history and practice of worship as seen either ecumenically or from within particular traditions. Among these, the following are notable contributions (listed in the order of their traditions):

O. C. Quick, *The Christian Sacraments*, London 1927 (Anglican).

E. Underhill, *Worship*, London 1936 (Anglican).

N. Clark, *An Approach to the Theology of the Sacraments*, London 1956 (Baptist).

W. Hahn, *Worship and Congregation*, London 1963 (Lutheran).

V. Vajta, *Luther on Worship*, Philadelphia 1958 (Lutheran).

J. A. Kay, *The Nature of Christian Worship*, London 1953 (Methodist).

A. Schmemann, *Introduction to Liturgical Theology*, Leighton Buzzard 1966 and *The World as Sacrament*, London 1965 (Orthodox).

P. Verghese, *The Joy of Freedom: Eastern Worship and Modern Man*, London 1967 (Orthodox).

J. D. Crichton, *Christian Celebration*, London 1973 (Roman Catholic).

N. Lash, *His Presence in the World*, London 1968 (Roman Catholic).

J. J. von Allmen, *Worship: Its Theology and Practice*, London 1965 (Swiss Reformed).

G. Dix, *The Shape of the Liturgy*, Westminster 1945 (Ecumenical).

But the present book is not an addition to those on worship and liturgy; it has been concerned specifically with the praise of God, and has sought to trace its presence within many other movements of the life of man through his life with God. It is, of course, true that praise appears, perhaps most specifically, in worship, and we have recognized this in chapter 2, however briefly. But confining it to its appearance there tends to reduce its importance: if it is one activity of worship, its centrality to worship is readily lost; and if worship is seen as separate from life, as it is very commonly today, then praise is separated from life – and all the activities of life, including knowledge and action – as well.

The same arguments tell against a book of theology from the perspective of worship; praise may then be seen to be incidental to life, or on the margins of life. Of course, such problems can be avoided by making it central to the basic activities of life, as they are in the one notable attempt to write theology from the perspective of worship which has appeared, Geoffrey Wainwright's *Doxology: The Praise of God in Worship, Doctrine and Life*, London 1980. We will do well to pause to consider the present book in relation to his.

Despite his specific attempt to integrate worship, doctrine and life through the understanding of praise, and despite the breadth of scholarship with which Wainwright does so, two problems arise in particular which require another kind of work to be undertaken: (1) Worship (which is to be tested by considerations of origin, spread and ethical correspondence) is there treated as 'a source of doctrine in so far as it is the place in which God makes himself known to humanity in a saving encounter, the human words and acts used in worship being a doctrinal locus in so far as either God makes them the vehicle of his self-communication or they are fitting responses to God's presence or action' (pp. 242f.). Now this way of proceeding rests on the use of a notion of encounter, which Wainwright does not develop. The need to establish an adequate notion of encounter itself justifies the additional work which the present book undertakes; it is necessary to establish the inner movement or 'grammar' of God's relationship with man. In the end, through the consideration of praise, we find a notion of encounter which is far more specific in content than that used in Wainwright's book, and in much other current theology.

(2) The material which is considered in Wainwright's book is gathered as the expressions (in the form of ritual, teaching and behaviour) of the experience of man which arises in this saving encounter. Unlike treatments which give more prominence to doctrine or ethics, Wainwright's requires that forms of worship (rituals) be examined as the focal expression of the teaching and behaviour which also manifest this encounter. In so doing, it follows the line of current phenomenology (in the English sense) of religion, but with rituals being given primacy; its purpose is sometimes described by the author as theology from the standpoint of liturgy. (a) One problem with this is that the notion of experience which lies at the heart of it is undefined and undelimited, which brings, on

the one hand, an unwillingness to evaluate the materials considered (liturgies, doctrines and ethical positions) – a tendency to 'have things both ways at once', and on the other hand, an avoidance of the question of how worship is related to doctrine and ethics. (b) Another problem is that the inner dynamic of experience in relation to God goes unexplored; for this reason, the book lacks the criterion which is necessary for the production of a systematic theology, and tends therefore to be intelligent humanism making use of Christian materials. That is not to say that it does not take the integrity of Christian worship and belief and life seriously; it simply does not show how they arise from and concentrate the life and power of God for man.

So, by comparison with Wainwright's book, we have attempted to explore the inner movement of God's relationship with man through the life of praise, and to allow that to show how worship operates, and how knowing and behaving (including their doctrinal and ethical form) arise. We also make that movement the criterion for the examination of Christian materials, and for a systematic theology. Thus, our focus is not simply on 'encounter' and 'experience', but on the activities which occur in the life of praise, as they comprise man's life in the world – particularly his knowing and doing, whose quality improves or deteriorates as he moves closer or farther from the one who is the source of truth and goodness. Our purpose is therefore altogether different from Wainwright's.

On Reading Books

As we have pursued the purpose just described, during the course of the book, one main intention has been to provide a different way of understanding the tradition and life of Christianity. As we have unfolded the meaning of praise during the course of the book, we have therefore tried to assist the reader by giving him 'practice' in the reading of important sources from the past in a particular way. In this Appendix, we shall extend the list of such sources. But we must recognize that they themselves will only yield their benefits if the reader brings to them the 'dynamic' of reading which we have sought to develop. Reading them will require participating in the same movement of praise which has been the main theme of the present book. Ideally, perhaps, we might be able to cite existing comment on them which would make clear the praise which is implicit in them, but in most cases such comment has still to be written. Nor is there space here to provide this comment; we can do little more than list some of the works which will most repay the use of the 'praise-reading' which we have tried to exemplify.

Furthermore, even if we were to provide the comment which would make clear the praise which is in them, that would not meet the reader's responsibility, which is his alone, to read them in the dynamic of praise.

Finding the Movement of Praise in Literature

It would be a mistake to think that one can simply go back to 'classical' expositions of praise, there to find a notion which remains self-same afterwards. While one can get an approximation of praise in that fashion, which will help in identifying it thereafter, praise is rather more elusive than that, since it is interwoven in the history of God with man, and in every moment of that movement. It is, shall we say, the moving strand which underlies – somewhat like grammar in language or a *cantus firmus* in music – all of the movements in that history, just as we saw it to be the thrust of attention and determination or affirmation (see Appendix A). So it is always to be found at the heart of the thought and practice of particular eras of history, and at the heart of the dynamic of life as it moves from era to era. It can therefore be construed and expressed very differently, so much so that one can easily lose sight of its presence and central importance.

For example, one can say that there is a central strand which underlies all ontology (science of being or existence) and epistemology (theory of knowledge), the wish to attend to 'what is' and to find or establish 'it' as it truly is, and thus to accord it recognition and respect as such, among other things by understanding it and acting properly towards it. These things are to be achieved by freeing oneself from attachment to lesser objectifications of it, or from techniques by which to take possession of 'what is'. However variable are the means employed in ontology and epistemology, and they have varied widely through the ages, this central strand has always been present, even if rendered effective in different ways. This strand, of course, is the appearance in ontology and epistemology of the movement of praise.

There is a comparable situation in history and hermeneutics (the art or science of interpretation). Despite all its failures, history seems to be characterized by an inner thrust, not to be identified with the notion of progress, towards what is true, in order to be able to approximate to it more and more (cf. the Kingdom of God). And that is sought, however indirectly or haltingly, through interpretation, both as a movement of knowledge and as one of life (i.e. an art). This thrust is fulfilled through the movement of freeing oneself from attachment to, indeed imprisonment by, lesser versions and techniques. History, of course, is filled with variations of these versions and techniques, but this inner thrust towards an unconditioned truth and freedom has always been present in human interpretation, whether in the form of understanding or that of life. And this thrust is the appearance in history and hermeneutics of the movement of praise.

We use these two examples to show that praise is more often than not mediately present – present in the inner movement of mediations, in ontology and history in the cases earlier discussed, and present for human beings through their participation in the movement, by their attempts to know and act. Though there are many times when it surfaces, and is seen for itself, it has properly to be seen as the surfacing of something which is operative within other movements. Not to do this will marginalize praise, by treating it as a surface activity whose relation to the inner movements of being and history is only accidental, treating it, in other words, as an essentially arbitrary activity, a human game, even an entertainment, detached from (perhaps even concealing) truth and history. Sadly, this is exactly what has happened; it has become normal to marginalize praise, separating it from its presence within other movements: (1) For example, praise, as we have already mentioned, is most often seen as equivalent to worship, and worship is seen as separate from the deepest and most natural movements of truth and history. Properly speaking, the expression of praise should be the surfacing or acknowledgement of its movement in the other movements of life, not a separate activity. (2) Another way of marginalizing praise is to consider it a special kind of experience, which one may or may not have or do, like an activity which one may or may not do depending on one's circumstances or intentions. This is not only to fragment experience, but also to divorce it from the inner movements of truth and history. Properly, truth and history should be seen to have their own dynamic, in which one participates by the experience of praise.

The Resources for Praise

The resources for the consideration of praise, then, are not simply those in which the acknowledgement or discussion of praise is explicit. They must also include those which successfully identify the inner movements of life as the movements of God's life with man; these are instances where there is a genuine enhancement of human truth and life by drawing their movement into the praise of God – a fulfilment of truth and history by recognizing their fulfilment in praise.

Alongside these, however, there have almost always been competing movements which in various ways undermine this movement of God's life with man; some do so purposefully, in open disagreement, others accidentally. (In modern times, the prominence of such competing movements has become increasingly great, as time and time again alternative standpoints have been presented which suggest that these inner movements of life are alienated from their proper nature by being associated with the movements of God's life with man.) These often, though not always, propose a radically different direction for the proper life of man, and are associated with drastically different proprieties for praise. Since they are such a challenge, they too must figure in our review of the resources for praise.

In still more recent times, these – together with the more traditional views earlier discussed – have been dislocated by new perplexities about what are the movements of life. New ways of approaching and understanding the nature of life in the world are afoot, and their implications are so far unclear. These new openings, and their possible use in praise, must be considered, too.

Our treatment of the resources will therefore be divided into two parts: (1) the creative retrieval of praise, and the hindrances to it which have arisen, and (2) new possibilities for praise.

The Creative Retrieval of Praise and Its Hindrances

THE NOTION OF PRAISE IN THE BIBLE

1. Despite our earlier warning that one cannot return to a classical notion of praise which remains self-same thereafter, it is possible to find classical instances of praise. And these are valuable for the preliminary approximation which they provide. The study of the Psalms is of great importance in this connection: Psalm 113, for example, offers praise in such a way as to make clear the features which comprise its praise. There, the following elements appear:

(a) the one to whom praise is addressed is attended to, determined or 'thought', and praised as such;

(b) the determination of this one is expressed in descriptive or metaphorical terms – using statements of his attributes or deeds, or metaphors;

(c) those who so address and render praise are identified imperatively or self-involvingly;

(d) when praise is offered is specified, at particular times and also continuously;

(e) where praise is offered is specified, at particular places and also everywhere;

(f) for what reasons, or why, praise is offered (this is intimately related to (b) above; thus praise is addressed to one who is determined in a particular fashion, rather than 'for' what he has done);

(g) by what movements or modes of activity praise is offered, whether external (offerings, fastings, physical activities, utterances, silence, etc.) or internal ('all that is within me').

See: J. H. Eaton, *Psalms: Introduction and Commentary*, London 1967.
A. R. Johnson, 'The Psalms' in H. H. Rowley, ed., *The Old Testament and Modern Study* (Oxford 1951), pp. 162–209.
S. Mowinckel, *The Psalms in Israel's Worship*, Oxford 1962.
G. von Rad, *Theology of the Old Testament*, i, London 1975.
C. Westermann, *Praise and Lament in the Psalms*, Atlanta 1981.

2. It is especially noticeable, in the features of praise listed above, that praise is the comprehensive activity for man in relation to God. It is to be in each place and time and in every place and time, in each and every activity of man. It is therefore mistaken to limit the notion of praise to those situations where it is explicit, as in the Psalms, and thereby to lose sight of its presence as the essential dynamic of man's relationship with God. For this is to 'frame' praise, both as a notion and a complex of activities, by reference to some more primary reality, and thus to delimit the sphere of praise to a place within this reality, instead of understanding that it is the essential dynamic of reality itself. This 'framing' of praise is what is done when, for example, the everyday life-world of man is seen as 'reality', and praise seen as something done within that. It is exactly this which the Psalms attempt to defeat, as they make it clear that praise is due always and everywhere. There is nothing, in other words, which stands outside praise.

Seen in this way, there is nothing, whether in nature or human life and history, which stands outside praise (and in so doing frames it as a special activity within). It is particularly important to understand this where matters like cosmology and history are discussed; they are not of interest for their own sake, but for their manifestation of the affirmation of the world and man by God through the whole of conceivable history, and for the possibilities which this affords man to respond to God (which include the interpretation of God's action in history and righteousness of life). For this reason, all of the Old and New Testaments are as relevant to praise as the Psalms, and the only difference is in exactly how (and how far) they make praise explicit as the essential dynamic of man's relationship to God, or in how far they identify this essential dynamic and integrate other movements of life in that. They do, of course, vary in the content which they associate with this dynamic, particularly as their historical situation alters and as the depth of their understanding grows, but their importance lies not so much in that as in the rightness of their appreciation of the essential characteristics of the dynamic itself.

This has not been fully recognized in comment on the Bible, and much scholarship has been concerned with praise as a matter of literary form rather than as the central feature of the dynamic between man and God, but there is some helpful literature available none the less.

See: (General)

G. J. Botterweck and H. Ringgren, eds., *Theological Dictionary of the Old Testament*, trans. J. T. Willis, Grand Rapids 1974–80.

G. Kittel and G. Friedrich, *Theological Dictionary of the New Testament*, trans. G. W. Bromiley, Grand Rapids 1964–76.

D. Senior and Carroll Stuhlmueller, *The Biblical Foundations for Mission*, London 1983.

L. Scheffczyk, *Creation and Providence*, London 1970.

C. Westermann, *Blessing in the Bible and the Life of the Church*, Philadelphia 1978. (Old Testament).

J. H. Eaton, *Vision in Worship: The Relation of Prophecy and Liturgy in the Old Testament*, London 1981.

J. H. Eaton, *Festal Drama in Deutero-Isaiah*, London 1979.

H. H. Rowley, *Worship in Ancient Israel*, London 1967.

3. After having seen praise in a preliminary approximation in the Psalms, and recognized it as the essential dynamic between man and God in the varying situations with which it is associated, it is important to see the transition which it undergoes in the New Testament, as it is given its primary content by Jesus, so that, in the words of one of our chapter titles, 'Jesus is our praise'. Accordingly, praise thereafter is 'in' him and receives its characteristics from him, and in so far as this praise identifies God and those who render praise (cf. the elements of praise seen in Psalm 113 as listed above), God and man are freshly specified in him, though in such a manner that all the Old Testament Scriptures are now seen to point to or concern him (cf. Luke 24:25–7). The identification of the essential dynamic between God and man with Jesus is well seen in the Letter to the Hebrews, its consequences for God well seen in Revelation, and those for man well seen in 2 Corinthians.

The matter, of course, is not so simple. For one thing, the reconstitution of the dynamic of praise by Jesus, as it appears in the New Testament, is not in a simple time-frame, 'framed off' from the historical reality before and after. It does appear in time, but as the fulfilment of time, and thus as the heart of the dynamic of God with man in his history, before and after. And as such, it reconstitutes the meaning of the past and awakens movement towards the future, freeing men to live for the anticipated commonwealth in heaven – 'an eschatological illumination of existence and the world' (Käsemann). Nor does it appear simply 'in' creation, to be enclosed thereby. Though it happens as creation, it happens as the redemption of creation (therefore as a 'second' or 'new' creation), thus reconstituting the truth of creation and freeing men to know the truth of nature and themselves. The relevance of praise to this is well seen in the Letter to the Philippians (see chapter 3 of the book).

Second, it is not that Jesus alone is agent in this dynamic. He is attended and affirmed or determined (in the sense discussed in Appendix A) by God as the principal agent in the struggle against evil, and this affirmation – as well as the placing of Jesus in the conflict with evil – is accomplished by the Spirit (cf. Mark 1:1–15). In other words, there is a triple agency operative with Jesus, not the singular agency of one man. But at the same time, this agency is not indicated in conceptual terms, but in terms of what is done in historical events (e.g., the Spirit drove him out into the wilderness).

Third, this scenario is vitally concerned with the problematic of man's entrapment by evil, again not in conceptual terms but as genuinely historical. And it is made amply clear that the possibility for resistance to this rests on the authority of Jesus and immediate response to it, which are seen primarily as the recognition of Jesus' authority through the action of following him (discipleship) – again not as an abstract intellectual act of belief, but as following in life. For this gift of freedom from the shame of man, God alone is to be praised (cf. Rom. 11:33–6).

Fourth, it is abundantly clear how central to man's participation in this is his honouring and thanking of God. The change of lordship for man which is involved in honouring and thanking God, and doing so through recognition of Jesus, is a change of existence for man. In other words, it is through the movement of praise for God through Jesus, that God is God for man, and man is himself.

Some recent comment on the New Testament has fastened helpfully on the movement which is thus seen, while not fully grasping the centrality of praise.

See:

G. Bornkamm, *Early Christian Experience*, London 1969.
E. Käsemann, *Jesus Means Freedom*, London 1969.
E. Käsemann, *Commentary on Romans*, London 1980.

C. F. D. Moule, *The Birth of the New Testament*, London 1966.
L. Scheffczyk, *Creation and Providence*, London 1970.

4. It is already obvious that a principal problem in viewing the movements of praise in the Bible is the ease with which one is distracted by the intricacies of material. Material, historical or cosmological or whatever, in which the movement of praise is mediately present, is seen as important in its own right, and thus distracts. This problem is much magnified by the norms which operate in and upon the modern interpreter, for example those of modern preoccupations with the proprieties of historical and scientific investigation. Hence, the combination of unfamiliar historical material and historical-critical norms tends to lead one away from the inner movement of praise to surface-historical, -personal or -cosmological studies. The rediscovery of means more appropriate to the movement of praise is dealt with later in the section on new possibilities for praise.

THE MOVEMENT OF PRAISE IN TRADITION

1. The same problem of distraction afflicts discussions of post-biblical material. A sharp distinction is commonly made between the historical mode of thought and presentation which is considered to be characteristic of biblical writers and the preoccupation with ontological and conceptual ones which is thought (at least by those committed to the historical mode) to mark the early Church's continued treatment of the issues. And it is not infrequently said that concern with the ontological-conceptual issues of the essence and Trinity of God was a 'switching to the wrong track', a distortion of the purely historical character of the gospel (Käsemann). As if further to confirm this, modern historical-critical methods are then applied (as by Wiles) to the ontological-conceptual discussions in order to show them as products of minds formed by habits of thinking (primarily neo-Platonic) which are alien to the purely historical modes of biblical thought, and which are relative to the situations in which they were written. Others, however, defend the movement to ontological-conceptual formulations as a move from gospels which are addressed 'to the whole person' to dogmatic presentation for those who 'can focus attention on the aspect of truth alone' (Lonergan), suggesting that these changes are not only a change in the ('objective') form of presentation but require a ('subjective') change in the thinker which must come about through a slow learning process. The controversy is very similar to that in the present day between devotees of consistently historical and consistently scientific thinking, and the parties as intransigent.

See: E. Käsemann, *Commentary on Romans*, London 1980.
   B. Lonergan, *The Way to Nicaea*, London 1976.
   M. Wiles, *The Making of Christian Doctrine*, Cambridge 1967.

The question remains whether the two parties are not so distracted by the intricacies of their self-appointed tasks that they fail to see the movement which is common to both kinds of thought. This is the movement of praise mentioned earlier ('Finding the Movement of Praise in Literature'), seen in history as the thrust towards what is true and free – and participated in by interpretation as understanding and life, and seen in ontology as the wish to attend to 'what is' by recognizing it as it truly is – through appropriate self-corrective movements of thought and action. Each of these two is deeply interwoven in the other, almost inextricably so. While they may be notionally formulated as separate options, their inner dynamic – that of praise – is remarkably similar. And each, in the end, rests on truth realized in free thought and action – thought, freedom and action which are dependent for their realization on the truth which comes to light in them.

See: W. Pannenberg, 'Analogy and Doxology' in *Basic Questions in Theology*, vol. i, London 1970.

2. There was normally no such clear gap between the ways of biblical presentation and those of post-biblical writers as is so often supposed. Common to them was the supposition of a dynamic unity of God and man, whose basis in the nature of God himself was enacted for man in Jesus and the Holy Spirit. But, if this was set out in discursive or narrative form in the Bible, it was now set out in close-knit conceptual form. It was no less the attempt to attend to it and determine it in such a way as more exactly to participate or follow in it, and to do these by participating in God's own affirmation of man. Furthermore, these were undertaken specifically as the attempt to see the glory of God through thinking the truth:

'Therefore we worship the Father of truth and the Son who is the truth, two things in respect of hypostasis, but one thing by harmony and concord and identity of will; in such manner that whoever sees the Son, who is the splendour of his glory and the figure of his substance, in him, who is the image of God, sees the Father also' (Origen, *Contra Celsum*, trans. H. Chadwick, viii, 12, Cambridge 1953).

See: B. Lonergan, *The Way to Nicaea*, London 1976.
   J. Pelikan, *The Emergence of the Catholic Tradition (100–600), (The Christian Tradition: A History of the Development of Doctrine*, vol. 1), Chicago 1971.
   G. L. Prestige, *God in Patristic Thought*, London 1936.

3. The most difficult issues surrounded the adequacy of particular notions as means of attending to and thinking the truth. But the truth which was the focus of attention was not simply that which had derived from the gospel, but that truth as the truth underlying the 'truths' held by those who had not yet heard the gospel – those in the wider world in which Christianity was now present. So all the central content of the truth of the relationship between God and man had to be considered, and at times painfully negotiated. Even where some progress was made in developing notions for the purpose, problems emerged. Some, of course, produced obvious distortions; and these heresies could be identified fairly quickly. Others introduced limitations both more subtle and more long-lasting. Since the issues at stake were vast (what are sometimes called 'limit questions'), it is not surprising that such problems were difficult to identify and correct. There is a vast deposit of literature which arose in this situation, and an even more vast amount of secondary discussion dealing with it either in historical-conceptual terms (Kelly) or against its historical background.

See: J. N. D. Kelly, *Early Christian Doctrines*, London 1958.
      F. M. Young, *From Nicaea to Chalcedon*, London 1983 (includes a valuable bibliography).

4. The intricacies of the discussion, historical and conceptual, are so great that it is easy to lose sight of the central position of praise. It was not simply a discussion about theoretical formulation, but was based on a central thrust of attention, determination and praise. It was, therefore, a movement combining the most fundamental human abilities, and indeed the whole of life, but one which was carried upward (so to speak) by its object, and whose proper context is 'the confession of the praise of God' (Augustine). And this brought concern for the means by which that movement, as distinct from contrary movement, was constituted and made possible through repentance and witness to Christ; these were the issues of the 'economy of salvation'. Beyond these, there were the questions of the presence of God himself in the economy, and how God was constituted himself; what, for example, was the nature of the infinitude of God – fixed or dynamic, bounded or boundless? Two figures are particularly interesting and important in this connection: Augustine and Gregory of Nyssa.

5. Augustine and Gregory of Nyssa, the Latin West and the Greek East, present a nice contrast. Augustine, both as a man and in his theological work, 'found the light, life and joy of his intelligence in faith' (Congar, p. 45), and correspondingly saw faith to be the

gathering of all human capacities in a movement into the eternal realm by which there could finally (after preliminary attention and determination) be understanding of God. So knowledge and human activity were fulfilled in faith, and were purified in the loving movement of faith to God; there could be no autonomous thought (philosophy) or action (ethics). At the same time, God was, it seemed, treated as a terminus of movement, the 'Self-same Holy, Holy, Holy, Lord God Almighty' (*Confessions*, xii, ch. vii), unchangeable in his counsel and will and foreordination. Gregory, on the other hand, finds the necessity of infinite growth, which also includes all of man's capacities and life, because of the ineffable and inviting God: 'for those rising in perfection, the limit of the good that is attained becomes the beginning of the discovery of higher goods' (Daniélou, ed., p. 213). And it is evident that for him the transcendent, the infinite beauty and goodness of God, is 'always seen as something new and strange in comparison with what the mind has already understood' (Daniélou, p. 247), very much like the 'expanding' nature of God discussed in Appendix A. It is quite clear that both gave much importance to the gathering of all human capacities, and all human history, into a movement towards God, an ascent, and that for them there was no divorcing of thought and action, or history, from the movement of praise – an issue of central importance in discussions of the tradition in Christianity. But it is also clear that they construe the economy of God differently, the one predominantly emphasizing self-sameness, the other the dynamics of the infinite.

See: J. Pelikan, *The Spirit of Eastern Christendom (600–1700)*, (*The Christian Tradition*, vol. 2) Chicago 1974.

Augustine, 'On Christian Doctrine' (*Nicene and Post-Nicene Fathers of the Christian Church*, ed. Philip Schaff, vol. ii), Grand Rapids 1977.

Augustine, 'Of True Religion' in *Augustine: Earlier Writings*, ed. J. H. S. Burleigh (Library of Christian Classics, vol. vi), London 1955.

Augustine, *Confessions and Enchiridion*, ed. A. C. Outler (Library of Christian Classics, vol. vii), London 1955.

Augustine, 'On the Trinity' (*Nicene and Post-Nicene Fathers of the Christian Church*, ed. Philip Schaff, vol. ii), Grand Rapids 1979.

Augustine, 'Commentaries on the Psalms' (*Nicene and Post-Nicene Fathers of the Christian Church*, ed. Philip Schaff, vol. viii), Grand Rapids 1979.

Gregory of Nyssa in *Christology of the Later Fathers*, ed. C. Richardson (Library of Christian Classics, vol. iii), London 1954.

Gregory of Nyssa, *The Life of Moses* (Classics of Western Spirituality) New York 1978.

J. Daniélou, *From Glory to Glory. Texts from Gregory of Nyssa's Mystical Writings*, New York 1961.

D. F. Winslow, *The Dynamics of Salvation*, Philadelphia 1979.

6. Yet, for all their similarities, there are serious and important differences between them, not only about the way to God but also about the nature of God. (a) Augustine finds the way to God through the desire of the soul and self-knowledge; man, in memory, understanding and will, should cleave to God in order to be reformed into the image of God, and this constitutes his return to God through a long process of purification. While also being concerned with the virtue of the soul, Gregory, however, finds another kind of approach to God, in an ascent by man which has both contemplative and active sides, which are purified in the ascent to the perception that God alone truly exists; this is a withdrawal from wrong ideas of God, a transition therefore from darkness to light, followed by a closer awareness of hidden things which guides the soul 'through sense-phenomena to the world of the invisible' and accustoms the soul to look towards what is hidden, allowing it to make progress still higher and 'enter within the secret chamber of the divine knowledge, there to be cut off on all sides by the divine darkness in order to contemplate the invisible and incomprehensible' (Daniélou, p. 247). Gregory's understanding of the way to God is, as we see, strikingly different from Augustine's, Augustine's being a purification of man *in situ* by the gift of God, and Gregory's an ascent of man to divine knowledge which is never fully complete. It is not particularly helpful to term either of these ways 'mystical', as do many scholars, for they are dynamic ways of knowledge (even if different), and both suggest that the culmination of knowledge is in the proper recognition and respect, or praise, of God. (b) The other, perhaps even more important, difference between the two men is in their conception of the infinite which is God. Augustine's understanding of God, as previously hinted, emphasizes the self-sameness of God as Trinity who condescends to give himself in Christ and the Holy Spirit to man, who yet remains 'unchangeable over all' in the very disclosure of himself in man's soul. Gregory's understanding of God, however, is one of an ever-deeper, and an ever-new, infinite – an infinite which by its nature is dynamic, even expanding (as was suggested in Appendix A), which by its nature draws man continually out of himself in knowledge and love (action) into closeness with the infinite presence of God.

See: R. E. Heine, *Perfection in the Virtuous Life: A Study in the Relation-*

ship between Edification and Polemical Theology in Gregory of Nyssa, Philadelphia 1978.

A. Louth, *The Origins of the Christian Mystical Tradition*, Oxford 1981.

R. Williams, *The Wound of Knowledge: Christian Spirituality from the New Testament to St John of the Cross*, London 1979.

7. The concern with a close-knit method for Christian theology, already evident in Augustine, became much more strong – perhaps even overwhelming afterwards. Perhaps partly because of the majority-position of Christianity, and partly because of the intrinsic characteristics of Latin culture, there was a strong wish for a methodical resolution of issues about the interrelation of Scripture and theology, and of faith and reason, and for the development of a systematic dialectical method which could be used as a standard procedure in controversies. Discussion of these matters took place, furthermore, with the supposition (fostered by Augustine) that the sciences and the arts should be put to the service of Christ in theology, and as Christians became involved in education. A still further influence came from the introduction of Aristotle to the West by Boethius as early as the sixth century. Altogether, there is evidence that concern with the niceties of these questions, perhaps very important in themselves, overwhelmed the movement necessary to theology; theology, one might say, became 'seized up', and few even of the experts could escape the disorientation induced by methodicalism.

See: Y. M.-J. Congar, *A History of Theology*, Garden City 1968.

J. Pelikan, *The Growth of Medieval Theology (600–1300)*, *(The Christian Tradition*, vol. 3), Chicago 1978.

8. Before touching on the major figures who perhaps succeeded best in continuing to preserve the inner dynamic of praise in their understanding, something must be made clear about the situation in which they lived and worked. For them, the context of monastic life, with its daily round of manual work and study and worship, was extremely important – so much so that we can hardly understand the character of their work without taking this into account. It is noticeable, in fact, that the discipline of this religious life was itself the movement of attention in understanding and action to their fulfilment in praise – that combination of the central elements of life in praise which we have frequently indicated as the movement of praise. Correspondingly, when we attempt to understand such major figures as Anselm of Canterbury, or Thomas Aquinas, we must remember that their work was 'enclosed' in a corporate life of praise; and even those who were not themselves 'religious' like

Dante Alighieri, lived within surroundings deeply affected by the presence of the same ideals as those which shaped monastic life. For life itself, with all the sciences, arts and forms of behaviour of which it was made up, was seen to achieve its truth as and when it was fulfilled in the glorification of God who had created and redeemed it and would bring it to its final shape. Such a vision alone, for example, could have resulted in the art of the pre-Renaissance era.

9. Among the most remarkable figures in any history of praise in theology would be Anselm of Canterbury, who is both an expert in the theoretical matters of the logic of knowledge and of action, and also one who integrates them in their fulfilment in praise. Nor do his endeavours result simply in a description of how this is so; they carry the reader into the movement of praise: 'And now, my soul, arouse and elevate your whole understanding; ponder as best you can what kind of good this is and how great it is. For if the individual good things are enjoyable, reflect attentively upon how enjoyable is that Good which contains the joyfulness of all good things. This is not the kind of joyfulness experienceable in created things but rather a kind as different from that kind as the Creator is different from the creature. For if created life is good, how good must be that Life which creates!' His purpose, therefore, is to bring the understanding to ascend to the contemplation of goodness, and to the wonderful Good which creates. In doing so, he traces the logic of his 'ontological' argument, whose content he finds is that of the Trinity, the incarnation, and the movement of God's Spirit, and carries us with him to find the supreme joy in God, a God whose own nature is unlimited joy: 'For I have found an abundant joy – even a superabundant joy. Indeed, when the heart, the mind, the soul – when the whole man – is filled with joy, there will still remain joy without limit. Therefore, the whole of Your joy will not enter into those who are rejoicing; instead they will all enter into Your joy . . . O Lord, I ask for what You counsel through our marvellous Counsellor; may I receive what you promise through your Truth, so that my joy may be full. Until then, let my mind meditate upon [what You have promised], let my tongue speak of it. Let my heart love it; let my mouth proclaim it. Let my soul hunger for it; let my flesh thirst for it; let my whole being desire it until such a time as I enter into the joy of my Lord, the triune God, blessed for ever. Amen.' (*Proslogion*, chs. 24–6). For Anselm, true knowledge and righteousness of life are thus found through the restoration of God's honour by Christ, by which it becomes possible for man to give due honour to the overflowing perfection of God. God himself is dynamic and limitless perfection.

See: *Anselm of Canterbury*, vol. 1, ed. and trans. Jasper Hopkins and
     Herbert Richardson, London 1974.
     Anselm of Canterbury, vols. 2, 3, 4, ed. Jasper Hopkins and
     Herbert Richardson, Toronto 1976 (including *Why God
     Became Man*, available separately).
     John McIntyre, *St Anselm and His Critics: A Reinterpretation of
     the 'Cur Deus Homo'*, Edinburgh 1954.

10. The trend of subsequent medieval philosophy and theology was
to give much more prominence to the world and human experience.
Whereas for Augustine, all things, even in their material nature,
were to be referred for their truth to God who was their beginning
and also their final goal, St Thomas Aquinas, partly as a result of
his assimilation of Aristotelian philosophy, was concerned with
things as they were in themselves, without simply referring them to
God. So it was important to acquire knowledge of things for themselves, beginning from sensory knowledge, and proceeding to define
them and understand them for their own intelligibility, and only
then finding their order in relation to God. Thus they retained their
nature even while it was perfected when brought into relation with
God, lest his work in grace conflict with his work in creation.
Furthermore, the prominence thus given to nature raised the question of how God himself was to be spoken of, an issue which Thomas
resolved by the notion of analogy, whereby an idea applied in the
world might be transposed for application to the transcendent
reality of God through applying it to him 'eminently' without
depriving it of its worldly meaning. The serious problem which
confronted Thomas's theology throughout was whether it did not
draw the content of theology down into worldliness, with a very
serious consequence for praise and its dynamic: while apparently
valuing things more for their nature in the world, it might value
them less for their 'proper' nature in relation to God.

11. Two fundamental and long-term problems appear here. (a) One
is the very difficult question whether Thomas's understanding of
knowledge distorts praise, justifying the harsh critique later made
by Luther: 'the philosopher's eye [Thomas's, that is] is so focused
on the presence of things that all he sees are their quiddities and
qualities, whereas the Apostle lifts up our eyes from the presence
of things, from their essences and accidents, and directs them
toward the future of these things . . . in a new and wonderful theological vocabulary he speaks of the expectation of creatures' (*Epistle
to the Romans*). But the issue is not so easy. For Thomas may
have sought to look through knowledge to the very possibility of
intelligibility at all, and thus to find for each thing its production

and final end – the source of its intelligibility. So Thomas, at least in intention, sought to fulfil knowledge through carrying it to its 'ground' in God, the source of its intelligibility – fulfilling knowledge ultimately in praise. 'St Thomas divides the entire teaching of his *Summa Theologiae* according to the threefold consideration of the causality of God, that is to say, of God as the effecting principle, of God as the beatifying end, of God as the repairing saviour. And thus, proceeding from God as he is Himself and in His being, proceeding through God as he effects, and finalizes, and saves, there is a return to God to be enjoyed in Himself through the ultimate glory of the resurrection, which is evidently to complete the golden circuit of theology, which the divine *Summa* of St Thomas follows out' (*John of St Thomas*). If so, Luther's criticism may be the result of underestimating the importance and function of knowledge in Thomas, if not elsewhere also. (b) The other equally difficult and fundamental question, however, has to do with the very notion of being which Thomas uses of God and of his world; the analysis which Thomas employs starts from what things are, and traces them through their coming-into-being, contingency, etc., back to their prerequisite necessities and thus to the pure Being of God. But the question which must be asked of this is whether this does not concentrate unduly on the possessed attributes of things up to and including (though in a special sense) God himself. Does it not always locate the nature of a thing in itself, and then qualify it by its relation to what is higher, refusing to qualify only where God is concerned, in effect saying of lesser things 'yes, it is itself, but no, it is contingent', and of God alone, 'yes, he is fully himself'? The problem here is twofold: does this not 'fix' the importance of things in too static a way, and also limit the nature of God to static changelessness? If so, there are problems for the dynamics of praise: the praiseworthiness of things in the world may lie in their intrinsic qualities (cf. Appendix A); and the praise due to God is limited by the fact that his is not a dynamic infinite (cf. para. 6 above, in reference to Gregory of Nyssa).

See: St Thomas Aquinas, *Summa Theologiae*, first part, ed. and trans.
    Thomas Gilby *et al.*, London 1964–75.
M. D. Chenu, *Toward Understanding St Thomas*, trans. A. M.
    Landry and D. Hughes, Chicago 1964.
E. Gilson, *The Spirit of Mediaeval Philosophy*, New York 1940.
P. E. Persson, *Sacra Doctrina: Reason and Revelation in Aquinas*,
    trans. Ross Mackenzie, Oxford 1970.

12. Though it comes from the same 'world' as that of Aquinas, the work of Dante Alighieri is also remarkably different, perhaps partly

because it is subject to wider and different influences, but more because it is art intended to 'change the state of being of the enjoyer, to awaken his sensitivity to others, to reveal the unity underlying his own nature, and to fructify and refresh through the integration of his psychology his capacity for insight, understanding and joy' (Anderson, p. 6). In this, it has been said that Dante's poetry constituted a great leap forward, like Augustine's *Confessions*, in the realization of man's inner life; it is this upon which the *Vita Nuova* focuses. In the *Divine Comedy*, much later, the same expansion of self-understanding and the means of self-purification reaches far greater depths as it is portrayed as a matter of salvation; the whole quality of one's life depends on the arrival of the Kingdom of Heaven. Following the views of Augustine and Bonaventure, he portrays man's ascent through sense, imagination, reason, intellect, intelligence to perfection by wisdom in contemplation, these being represented by Virgil, Cato, Statius, Matelda, Beatrice, St Bernard, and the vision of the Trinity. It is fascinating to watch – and participate in – the process by which the 'raw energy' of man's lower life is transformed into 'finer energy' by the ascent to contemplative vision in salvation; man's attention and knowledge and action are progressively drawn to purification in praise.

See: Dante Alighieri, *La Vita Nuova* (many versions).
  Dante Alighieri, *The Divine Comedy* (many versions).
  William Anderson, *Dante the Maker*, London 1980.

13. The preoccupation with the subtleties of the ways of knowledge which characterized the medieval period, and the concentration on forms seen in Thomas Aquinas, brought penalties. On the one hand, they tended to separate human understanding from the object of religion. On the other hand, they led to submersion in rules, and a satisfaction found through conformity to them. These, when tested against a yearning for another kind of religious understanding and another sort of righteousness, in the context of praise, are shown to be radically deficient – false intellectualism, false asceticism and a false satisfaction. While he was already well-versed in the nominalism, humanism and mysticism which were characteristic of educated people of his time, it is significant that it was with these worries that Martin Luther began. He became aware of the insufficiency of reason, and he was convinced by his own experience that rules could not bring righteousness or certainty; his study of the Psalms and Romans brought these worries into clear focus. 'I was indeed a good monk, and kept the rules of my order so strictly that I can say: if ever a monk got to heaven through monasticism, I should have been that man.' 'Yet my conscience could never give

me certainty.' 'Meanwhile I had once again turned to the task of interpreting the Psalms . . . I had certainly been seized with a wondrous eagerness to understand Paul in the Epistle to the Romans, but hitherto I had been held up – not by a "lack of heat in my heart's blood", but by one word only in chapter 1: "The righteousness (*justitia*) of God is revealed in the gospel." For I hated this word "righteousness of God", which by the customary use of the doctors I had been taught to understand philosophically as what they call the formal or active righteousness whereby God is just and punishes unjust sinners . . . At last, as I meditated day and night, God showed mercy and I turned my attention to the connection of the words, namely – "The righteousness of God is revealed, as it is written: the righteous shall live by faith" – and there I began to understand that the righteousness of God is the righteousness in which a just man lives by the gift of God, in other words by faith . . . And now, in the same degree as I had formerly hated the word "righteousness of God", even so did I begin to love and extol it as the sweetest word of all; thus was this place in Paul to me the very gate of paradise' (*Autobiographical Fragment*). So Luther turned from a formalistic knowledge of the relationship between God and man to another kind of knowledge, that of the presence in the sinner's life by faith of the gift of righteousness. And, strikingly, he sees this very transformation of the sinner as the means by which God is glorified: 'How strange is the glory of God. He is glorified when sinners and the weak are received as friends. This is because it is his glory to be a benefactor to us' (*Lectures on Romans*, LCC, p. 411).

14. For this reason, the cross of Christ is central to Luther's theology: 'The cross puts everything to the test. Blessed is he who understands.' Luther's central conviction is that God's grace is seen in the death of Jesus, where we are met with absolute judgement and limitless mercy; and this is present where we live by faith, and are liberated or transformed from our self-centred fears, hopes and guilt. God's glory is present in our liberation; faith discerns that and praises, even amidst sin and death. So, for Luther, the subject-matter of Christianity is life in faith under the cross, a liberation which is itself also the glorification of God. Correspondingly, it has to be understood in a 'practical' way, not for the sake of understanding as such (which hides God) and not in order to achieve goodness (which produces legalism, and therefore hides the gospel), but in order more fully to realize this faith, and the glory of God's mercy in granting righteousness. Luther's view is therefore a fascinating alternative to the attempt to incorporate philosophical knowledge into praise, whether it be done after the fashion of Augustine or in the manner of Aquinas; it incorporates the life of faith under the

cross, in which there is transformation by the gift of righteousness, into the praise of him who gives salvation at such cost to himself. His view stands aloof from attempts to search out and objectify the glory of God, and from exercises in inwardness, and instead constantly emphasizes the movement of faith by adhering to the word of promise. That movement of faith is man's praise and the place where God's glory is truly found.

See: Martin Luther, *Lectures on the Psalms* (*Luther's Works*, vols. 10–14, ed. J. Pelikan), St Louis and Philadelphia 1955–67.

Martin Luther, *Lectures on Romans* (ed. and trans. Wilhelm Pauck, Library of Christian Classics, vol. xv), London 1961.

John Dillenberger, ed., *Martin Luther: Selections from His Writings*, Garden City 1961.

E. G. Rupp and B. Drewery, eds., *Martin Luther* (*Documents of Modern History*), London 1970.

Paul Althaus, *The Theology of Martin Luther* (trans. R. C. Schultz) Philadelphia 1966.

James Atkinson, *Martin Luther*, Harmondsworth 1967.

John M. Todd, *Martin Luther*, London 1964.

Vilmos Vajta, *Luther on Worship*, Philadelphia 1958.

15. The faith and theology of John Calvin were of a different sort, though also from the heart. The thrust of his work was always derived from his piety, and his intent, reflected in his *Institutes* (a word indicating 'instruction' or 'education') as well as his many commentaries, was to provide, for the benefit of the Church, 'the whole sum of piety and whatever is necessary to know in the doctrine of salvation'. So the central point in his work is always piety, 'that reverence joined with love of God which the knowledge of his benefits induces', which occurs when men 'recognize that they owe everything to God, that they are nourished by his fatherly care, that he is the author of their every good'. (*Institutes*, I.ii.1). This recognition of the overflowing goodness – the glory – of God should be seen for what it is, knowledge taken up into praise, praise for the inexhaustible richness of God. That was why this starting-point could be, not a foundational principle from which other things could be derived, but the total stance for man before God in which everything else was contained; the *Institutes* and the commentaries are then simply the elucidation of what is contained in this praise. Because praise does involve knowledge, not only the movement of faith as with Luther, Calvin can go on to elucidate the knowledge which is implicit in praise, and to provide a carefully-ordered exposition of it, protecting it at each step, by the structure of the *Institutes* as well as what is actually said, from the distortions which

may be introduced. The controlling 'principle' throughout is the conditioning of all knowledge, whether that of God or that of man, by man's living relationship to God in praise. In that living relationship, Calvin can proceed with a careful unravelling of man's consciousness, indelibly marked by the vestiges of the recognition of God in his self-understanding and in his understanding of the natural world; this is a recognition that is so much damaged by his heritage of sin that man cannot praise (and so know God and himself) except through the recognition in faith of God's self-revelation and redemption in his Word as found in Scripture. In other words, the controlling 'principle' for Calvin is life in the dynamic of praise for God, in which man is 'defined' by the praise and thankfulness which are made possible by God's goodness in and through the work of his Word. Falling away from this praise in his pride or self-love, man suffers a radical distortion in his knowledge.

See: John Calvin, *Institutes of the Christian Religion*, ed. J. T. McNeill, trans. F. L. Battles, two vols. (Library of Christian Classics, vol. xx, Book III, ch. 20, Book IV, ch. 17).

John Calvin, *Theological Treatises*, ed. J. K. S. Reid (Library of Christian Classics, vol. xxII), London 1975.

John Calvin, *Commentaries*, ed. J. Haroutunian (Library of Christian Classics, vol. xxIII), London 1979.

F. Wendel, *Calvin: The Origins and Development of His Religious Thought*, London 1965.

16. The traditions of Augustine, Gregory, Anselm, Aquinas, Dante, Luther and Calvin, all of them subjected at times to misunderstanding and misuse, sustained knowing in praise of God in the modern era. To follow the traditions which they constitute during modern times, however, is far too complex a task to accomplish in brief compass. More important is to recognize some of the factors which contribute to the loss of knowing in praise of God during the period. In some of these, the traditions of the past, for themselves or in distorted form, played a contributing role. For example, the persistence of scholasticism, associated with the continued use of Aristotelian-based educational methods in universities, brought a drastic reshaping of the praise-constituted theologies of pre-Reformation and Reformation alike. The consistent emphasis on the praise which occurs in the movement of life and knowledge, which marked earlier periods, now became a rigid system of belief whereby series of statements were derived deductively from a first cause. William Perkins's restatement of Calvinism for England, which followed the example of Theodore Beza (Calvin's successor at the Academy in Geneva), is a case in point, as a whole system of salvation was

derived from the decrees of election. Correspondingly, God the Trinity was fixed as the hidden cause for the decrees, losing the movement to God by Christ for man which was characteristic of Calvin's understanding. Nor was this an isolated case. Similar things happened elsewhere and in other matters, for example in the formalized use of Scripture.

See: *The Works of William Perkins*, Sutton Courtenay 1970.
    R. T. Kendall, *Calvin and English Calvinism to 1649*, Oxford 1979.
    J. B. Rogers and D. K. McKim, *The Authority and Interpretation of the Bible*, New York 1979.

17. As there came new developments in the theory of knowledge, and in supporting technology, powerful alternatives to the received traditions were provided, even if they were very slow to win widespread acceptance. Apart from that provided by Francis Bacon, which treated the 'book of nature' and the 'book of God's Word' as alike from God and to be understood in obedience to God, though requiring different kinds of disciplined handling for 'the advancement of learning', all the new developments dramatically reduced the dynamic of knowledge in praise. Even for Bacon the singular movement of knowledge in praise to God was lost, and in its place, the dynamic of human knowledge limited by experience (or in the case of Scripture by revelation) assumed more importance. But in others, whether they be John Locke, Isaac Newton, René Descartes or Benedict Spinoza or others after them, including Kant and Hegel much later, the movement of praise is radically displaced, usually with the aim of reducing man's knowledge and the universe to a unified and uniform whole, in so doing also displacing the object of praise (God) to a position in keeping with their 'systems'. This usually also avoided the traditional content and agency of the movement of praise, Jesus Christ and the Holy Spirit, either simply by omission or by treating them for their symbolic or educational value.

18. These were presented in sufficiently traditional language often to prove attractive to those not particularly well-versed in the movement of knowledge in praise of God. Furthermore, the explanatory power of the new systems succeeded in translating, if not alienating, the notion of God. A particularly influential 'translation' was the equation of God with the sensuously vast – the natural sublime, an equation which was made in different forms by Isaac Newton and Benedict Spinoza. The alternative was to 'translate' God into the position of guarantor of human knowledge (self-knowledge or knowledge of the world); Locke and Descartes (otherwise an unli-

kely combination) did this, while Hegel translated God into the self-fulfilling notion whose operation in history guaranteed the rationality of the whole of actuality. The strange function served in common by these translations was that, while they often took experience in and of the world very seriously, and appeared to provide an inclusive explanation of it, they also provided quasi-mystical substitutes for the infinite God of Christian tradition; this combination proved enduringly attractive, later reappearing among the Romantics.

See: Francis Bacon, *The Advancement of Learning*, Oxford 1963.

John Locke, *Essay Concerning Human Understanding*, London 1961.

Frank E. Manuel, *The Religion of Isaac Newton*, Oxford 1974.

Richard S. Westfall, *Science and Religion in Seventeenth Century England*, Ann Arbor 1973.

René Descartes, *Philosophical Writings*, ed. and trans. E. Anscombe and P. Geach, London 1970.

Benedict Spinoza, *On the Improvement of the Understanding and Ethics*, ed. and trans. R. H. M. Elwes, New York 1951–5.

H. A. Wolfson, *The Philosophy of Spinoza*, Cambridge and London 1934.

Immanuel Kant, *Critique of Pure Reason*, trans. Norman Kemp Smith, London 1933.

Immanuel Kant, *Critique of Practical Reason and Other Works of the Theory of Ethics*, trans. T. K. Abbott, London 1909.

Immanuel Kant, *Religion within the Limits of Reason Alone*, trans. T. M. Greene and H. H. Hudson, New York 1960.

Ernst Cassirer, *Kant's Life and Thought*, trans. James Haden, New Haven 1981.

G. W. F. Hegel, *Encyclopaedia of the Philosophical Sciences*, in Three Parts (Part One: *Logic*; Part Two: *Philosophy of Nature*; Part Three: *Philosophy of Mind*), trans. William Wallace and A. V. Miller, Oxford 1969–71.

G. W. F. Hegel, *Lectures on the Philosophy of Religion*, 3 vols., trans. E. B. Spiers and J. B. Sanderson, London 1968.

Quentin Lauer, *Hegel's Concept of God*, Albany 1982.

David B. Morris, *The Religious Sublime: Christian Poetry and Critical Tradition in Eighteenth Century England*, Lexington 1972.

Thomas Weiskel, *The Romantic Sublime: Studies in the Structures and Psychology of Transcendence*, Baltimore 1976.

19. Even under the pressure of such alien philosophies, strong as they were, there were significant attempts to restore the integrity of the movement of praise. Particular mention should be made in

this connection of those, such as Jonathan Edwards and Friedrich Schleiermacher, each of them in a very different geographical and conceptual environment, but alike attempting to rescue the movement of praise by use of the content and movement of experience. They too are an unlikely pair. Edwards was a great American philosopher-theologian whose context was the 'great awakening' in New England in the eighteenth century; a rigorist himself, he took his inspiration primarily from Calvin, John Locke, and the Cambridge Platonists. Schleiermacher, the 'father of modern liberal Protestantism' found himself in an era of unparalleled confidence in the achievements of modern German culture at the turn of the nineteenth century, and drew on Calvin, and more often Plato, modern idealism and romanticism. For both, religion was related to all aspects of life by their use of 'experience' as a mediating concept, though it must be stressed that they did not have in mind by that the rather empty notion of experience by which others more recently have sought to synthesize religion with other aspects of life. Their concern was much more for the 'affections', and their piety was as such in line with Calvin's stress on a relation of 'heartfeltness' to God; they were concerned not so much with experience in general, but with the special forms of experience which evidence for man the presence of God.

20. Edwards conducted a careful analysis of the affections, not because they were interesting in themselves, but because they manifested the operation of God's spirit convicting people of their sin and through that bringing them to a sense of God's justice and the 'excellency of the way of salvation by free and sovereign grace, through the righteousness of Christ alone, so that with delight they renounce their own righteousness' (A Faithful Narrative). Being thus caught into the dynamic of salvation, as Edwards thought, people were brought into relation with the fullness of being which was God. That was present for, and consented to, man in such a way that its perfections (existence and excellence, two kinds of beauty) were encountered through man's aesthetic sensibility, thought and will. The proper content of this 'fullness of being' was the Trinity, God in Christ and the Spirit perfecting man in thought and will, so that men could thereby enjoy God now and look forward to the coming Kingdom. Edwards found himself enjoying these benefits, and could therefore admire God's creative work in even the smallest creatures without being the less interested in what these actually were (cf. The 'Spider' Papers). His work, philosophical and theological, folds all its material into the amazing dynamic of the Trinitarian God with man, which is to be enjoyed by man by his senses, thought and action, all of which are therein gathered into praise.

See: Jonathan Edwards, *The Great Awakening*, ed. C. C. Goen (*Works*,
     vol. 4), New Haven 1972.
   Jonathan Edwards, *A Treatise Concerning Religious Affections*, ed.
     J. E. Smith (*Works*, vol. 2), New Haven 1959.
   Jonathan Edwards, *The Philosophy of Jonathan Edwards from His
     Notebooks*, ed. H. G. Townsend, Westport 1972.
   R. A. Delattre, *Beauty and Sensibility in the Thought of Jonathan
     Edwards*, New Haven 1968.

21. Schleiermacher is no match for the lucidity of expression to be
found in Calvin or Edwards, and what he makes of the affections
is rather different in any case. For him, they are closely allied with
feeling or self-consciousness, not understood in a psychological sense
but as a prereflective apprehension of ourselves in relation to what
is beyond ourselves. That, of course, might apply to our relation to
anything or anyone beyond ourselves, and be discussed as the
basis of thought or action; and these were particularly important to
Schleirmacher while he was concerned with establishing the relation
of religion to culture – the prereflective was precisely the bond (or
mediating concept) between culture and religion, he thought. But
he quickly occupied himself with expounding the particular 'determination' of this prereflective 'consciousness' which was religious,
the consciousness of ourselves as utterly dependent, i.e., the consciousness of ourselves in relation to God. Thus he saw this consciousness to be fundamentally relational. Its character as such was to be
seen in its historical and cultural manifestations, but always by
looking beneath the surface for the 'essence' (the religious determination of consciousness) present in the varying manifestations of
history and culture; here Schleiermacher was pressed by his *a
priorism* into a kind of 'proof-text' method of expounding history,
which brought a certain vulnerability to the accusation that he was
not in fact a very careful historian. Looking 'through' history in this
fashion, Schleiermacher identified the gradual maturation of this
determination and the particular content which it acquired in Christianity. After this 'historical' analysis, he undertook a 'systematic'
statement of the Christian form, unravelling the various implications
of the determinate Christian religious affections, keeping as strictly
as possible to the very careful restrictions he had set himself – to
make all doctrine and ethics an explication of these religious affections, thereby to avoid making the affections into science or ethics.
This he did by providing a new arrangement for the contents of
doctrine, based on his definition of Christianity as 'a monotheistic
faith, belonging to the teleological type of religion, and essentially
distinguished from other such faiths by the fact that everything in
it is related to the redemption accomplished in Jesus of Nazareth'

(*Christian Faith*, para. 11). The new arrangement, loosely corresponding to Calvin's double knowledge of God as creator and
redeemer, orders the contents into consciousness of sin and that of
grace, considering in each case the state of man or the Christian,
the attributes of God and the constitution of the world, with the
whole being prefaced by a consideration of what is presupposed
(about man, God and the world) by this double consciousness.
Though it is easily lost in the intricacies of this structure and the
enormous amount of technical material which it contains, Schleiermacher was always deeply concerned with the dynamic of movement, particularly the 'rise of your consciousness' through the
'desire to be identified with the Universe' (*Second Speech*), and the
gradual discrimination of the whence and whither of this, which for
the Christian has its content exclusively in the redemption by Jesus
of Nazareth. But strange things have happened: Schleiermacher has
moved away from the world and history to their meaning, moved
from knowledge and duty to the prereflective and intentional, and
from the being and activity of God to man's consciousness of them.
In other words, the dynamic of knowledge (and action) in the praise
of God has been dislocated at nearly every point, and ends in a
kind of formalism of the affections, where they are detached from
their own constituent elements and lose their realism and their
dynamic.

See: F. D. E. Schleiermacher, *On Religion: Speeches to its Cultured
    Despisers*, trans. John Oman, New York 1958.
    F. D. E. Schleiermacher, *The Christian Faith*, ed. H. R. Mackin-
    tosh and J. S. Stewart, Edinburgh 1928.
    R. R. Williams, *Schleiermacher the Theologian: The Construction of
    the Doctrine of God*, Philadelphia 1978.

22. As was the case with Calvin and Luther in the wake of the
Reformation, the dynamics seen in the experiential theologies of
Edwards and Schleiermacher, different though they were, were
subjected to kinds of 'scholastic' transformation, seemingly to make
them more manageable. The fate of Edwards's views was for them
(or at least those which were known, for many were never made
public in his lifetime) to be translated into something considerably
less demanding, which people could combine with the rising
American convictions about individual rights and achievements; in
effect, the dynamic of praise was 'losing its reality as human experience and, therefore, its appeal to the hearts and minds of men and
being transformed into a vast, complicated, and colorless theological
structure, bewildering to its friends and ridiculous to its enemies'
(Haroutunian, p. 71). Much the same could be said of Schleierma-

cher's theology, as it sponsored whole approaches to religion through history and cultural studies, or as 'personal' or 'transpersonal' experience which required study by 'phenomenological' or 'hermeneutical' means, while at the same time losing its own credibility as an exposition of religious experience. So Edwards was transformed into what is sometimes called 'moralism' and Schleiermacher was emasculated into 'religionism'; the dynamic of experience which they had attempted to trace was thereby turned back on itself – the task for man was now to be moral or to be religious, rather than through experience to be himself in the recognition of God. Experience thereby lost its location in the dynamic of praise.

See: Joseph Haroutunian, *Piety versus Moralism: The Passing of the New England Theology*, New York 1970.

P. J. Cahill, *Mended Speech: The Crisis of Religious Studies and Theology*, New York 1982.

23. That rather detached view of 'morality' and 'religion' accorded nicely with the idealist and rationalist approaches of Kant and Hegel in the eighteenth and nineteenth centuries (see paras. 17 and 18), which were the principal philosophical influences of the time. The natural sciences tended in the same direction also. Physics, following the lead of Newton, was concerned with the mechanisms of the world as part of the sensuous vastness (the sublime). Geology tested biblical accounts as 'scientific' hypotheses, and found them faulty. Biology, particularly as evolutionary views took hold, seemed to be at odds with established religious views. Psychology found itself convinced that man's mental processes, including his moral and religious inclinations, operated through a kind of mechanistic association of ideas (a view continued today, though in transmuted form, in behaviourism). The social sciences were founded on the basis of Comte's supposition that the human spirit (society) had passed through the ages of theology and metaphysics to its culmination in 'positive' science. The pressure from all these directions confirmed the supposition that morality and religion were rather peculiar human activities, with their own inner dynamic whose operation had very little to do with 'real' knowledge. Increasingly, their particular content and value, such as they were, were seen to be symbolic.

See: C. G. Gillispie, *Genesis and Geology*, Cambridge 1951.

N. C. Gillespie, *Charles Darwin and the Problem of Creation*, Chicago 1979.

Michael Ruse, *The Darwinian Revolution*, Chicago 1979.

M. Mandelbaum, *History, Man and Reason*, Baltimore 1971.

24. After we have reviewed the complexities of the history of the life of praise, and the regular dislocations and distortions to which this life has been subject, it is little wonder that man today appears anxious and perplexed. Far from understanding himself, his thought and action, as caught up in a movement of praise for God – one which should make him relaxed and hopeful – his activities seem fragmented, bound together only by the fact that they are his, for what he can make of them. And, so far as his history is concerned, far from being a thrust towards an unconditioned truth and freedom in which there arises genuine hopefulness through anticipation (which, as we saw earlier, is another form of praise), it is more frequently seen as a series of complex accidents. What are the resources available today for the recovery of the movement of knowledge in the praise of God?

New Possibilities for Praise

1. It is best to begin by again clarifying the basis of our understanding of the movement of praise, with some of the lessons learned through our review of the history of the life of praise. Central to this has been the strange 'fact' that we find the perfection of the infinite in attending, determining (or recognizing) and praising, even where these are directed to 'places' where that perfection is only mediately present. The parallel to this for action or behaviour is where we find the perfection of the infinite through action directed to goals in which that perfection is affirmed or praised, even where the perfection is only mediately present in the goals. And it has been evident that, even if much can be gained by either as an instantaneous deed (that is, as an attending-determining-praise, or as a goal-affirming-in-action, which is limited in duration to a 'one-off' deed), whether directed to the mediation of perfection or reaching through it to appreciate the perfection itself, properly speaking what is required is an ascent to the perfection by a process of something like purification, in which one participates in the perfection in the process of 'finding' it. Hence perfection is praised through the very dynamic in which it is already present.

2. If this is so, much stress is laid upon the dynamic and multifaceted bond which arises between human beings in their knowing and action, and the infinite perfection which is present therein. But the bond is not seen to be 'graspable' in any simple way, because it is only understandable or 'actable' by one's movement within it, and even then very diversely because the 'grasping' and 'acting' of it are themselves composite (attending, determining and praise in

the one case, affirming and moving towards goals in the other case) and fluid. What is more, the bond is that between the perfecting of man and the expanding perfection of the infinite God, and that too prevents any simple grasping or acting in praise on man's part; there is no terminal point in the process, but rather an expanding economy of closeness between man and God which leaves behind no aspect of man's knowing and doing in so far as they are true and good.

3. The most significant contributions in the history of praise have fastened on one facet or the other of this fascinating bond. And the fact that they have done so has usually led to distortion of the nature of the very bond which they have tried to ascertain. This seems to be because while the perfection in which praise participates may be mediated through these facets, it cannot be uncovered fully through any one; the consistent use of one facet, while an attractive way to proceed, is inconsistent with the kind of bond which it is. One cannot therefore, for example, simply explore memory, knowledge, existence, experience, perfection, etc., without doing damage to the bond between the world, man and God as that is found through praise. The deficiency of such ways, taken in themselves, has been one of the chief lessons of the history of praise. Not only do they fall short; the very attempt to make them do what they cannot do eventually makes them ends in themselves, and severs them from other constituent factors in the bond of which we have been speaking. Praise, on the contrary, glories in the growing fulfilment of all the activities of knowledge and action by their movement together, and anticipates their completion by the presence of the perfection which they seek.

4. The most important resources for praise in the present century are those which have, in some degree at least, escaped the limitations just mentioned. One feature in particular marks them all, their emphasis on interaction, our interaction with the world or others, and the necessity of constituting that interaction appropriately, whether in history, nature, human relationships or theology. The fact that we know or act interactively is now seen, not as a temporary barrier preventing us from having purely objective knowledge (of the sort which answers questions of the form 'What is. . .?) or goals, or one making all knowledge (or goals) fully subjective but as the way in which things (goals) are knowable (realizable) if they are so at all. That has led to certain fundamental convictions, among them that knowledge must interact with its object, that it is inescapably personal but also social, that it is affected by biological factors, and yet that it is dependent on its object, etc.

See: Werner Heisenberg, *Physics and Philosophy: The Revolution in Modern Science*, London 1959.

M. W. Wartofsky, *Conceptual Foundations of Scientific Thought: An Introduction to the Philosophy of Science*, New York 1968.

K. R. Popper, *Objective Knowledge*, Oxford 1972.

M. Polanyi, *Personal Knowledge: Towards a Post-Critical Philosophy*, London 1958.

T. F. Torrance, ed., *Belief in Science and in Christian Life: The Relevance of Michael Polanyi's Thought for Christian Faith and Life*, Edinburgh 1980.

Melvin Konner, *The Tangled Wing: Biological Constraints on the Human Spirit*, London 1982.

W. Pannenberg, *Theology and the Philosophy of Science*, London 1976.

David Tracy, *The Analogical Imagination*, New York 1981.

5. The wealth of fresh understanding of the human factor in knowledge and action has tended frequently to obscure their relation to the object, whatever it may be; and it has often been suggested that they are 'merely' subjective, personal, social, biological, etc. This, however, is to prejudge not only the existence but also the nature of the very interaction which is so basic to modern understanding. In less extreme views, in cases where the 'object' is not so 'hard', at least by comparison with material objects – for example, in the case of personal identity, moral goals or God – the tendency is to consider these as special forms of experience within the general class of experiences, distinguished from other kinds of experience by the way in which they present themselves (cf. Edwards and Schleiermacher, paras. 19–21) or the way in which they are to be interpreted. This is a way of specifying the interaction between subject and object, however, which in the first case rests the interaction entirely on the presence of a felt experience, and in the second case rests it on the justifiability of interpreting in a particular way. Both implicitly defend the presence of an interaction between subject and object by appealing to the evidentness of the interaction to human beings. This leaves the human factor primary, and in doing so tends to turn religious experience back on itself (see para. 22), making religious experience the criterion for the existence of religious experience. It has the added disadvantage that it does not allow for differences in the truth which may be present in the interaction; they are all at the same level, being differences of felt experience or of interpretation.

See: John Baillie, *The Sense of the Presence of God*, Oxford 1962.

A. R. Peacocke, *Creation and the World of Science*, Oxford 1979.

J. H. Hick, *God and the Universe of Faiths*, London 1973.

M. Goulder and J. H. Hick, *Why Believe in God?* London 1983.

6. But, in the interaction, there is also the possibility of finding the 'balance' otherwise, and more in favour of locating the proper interaction between subject and object – as a function, it might be said, of both subject and object and the proper relation between them. This is a matter which requires sensitive handling, without rushing too quickly into the business of knowing and acting. It has been approached from many different directions, largely unheard by those too much obsessed by the technological-manipulative ideal of knowledge and action. In terms of being, it requires one to 'let be'; in action, it requires one to 'attend'; in thought, it requires an 'intellectual contemplation', etc. All of these suppose that one has the 'space', including the power and time, to allow the other to be, and to enjoy that, without immediately carrying this contact into productive work. Herein, as we have seen in the text (in the discussion of recognition and respect, and in the discussion of attention in Appendix A), is one main thrust of praise.

See: Josef Pieper, *Leisure the Basis of Culture*, trans. Alexander Dru (Preface by T. S. Eliot), London 1965.

Simone Weil, 'Reflections on the Right Use of School Studies with a View to the Love of God' in G. A. Panichas, ed., *The Simone Weil Reader*, New York 1977.

Martin Buber, *I and Thou*, New York 1958.

Gabriel Marcel, *Being and Having*, London 1965.

Gabriel Marcel, *The Existentialist Background of Human Dignity*, Cambridge 1963.

Emmanuel Levinas, *Totality and Infinity: An Essay on Exteriority*, trans. Alphonso Lingis, Pittsburgh 1969.

Paul Ricoeur, *History and Truth*, Evanston 1965.

R. H. Lauer, *Temporal Man: The Meaning and Uses of Social Time*, New York 1981.

Martin Heidegger, *On Time and Being*, trans. J. Stambaugh, New York 1972.

7. But precisely by 'giving space' to the other, an interaction comes into being which is not simply dominated by the subject; there is an expansion of the interaction to allow for the other to 'be'. While this constitutes that being as truth for the subject also, it does not necessarily have to be seen simply in its effect on the subject. As the bibliography above shows, this has been a special concern for existential and phenomenological understanding. But the truth of the being of the other as it arises in the interaction with the other can equally well be spoken of objectively, as the truth which emerges through the 'self-utterance' or self-presentation of the other, so far as it is given primacy by the subject and so far as the relation

between them is corrected by its self-presentation. (In other words, the objectivity of the other is not a 'brute objectivity' but one which occurs in its interaction with the subject.) It is important to notice that in this respect there is a commonness between the existential-phenomenological and the objectivist views. Both are centred on the act of 'giving space' to the other, which is the act of praise. This central feature can then be seen in terms of knowledge or of human activity in relationships, or as the emergence into language of the other.

See: T. F. Torrance, *Theological Science*, Oxford 1969.
Dietrich Bonhoeffer, *Sanctorum Communio*, London 1963.
Dietrich Bonhoeffer, *The Cost of Discipleship*, London 1964.
Eberhard Jüngel, 'God – As a Word of Our Language' in *Theology of the Liberating Word*, ed. F. Herzog, Nashville 1971.

8. The same considerations are at issue in the approach to history, where the truth of the past emerges through interaction established by giving space for the past to be itself, as against the subsuming of the past within what are seen to be proprieties of present inter-pretation (as characterizes the 'domination' of the past by the modern in experience-centred or positivistic history). Again, there is a surface distinction between existential-phenomenological and objectivist interpretation, the one finding the truth of the historical past by ascertaining the existential position of its participants in its effect on the later interpreter, and the other by allowing the histor-ical objectivity of the past to emerge through its presentness for the modern critic. But both are united in their concern for the interac-tion which alone can make historical investigation possible, and this interaction is seen by both to arise in the 'letting-be' of the past which also constitutes its 'presentness' for the interpreter. Here again, the interaction – presence through letting be – occurs as an activity of praise.

See: Rudolf Bultmann, *Faith and Understanding*, trans. L. Pettibone Smith, London 1969.
Rudolf Bultmann, *Theology of the New Testament*, 2 vols., trans. Kendrick Grobel, London 1951, 1955.
Wolfhart Pannenberg, *Basic Questions in Theology*, 3 vols., trans. G. H. Kehm and R. A. Wilson, London 1970–73.
Hans-Georg Gadamer, *Truth and Method*, London 1975.

9. But, as is readily apparent, there is no necessary interaction between the self and the other, either in a moment or through history; or if there is, it is not clearly ascertainable. The very absence of such sponsors anxieties about the correct approach, the modern

obsession with 'method' in knowledge and 'hermeneutics' in history, and the seemingly endless – and very different – attempts to 'reach through' them to find an underlying interaction. All allow for fragmentation and contradiction within the interaction, a breaking of the interaction within it. And the principal issue is whether, after this 'breaking', there is an interaction possible at all. (a) The extreme of 'brokenness' is represented, perhaps, by those who, much aware of the benefits of idiosyncrasy and the presence everywhere of ambiguity and instability, stand for methodological anarchy or something very close to it (e.g., the 'deconstruction' of all conceptions of reality which build its rationality on its wordlikeness). Strangely enough, and also importantly, this – and the anti-traditionalism which often accompanies it – can produce a sensation of liberation and even playfulness. And this may be an affirmation of the very non-order in reality discussed in the text of this book, in other words an affirmation of a freer kind of interaction with the object (in knowledge or history) than has usually been conceived, to match its more dynamic character. (b) Less obviously extreme are those who find an interaction in the brokenness, and seek to use it constructively. There is bewildering variety in such attempts, but the range is indicated by these examples: (1) the 'methodological pragmatism' of some philosophies of science; (2) the finding of existential salvation through the very questionableness of all existence (Bultmann); (3) finding a bond between God and man whose content is Christ through the frail human process of 'loving him in the mystery in which he gives himself to be known by us' (Barth); (4) the finding of Christian hope in the 'pain of the negative' (Moltmann); (5) the finding of the freedom of God through following the pure contingency of his action in history (Pannenberg); (6) the finding of the unknown through the actual pursuit of knowledge as grasped through man's self-appropriation (Lonergan); and (7) the finding of God through man's openness to transcendent mystery (Rahner). The means by which these approaches are commended are so various that it is extremely difficult to see what runs through them all. But it is precisely the issue of finding an interaction which does not violate an acknowledged brokenness, finding a firm bond which is at the same time one which allows for the mystery which is present. Hence it is common to find such approaches advocating an open, dynamic relation between subject and object, while at the same time finding that it is a firm enough relation to provide what is seen to be necessary. What is desired through such an interaction is not always knowledge; it may be the possibility of existing authentically, life in hope, or freedom.

See: (a) Paul Feyerabend, *Against Method: Outline of an Anarchistic Theory of Knowledge*, London 1975.

Robert D. Cumming, *Starting Point: An Introduction to the Dialectic of Existence*, Chicago 1979.

T. J. J. Altizer *et al Deconstruction in Theology*, New York 1982.

(b) (1) Nicholas Rescher, *Methodological Pragmatism*, Oxford 1977.

(2) Rudolf Bultmann, *History and Eschatology: The Presence of Eternity*, New York 1957.

(3) Karl Barth, *Church Dogmatics*, vols. i and ii, ed. and trans. G. W. Bromiley and T. F. Torrance, Edinburgh 1975 and 1957.

(4) Jurgen Moltmann, *Theology of Hope: The Crucified God*, trans. J. W. Leitch; R. A. Wilson and J. Bowden, London 1967 and 1974.

(5) Wolfhart Pannenberg, *Basic Questions in Theology*, vol. ii, trans. G. H. Kehm, London 1971.

(6) Bernard Lonergan, *Understanding and Being: An Introduction and Companion to Insight*, ed. E. A. and M. D. Morelli, New York 1980.

(7) Karl Rahner, *Foundations of Christian Faith: An Introduction to the Idea of Christianity*, trans. W. V. Dych, London 1978.

10. The brokenness is not by any means limited to such 'clean' issues as those which are handled in methodological discussions. The brokenness is also located in the damaged identity of people, in social and economic and other fragmentations which beset life in the world, those which induce such self-protectiveness and violence towards others that there is little possibility for them to engage in the 'letting be' earlier discussed. The fact is that, for a lifelong-dispossessed person to be able to 'play' in the creative contemplation of the other, or to find an appropriately dynamic interaction with the other, is very nearly impossible. More frequently, the very violence which he has suffered prevents him from having the kind of freedom by which to appreciate the order or the non-order in reality; such freedom is for others who have not been subject to such disadvantaging. So for a 'damaged' person, his life and history are not disconnected from his interaction with the other; they are a necessary mediation of the interaction. And exactly this is also true of communities. For the individual or the community to achieve a dynamic interaction with the other requires the presence of something of such power as to preserve for them the possibility of achieving this, or, failing that, the coming of a radical transformation in their life and history. The most important thing to notice, however, is how the necessary preservation or transformation

occurs. It is by someone, or some community, holding that person/community in praise, and by that attention and affirmation – which need, of course, to be expressed materially – reversing the history and presence of the 'damage'. Praise thus creates a new mediation for the interaction with the other.

See: Jürgen Moltmann, *Religion, Revolution and the Future*, trans. M. Douglas Meeks, New York 1969.

Jürgen Moltmann, *The Crucified God*, trans. R. A. Wilson and John Bowden, London 1974, chs. 6–8.

Hans Urs von Balthasar, *The God Question and Modern Man*, trans. Hilda Graef, New York 1967.

Hans Urs von Balthasar, *Love Alone: The Way of Revelation, A Theological Perspective*, ed. Alexander Dru, London 1968.

11. If this interaction can be sustained in such brokenness as we have seen, what form may it take? If there is such widespread 'play' with 'non-order', the constant emphasis on correction and questionableness, on the frailty and contingency of all that is said or done, on the 'open' and surpassable character of all that is found, can there be any appropriate form for the interaction which does not contradict these emphases? This is a question which is implicit even in the activity of 'attending' or 'letting be' already considered, for how can one attend or let the other be without in some degree already establishing its/his place or condition? But the issue becomes very much more acute when one hopes to 'determine' or 'affirm' it as object or goal; can one produce more than contingent and relative approximations? Again, the extreme view, particularly apparent in religious discussions, is the position of relativism and individualism which is taken up and magnified through self-conscious espousal of it as a position; like methodological anarchism, even it can be considered an affirmation of non-order, and not therefore so threatening. But a more balanced position, one which is not so much focused on movement, 'reaches through' this very relativism, suggesting that the structures of scientific understanding are properly 'open-textured' or 'incomplete symbols' but also serve to simplify and unify knowledge of the physical world (they are thus remarkable combinations of contingency and intelligibility) and in turn require 'intelligible contingent relations' to the constitution of the world by God (Torrance). Thus the form of man's understanding of nature is itself a mixture of contingency and intelligibility, and this implies an interaction not simply with nature but also (through that) with what makes nature contingently intelligible; and this is itself appreciated through an interaction of contingent intelligibility.

See: George Rupp, *Beyond Existentialism and Zen: Religion in a Plural-
istic World*, New York 1979.
  T. F. Torrance, *Divine and Contingent Order*, Oxford 1981.

12. It is important to recognize the diversity of 'forms' available for
such use; they include those of nature, aesthetics, feeling, cognition,
action, freedom, etc., but also the modes by which life itself is lived
and perpetuated by each person as well as by people together.
There is a vast variety of materials which assist in recognizing and
appreciating these, and the study of them is by definition never-
ending. Some of the most useful approach the issue as: an 'aesthetic'
question of 'seeing the form' (von Balthasar), one of feeling and its
forms (Langer), the existential one of 'symbolizing' mystery
(Rahner), the search for freedom (Pannenberg), and the eschatological and practical one of finding hope in despair (Moltmann). All
alike find the possibility of form in brokenness, and all guard against
tendencies to 'come to rest' by eliminating contingency; but some
excessively devalue knowledge as such. Two things are common to
them all: they all attempt, against relativism, to maintain the legit-
imacy of some kind of form even if always as incomplete; and, in
doing so, they find an interaction with the true nature of things,
reaching beyond them – in praise – to their truth. If, as we saw
earlier (para. 10), praise creates a new medium for the interaction
with the other, this praise also achieves an appropriate form: there
is form for intelligence (knowing) and for action (goals) in praise.
But these are never complete; they require perfecting.

See: Hans Urs von Balthasar, *The Glory of the Lord: A Theological
Aesthetics*, 1. I: *Seeing the Form*, trans. E. Leiva-Merikakis,
Edinburgh 1982.
  Susanne K. Langer, *Mind: An Essay on Human Feeling*, vol. I,
Baltimore 1967.
  Karl Rahner, *A Rahner Reader*, ed. Gerald A. McCool, London
1975, esp. ch. 6.
  Wolfhart Pannenberg, *What is Man?*, Philadelphia 1970.
  Jürgen Moltmann, *Theology of Hope*, trans. J. W. Leitch,
London 1967.

13. We have seen that interaction with the world or others is
central to modern man's understanding, and that this interaction is
appropriately construed as 'attending' the other or 'letting be' – the
action of praise in giving 'space' to the other which also makes
it/him present. We have also seen that this interaction is not necessary or clearly ascertainable, but that, notwithstanding brokenness
and fragmentation and damage, it may occur, again through praise,

and may take form in knowledge and action which are incomplete and require perfecting. Whether such 'forms' do in fact go beyond relativism depends in the last resort on their content, on whether they provide a means of interacting with the other in such a way as to establish what it is. If they do, they do not function as empty forms, but are appropriate to the content of the other; in effect, they become praise of the other as they 'raise' it/him for the one who knows and acts. And this 'raising' has a 'feedback', in that it requires further development of the content of these 'forms' to make it more adequate to the one now better found in praise. This process of perfecting can go on, as a movement towards perfection, continuing in praise, and drawing man to fuller knowledge and life as he knows his neighbour more and more fully in praise. It can also be broken, however, and constantly is, when the whole enterprise of knowledge and life is scaled down to 'manageability'. For example, some human beings can (because they are privileged enough to be able to do so) and do secure for themselves the possibility of carrying on with 'clean' methodologies, unimpeded by brokenness in knowledge and life. By doing so, they suitably restrict objects and goals, and convince that they are attainable. Much of the implicit secularism of modern life adopts this strategy: less necessary, less attempted, less achieved. But praise directed to expanding perfection has no such restricted strategy: it can grow, and give a progressively much higher vision of the kind of interaction which is desirable and can be achieved. This happens on two levels: (a) there can be, within each situation within which we interact with others, an expanding vision which draws us to fuller and fuller interaction, to expanding forms of knowledge and action; (b) through praise, there can also be an expanding attending, determining and praise for the content of the vision. The one is an effective vision, the other an originative or terminal one.

14. It is difficult, if not impossible, to keep the two separate. Both are matters of doctrine and ethics. Both are pursued through systematic and historical modes. Both are concerned with what is the truth and with how that truth may become manifest. But one will give primacy to the practice of the truth, where the other will give primacy to the truth in practice. The 'primacy of practice' rests on an expanding vision of the future found through repentance and the constant changing of existing conditions. It is this which is the following of the crucified one, and this by which the vision of God comes to life. 'Repentance is joy' (Moltmann), and permanent repentance and change are the only way to achieve the vision of God. This way is a frequent feature of the lives of those engaged in direct action to bring about the needed change, but the forms vary

widely, from the simply Bible-based (Wallis) to those which employ
dialectical-historical understanding (Moltmann, Gutierrez) to those
which use modern scientific understanding (Segundo). What is
common to all are the radical practical implications of an expanding
vision of man which has its roots, implicitly if not explicitly, in
praise. What is perhaps less common is the conviction of joy which
should result.

See: Roger Schutz, *Festival*, Taizé 1973.
   Jim Wallis, *Call to Conversion*, Tring 1982.
   Jürgen Moltmann, *Theology and Joy*, trans. R. Ulrich, London
      1973.
   Jürgen Moltmann, *The Church in the Power of the Spirit*, trans.
      Margaret Kohl, London 1977.
   Gustavo Gutierrez, *A Theology of Liberation: History, Politics and
      Salvation*, trans. C. Inda and J. Eagleson, Maryknoll 1973.
   Juan L. Segundo, *A Theology for a New Humanity*, vol. 2 (*Grace
      and the Human Condition*) and vol. 3 (*Evolution and Human Guilt*),
      trans. John Drury, Dublin 1980.

15. The 'primacy of truth in practice' is pursued in two ways, one
systematic and ethical, the other hermeneutical and ethical. The
first of these involves an ongoing praise, in which are included
attending and determining, through the form of 'incomplete symbol'
or 'contingent intelligibility', of the perfection towards which man
moves in knowledge and history. This perfection, as we saw earlier
(Appendix A), has as its own characteristic an economy in expansion which is at the same time 'close' to man in his created nature
and also in his brokenness, in such a way that his life (knowledge
and action) are reconstituted. This suggests that the perfection of
God is not that of a simple 'absolute', whose nature is remote and
paradoxical, but rather one of praise perfected in order and freedom.
Such a God could gracefully create man and remain with him as
he denied this praise in his attempt to take order and freedom for
himself, and could take upon himself the disorder of mankind,
thereby to perfect man in his praise. Hence the central issue is the
content of the perfection which is God, as that is found in every
praise rightly directed towards others: the Trinity of God as a
dynamic of praise in order and freedom.

See: William J. Hill, *The Three-Personed God: The Trinity as a Mystery
      of Salvation*, Washington, D.C., 1982.
   Eberhard Jüngel, *The Doctrine of the Trinity*, trans. Horton
      Harris, Edinburgh 1976.
   Colin E. Gunton, *Becoming and Being: The Doctrine of God in
      Charles Hartshorne and Karl Barth*, Oxford 1978.

Jürgen Moltmann, *The Trinity and the Kingdom of God*, trans. Margaret Kohl, London 1982.

Karl Rahner, *The Trinity*, trans. Joseph Donceel, New York 1970.

16. There are important connections between such visions of the perfection of God and non-theological discussions. The large issues of modern cosmology, wherein scientists try to grasp the universe and its history as an intelligible whole, frequently force these scientists to the limit of their powers and beyond. Questions about order and energy, synergy, time and space, etc., bring illuminating discussions of extremely fundamental and important issues in which there is no clear division between what is scientific and what is theological. Since such issues bear importantly on fundamental issues of knowing in the praise of God, they are no longer to be considered 'optional' for theologians, and will require integration into the vision of praise.

See: Carl F. Von Weizsacker, *The Unity of Nature*, trans. F. J. Zucker, New York 1980.

Manfred Eigen and Ruthild Winkler, *Laws of the Game: How the Principles of Nature Govern Chance*, trans. R. and R. Kimber, London 1982.

Jeremy Campbell, *Grammatical Man: Information, Entropy, Language and Life*, New York 1982.

Peter A. Corning, *The Synergism Hypothesis: A Theory of Progressive Evolution*, London 1983.

David Park, *The Image of Eternity: Roots of Time in the Physical World*, Amherst 1980.

Paul Davies, *God and the New Physics*, London 1983.

17. The same content, the perfection of God, is ultimately the concern of historical-hermeneutical research. The purpose is to understand truth from and through history, not simply the past for the present but the truth throughout history in and through historical contingency (thereby avoiding pure relativism). Though there are many ways of 'scaling down' the enterprise, for example resting content simply with historical information or the dichotomy of 'facts' and subjectively-constituted 'meaning', the most thoroughgoing searches for the undercurrent of truth in history go far beyond this, to establish the content of the perfection of God as manifest through historical movement and events. This can involve careful discussions of past and present suppositions about interpretation (Frei, Kelsey), of hermeneutics as the foundation of understanding about God and Christ (Frei, Wood), of imagination and intentionality

(Hart, Ricoeur), of forms of language, meaning and rhetoric (Ricoeur), and of the meaning of revelation and historical truth (Ricoeur, Farley). While many allow room for the discovery of the perfection of God in praise, most are so much preoccupied by formal and anthropological questions that they fail to go on to find the possibility of joy and freedom arising from the content of what is found. It is this possibility which lifts the technology of their work to the place where it can 'contemplate' God himself, and so fulfil their hermeneutics in praise. 'Play is the clue to ontological explanation . . . The pleasure offered . . . is the joy of knowledge . . . The transformation is a transformation into the true. It is not enchantment in the sense of a bewitchment that waits for the redeeming word that will transform things to what they were, but it is itself redemption and transformation back into true being. In the representation of play, what is emerges. . . The being of all play is always realization, sheer fulfilment, *energeia* which has its *telos* in itself . . .' (Gadamer, pp. 101f.).

See: Hans Frei, *The Eclipse of Biblical Narrative: A Study in Eighteenth and Nineteenth Century Hermeneutics*, New Haven 1974.

Hans Frei, *The Identity of Jesus Christ: Hermeneutical Bases for Dogmatic Theology*, Philadelphia 1975.

David Kelsey, *The Uses of Scripture in Recent Theology*, Philadelphia 1975.

Charles Wood, *The Formation of Christian Understanding: An Essay in Theological Hermeneutics*, Philadelphia 1981.

Ray L. Hart, *Unfinished Man and the Imagination: Toward an Ontology and Rhetoric of Revelation*, New York 1968.

Paul Ricoeur, *Freud and Philosophy: An Essay on Interpretation*, New Haven 1970.

Paul Ricoeur, *The Conflict of Interpretations: Essays in Hermeneutics*, Evanston 1974.

Paul Ricoeur, *Interpretation Theory: Discourse and the Surplus of Meaning*, Fort Worth 1976.

Paul Ricoeur, *The Rule of Metaphor: Multi-Disciplinary Studies of the Creation of Meaning in Language*, London 1978.

Paul Ricoeur, *Essays on Biblical Interpretation*, Philadelphia 1980.

Paul Ricoeur, *Hermeneutics and the Human Sciences*, Cambridge 1981.

Hans-Georg Gadamer, *Truth and Method*, London 1975.

18. In the end, all questions of attention, knowledge, practice, history and hermeneutics find their fulfilment as they are brought more fully into interaction with the expanding perfection of God as

known in Jesus Christ and by the Holy Spirit. Philippians 4:4–9 sums it all up.

Index of Names

Index of Subjects